ENFORCING THE PEACE

ENFORCING

KIMBERLY ZISK MARTEN

THE PEACE

Learning from the Imperial Past

COLUMBIA UNIVERSITY PRESS
NEW YORK

Columbia University Press
Publishers Since 1893
New York, Chichester, West Sussex
Copyright © 2004 Columbia University Press
All rights Reserved

Library of Congress Cataloging-in-Publication Data

Zisk, Kimberly Marten
Enforcing the peace : learning from the imperial past /
Kimberly Zisk Marten.
p. cm.
Includes bibliographical references and index.
ISBN 0–231–12913–0 (cloth : alk. paper)
1. Peacekeeping forces. 2. Peace-building. 3. Imperialism.
I. Title

JZ6374.Z57   2004
341.5'84—dc22   2004048406

Columbia University Press books are printed on
permanent and durable acid-free paper

Printed in the United States of America

c 10 9 8 7 6 5 4 3 2 1

To my students

CONTENTS

Acknowledgments   ix

ONE   Peace, or Change?   1

TWO   Peacekeeping and Control   21

THREE   State Interests, Humanitarianism, and Control   59

FOUR   Political Will and Security   93

FIVE   Military Tasks and Multilateralism   119

SIX   Security as a Step to Peace   145

Notes   167
Index   193

ACKNOWLEDGMENTS

This project was made possible by the support of several organizations, to which I owe a great debt. A grant from the Carnegie Corporation of New York, via the Arnold A. Saltzman Institute of War and Peace Studies (IWPS) at Columbia University, funded a semester off from my teaching, supported two conferences that my colleagues and I organized at IWPS where I was able to try out my ideas, and paid for my research trips to NATO headquarters and SHAPE in Belgium, to Australia, and to briefings at U.S. Camp Bondsteel in Kosovo and at Ft. Bragg in North Carolina. Barnard College paid for an additional semester of leave for me, and my colleagues there have provided me with a congenial home-base throughout this entire project. My particular gratitude goes to Barnard Political Science Department Chair Richard Pious, Provost Elizabeth Boylan, and President Judith Shapiro, for their supportiveness throughout this project.

A Canadian Studies Grant from the Canadian Embassy in Washington, D.C. facilitated my research trips to the Lester Pearson Peacekeeping Center in Nova Scotia, and to speak with peacekeeping policymakers and military officers in Ottawa and New Delhi. A Council on Foreign Relations International Affairs Fellowship funded by Hitachi, Ltd. paid for my research in Japan, and the Institute for International Policy Studies (the Nakasone Institute) provided a headquarters for me there in summer 2000. The Council on Foreign Relations also gave me a second home in New York when I was a fellow there during the 2001/2 academic year, and I am very grateful to former president Leslie Gelb for giving me that opportunity. I also appreciate the additional occasions to present my work in progress that were provided to me by the Japanese National Defense Academy in Yokosuka (with a particular note of thanks to Takako Hikotani), the Japanese National Defense Agency, the Japanese National Institute for Defense Studies, Keio University, the Research Institute for Peace and Security in Tokyo, the Liechtenstein Institute on Self-Determination at Princeton University (with thanks to Wolfgang Danspeckgruber), the Summer Peacekeeping Training Seminar at the Columbia School of International and Public Affairs (with thanks to Naomi Weinberger), Canadian Forces Base Borden, the Center for Strategic and International Studies in Washington (with thanks to Celeste Wallander), and two International Studies Association annual meetings.

There are so many people whose ideas influenced this book, through their conversations with me, their criticisms of my work in progress, and their sharing of research contacts, that it is impossible to thank them all, and I apologize in advance to any I fail to recognize. I am particularly grateful to all of the military officers and policy officials I interviewed off-the-record in my research. The individuals I mention here may not agree with my arguments, and certainly should not be held responsible for any of my errors in either fact or analysis. They are listed in alphabetical order. Special thanks go to Edward Anselm, Deborah Avant, Gordon Bardos, Michael Barnett, Richard Betts, Rachel Bronson, Richard Butler, Simon Chesterman, Alexander Cooley, Christopher Donnelly, Michael Doyle, V. Page Fortna, Willis Hintz, Lise Morjé Howard, Robert McClure, Christopher Miller, Roland Paris, Dmitry Ponomareff, John Rollins, Alan Ryan, Stephen Saideman, Arturo Sotomayor, Dina Schorr, Jack Snyder, and an anonymous reviewer for Columbia University Press. At Columbia University Press, Peter Dimock has been a supportive and responsive editor, and Leslie Bialler has been a terrific copy editor. Ingrid Gerstmann at IWPS and Nell Dillon-Ermers in the Barnard Political Science Department provided administrative (and emotional!) support for my work that far exceeded what I could have reasonably expected. And as always, I am grateful to my parents, Gordon and Lynette Marten, for their support and love.

This book is dedicated to my students, whose curiosity and insight keeps me inspired.

Kimberly Zisk Marten
March 2004

ENFORCING THE PEACE

ONE

PEACE, OR CHANGE?

"Even the lowliest men prefer being subjects to men of their own people rather than to any aliens."
—Leo Strauss (as quoted by James Atlas in the *New York Times*)

"Alien rule is intrinsically inconsistent with liberal western values; but there are worse things that can happen to any people."
—D.K. Fieldhouse, *Colonialism 1870–1945: An Introduction*

In the weeks and months following September 11, 2001, the citizens of New York City found themselves surrounded by United States military personnel as they went about their daily lives. Soldiers guarded every bridge and tunnel leading into the city. As police pulled over cars and trucks on the George Washington Bridge for routine inspections, military teams took part. Uniformed National Guard troops stood at every airport security gate in the metropolitan area, and pairs of soldiers carrying automatic rifles walked through the passenger waiting area at Newark Airport during the holiday season that December. Throughout lower Manhattan, military personnel checked everyone's identification, even blocks away from the World Trade Center site; for awhile only those who could prove they were residents were allowed into the area. At the National Guard Armory on Manhattan's Upper East Side, stern-looking soldiers in combat fatigues glared at passersby on the sidewalks, and occasionally blocked off a neighboring street or two for security reasons. Eighteen months later when the U.S. invaded Iraq and government-declared threat levels went up again, many of these scenes were repeated. Soldiers with automatic rifles patrolled the Port Authority Bus Terminal, combat tanks stood outside the toll gates at the Lincoln Tunnel, and one Wednesday morning a half-dozen Black Hawk helicopters hovered over the Manhattan skyline during rush hour.

In one sense, these measures made the population feel secure. The troops were there to protect the area from what appeared to be the very pressing threat of terrorism. Virtually everyone in the New York metropolitan area had lost at least a friend of a friend—if not someone closer—in the World Trade Center attack, and the city was on edge. The soldiers weren't there to hassle the average citizen; they were there to deter attacks by the people who wanted to disrupt those citizens' lives. Yet at the same time the military presence caused real psychological discomfort and insecurity. It is unnerving to see heavily armed and uniformed military troops walking around on a sunny day among civilians going about their ordinary business. There is a tinge of menace inherent in the appearance of armed soldiers, something that no amount of goodwill can entirely dissipate. Their presence also made the threat seem more real. It was difficult to forget that the country felt under siege when combat troops became a normal part of the scenery.

Now change this scenario, so that the uniforms are worn by foreign soldiers, most of whom need interpreters to communicate with the locals. Make the military presence go on for years, and make it much more intrusive, with soldiers not merely stationed at bridges, airports, and depots, but actually engaged in regular foot and vehicle patrols in heavily armed units down city streets. Then put the area's laws and institutions—political, educational, and economic—under the control of the same foreigners who send in most of the troops.

These alterations make the mood a little different, even when the soldiers hail from liberal democratic states, and even when their stated goals—protecting society and making it more secure—are the same. The dangers and threats may be just as real, and the citizens may know just as clearly that the troops are there in order to keep the peace. But the psychological balance shifts. Who knows what really motivates the presence of armed foreigners on one's own soil, especially when they are directing everything from traffic to the conduct of judicial proceedings? And who knows what the citizens truly value anymore, when the country seems to function as it does only because the foreign guns are still present?

Keeping Peace and Forcing Change

This book examines the use of military troops by liberal democratic states to keep the peace and rebuild order in foreign societies. Its focus is on the operations carried out under United Nations Security Council authorization in Haiti, Bosnia, Kosovo, and East Timor in the 1990s, but it also begins a tentative exploration of the initially more unilateral U.S. occupations of postwar Afghanistan and Iraq. The lessons of the 1990s have clear relevance for these more recent American cases—and for the second round of peacekeeping intervention that began in Haiti just as this book was going to press. Indeed in spite of the suspicion that some Washington officials have of multilateralism in general, and of the UN as an organization in particular, the administration of U.S. President George W. Bush found itself under increasing pressure to reach out to the international community to help share the burden of peacekeeping after wars it had waged. By late 2003, the American-led coalition in Afghanistan was sharing space with peacekeepers from the North Atlantic Treaty Organization (NATO) who had UN authorization to deploy across the country, and the American-led coalition in Iraq finally gained an official multi-state peace mission component under UN approval.

Despite their many differences, each of these newer operations differs markedly from the older and more traditional understanding of United Nations peacekeeping that is carried out by troops wearing blue helmets. It is time for us to change our understanding of the concept of "peace-keeping," even though some in the UN community resist this transformation. It used to be that UN peacekeeping was only about ensuring that ceasefires held in various world hotspots, and about trying to prevent the immediate outbreak of renewed fighting in situations where peace agreements were fragile. (These traditional goals have still been pursued recently by UN peacekeepers in some isolated cases, like Cyprus and the Ethiopian/Eritrean border.) It also used to be that UN peacekeeping was done with the full consent of all the parties to the conflict. What sets these newer operations apart is that they were designed to go far beyond such traditional purposes. The international community for the first time took responsibility for the functioning of political societies destroyed by civil war or tyranny. In each of these newer operations the presence of foreign military troops was used by outsiders to try to control political outcomes. In each of these newer cases some parties to the conflict had to be coerced into accepting the foreign military peacekeeping presence under threat of military attack, or indeed after they lost a war to the states who then sent in peacekeepers. In several cases—including Bosnia, Kosovo, Afghanistan and Iraq—there are significant factions to this day who do not recognize the legitimacy of the foreign troop presence in their countries, despite the UN mandates that cover those troops under international law.

In order to provoke a reconsideration of the design of these complex peacekeeping operations and of whether they have a realistic chance of establishing lasting political change in war-torn or post-tyrannical societies, this book explicitly compares them to the colonial occupations carried out by liberal democratic states at the turn of the twentieth century. Comparing complex peacekeeping operations to this type of colonialism helps highlight the dilemmas associated with attempts to control foreign societies, especially since in both cases a fundamental goal has been to make these foreign societies look more like the West. While there are many crucial differences between peacekeeping and colonialism, which will also be explored in this book, the tendency of today's international community to shy away from the comparison out of fear of being tarred with the imperialist label actually clouds our ability to see and analyze modern operations clearly.

Complex Peacekeeping and Control

When new more complex peacekeeping operations were undertaken beginning in the mid-1990s, their goal was no longer limited to stopping the immediate threat of war. Instead, these operations were undertaken in an effort to move war-torn societies on to a liberal democratic path of political development. The hope was that by establishing new political values and institutions in these countries, the representatives of western society—since these operations have been uniformly led by states or coalitions representing western values—could create a more stable and secure international environment. By remaking societies, it was thought, the fundamental underlying causes of war could be removed. These operations have hoped to build global security by encouraging lasting political change in thorny world areas.

To distinguish this new type of operation from traditional peacekeeping, and to highlight its interwoven military, political, and economic components, I refer to these new kinds of missions as "complex peacekeeping operations." Others have called them peace enforcement, peace building, or peace maintenance operations (or sometimes just "peace operations"), but this proliferation of terms and the definitions that accompany them tends to confuse the issue rather than adding real analytic heft. The Brahimi Report, issued in 2000 by an expert panel convened by UN Secretary General Kofi Annan to evaluate these new missions, uses most of these terms interchangeably.[1] (Reportedly the question of whether to use the term "peacekeeping operations" or "peace operations" in the title of both the panel and the report caused so much controversy in the UN community that it almost undercut the group's work.) No two of these recent missions look exactly alike, since all of them have been structured in response to specific conditions on the ground where they are deployed. Yet all of them have evolved over time out of the first UN peacekeeping operations of the 1950s. Their designers have tried to learn from mistakes made earlier while adapting to contemporary circumstances. For these reasons, to keep the term "peacekeeping" while acknowledging the new complexity of these operations is a fitting choice.

The objectives of the international community in these new missions have been noble: to create stable, tolerant, more liberal and democratic regimes out of the wreckage of war-torn societies. In Haiti in 1994, the goal was to restore a nascent democracy that had been wiped out by a brutal military coup three years before, and to bring an end to the country's long history of violence and political mayhem under a series of malevolent dictators. In Bosnia in 1995 and Kosovo in 1999, the aim was to convince warring ethnic groups to lay down their arms, while staving off the temptation these groups faced to retaliate against each other for past wrongs. The hope was that the victims of ethnic cleansing could return to their homes and learn to live together in stable, integrated societies. In East Timor the objectives of international peacekeeping changed over time. The initial purpose of UN-backed intervention in 1999 was to rescue a newly independent territory from rampaging militias. The international community then followed this in 2000 with a plan to reinforce this territory's status as a newly sovereign state, separate from Indonesia, by helping it to create liberal democratic political and economic institutions from scratch. In Afghanistan and Iraq, the international community has wanted to shepherd in new regimes that would bring more stability and better human rights records to their countries than either the Taliban or Saddam Hussein did.

Intervention by military peacekeepers to help accomplish these goals seemed warranted in each case, because the societies in question would not move in these beneficial directions on their own after the trauma that they had undergone. Citizens needed to be protected from the bad actors among them who would otherwise undercut social and political progress, and both entrenched and emerging political leaders in these societies needed to be deterred from reverting to the intolerant and corrupt political and economic systems of the past. For these operations to be successful, the international community would have to act as a benevolent occupation force, serving to protect and oversee societies that were thought to be not yet ready to function by themselves. The goal has been to move these struggling societies toward the path of development that was taken by the liberal democratic states who dominate the international system today.

The international community, motivated by liberal democratic principles, in other words acted with the intention of controlling political developments in foreign societies. Yet to control a society from without, using force, brings up the specter of imperialism. The idea of making foreign societies look more like liberal western democracies is not new. Perhaps surprisingly to those who have not studied the subject before, it is one of the factors that motivated the imperialism practiced by liberal states—the United States, Great Britain, and France—at the turn of the twentieth century. A wide range of analysts have in fact remarked on the resemblance of peacekeeping to imperialism. Colonel Robert C. Owen of the U.S. Air Force notes, "The naked reality of peace operations is that they are the consequence of decisions by powerful outsiders to intervene in the affairs of less well-endowed local governments, groups, and factions. . . . [They] direct or facilitate the movement of the social, economic, and political affairs of others in directions that the intervening states believe they would not go without that application of power."[2] This sounds remarkably similar to the basic definition of empire proposed by Michael W. Doyle in his seminal book on the subject: "Empires are relationships of political control imposed by some political societies over the effective sovereignty of other political societies."[3]

Some more radical critics of today's peacekeeping go so far as to accuse the international community of practicing tyranny in complex peacekeeping operations, by forcefully imposing western liberal values on societies that are by nature based on patronage networks and nationalism.[4] Much of the population in each of the peace-kept countries of today may have initially welcomed in outside support, yet many have later resented the specific contours taken by peacekeeping operations as time has gone on. When control is exercised by foreigners, domestic preferences are not always heeded. It should be remembered, as well, that imperial occupations also relied for their success on the tacit support of at least segments of the colonized population.

Imperialism and Peacekeeping: A First Cut

There are many important differences between the imperialism of a century ago and the complex peacekeeping operations of the 1990s and beyond. Perhaps the most crucial is that imperialism was designed to take resources from the colonies for the benefit of the empires, while complex peacekeeping operations are designed with the intention of assisting target countries to become more self-sufficient. In those days intervention was carried out by states acting alone; today to be considered legitimate, intervention must be multilateral and carried out under the provisions of international law. Yet the idea of forceful intervention to create political and social change is common to both eras, and in both eras the powerful liberal democracies who led the interventions believed that such change would benefit both themselves and the target population. Their involvement in both eras was motivated at least in part by humanitarianism. Yet national interest in both eras played a significant role in their decisions.

Journalists now commonly argue that today's complex peacekeeping operations resemble imperialism.[5] John Laughland, in the British weekly *The Spectator*, compares the power of peacekeepers in Bosnia today to that held by British colonial officials from a century ago. Max Boot, former chief editorialist for the *Wall Street Journal*, argues that sending American troops on peacekeeping operations is like sending them to fight the small wars of the imperial era.[6] In 2002, Boot advocated the expansion of U.S. peacekeeping activities in Afghanistan to match those carried out by its quasi-colonial garrison in nineteenth-century Shanghai. Michael Ignatieff, in *The New York Times Magazine*, contends that UN agencies and humanitarian nongovernmental organizations (NGOs) in Afghanistan have an "inherently colonial" relationship with the local population. Even efforts made by international aid agencies to empower local people, he thinks, are just "the illusion of self-government joined to the reality of imperial tutelage."[7] In Bosnia, he suggests, "our need for noble victims and happy endings" is a "narcissistic enterprise," designed to force others to be like us. He asks, "what is empire but the desire to imprint our values on another people?"[8]

Calling UN-authorized peacekeepers "imperialists" isn't new. Peacekeeping troops from NATO in Bosnia and Kosovo have been branded imperialists by those who object to the politics of ethnic tolerance that the international community is trying to institutionalize there. Australian forces leading the INTERFET mission in East Timor in 1999 were labeled imperialists by their detractors, even though INTERFET included troops from a wide range of countries in Southeast Asia and the South Pacific and had the support of most local players. United Nations officials and representatives from the NGO community are often horrified that anyone might consider what they are doing the least bit colonial. They emphasize that their actions are humanitarian and are carried out with the cooperation of many countries, in accordance with international law. That hasn't stopped their critics.

To get foreign countries to do what the international community wants them to do, namely develop along liberal, democratic, humanitarian lines, peacekeepers have to use force to stop those who try to undercut them. They have to pick political winners and losers according to their adherence to particular values, and they have to monitor political behavior so that those who support particular outcomes in target societies can be selectively rewarded. While their ultimate goals and many of the means they used were different, that is exactly what the imperial powers of a century ago did, too.

These strategies usually failed to work over the long run. Picking new winners and losers according to their support for the occupying forces tended to disrupt long-standing social and political equilibria in foreign societies; and this bred resentment. When the imperial powers emphasized the desirability of liberal democratic ideals, they only highlighted the inconsistency of their own policies, where outsiders used force to control a foreign society rather than allowing it to determine its own path. Colonialism simultaneously often bred dependency on outside assistance to achieve societal and economic stability, even as that dependency was resented.

The complex peacekeeping cases discussed here have each faced those challenges as well. Yet if outsiders had not intervened, the populations of Haiti, Bosnia, Kosovo, and East Timor would have continued on their trajectory of violence and chaos—although in Haiti, the initial 1994 intervention failed to keep the country from reverting to that trajectory again a decade later. In postwar Afghanistan and Iraq, the belief was that power vacuums left in the wake of brutal authoritarian regimes go on attracting reactionary Muslim militants and stirring up longstanding ethnic conflict, while corrupt warlords and common bandits would remain unchallenged. The hope, perhaps misplaced, was that outside intervention could set these societies on a more stable and liberal political path. This is where the dilemma of complex peacekeeping arises. Liberal democratic publics believe that something must be done to stop the bloodshed that foreign societies inflict on themselves, especially when the victims are innocent people. Yet the notion that outsiders can control the direction of political development in foreign societies is very often illusory.

The Additional Dilemma of Multilateralism

It is hard enough to coax liberal democratic change out of a foreign society without seeming like an occupier. Beyond this, UN-authorized peacekeepers face an additional practical difficulty. To be considered legitimate, complex peacekeeping operations must be multilateral, representing the consensus of the international community that intervention is justified. This characteristic is what most separates them from imperialism in the eyes of many analysts. Drawing on the classic definition of multilateralism provided by John Gerard Ruggie, this means that they must be based on the participation of many different states (and in reality, of NGOs too) who have reached wide agreement on what the appropriate principles for conduct should be.[9] They must be nonexclusionary, welcoming all comers and not based on alliances of convenience. Yet this often makes coordination unworkable.

The foreigners involved in managing and carrying out these military interventions do not come from a single country or institution, but instead represent a diverse set of national and organizational interests and practices. Because they tend to be from liberal democratic states, the leaders are ultimately beholden to their domestic audiences. As Lisa L. Martin notes, multilateralism is usefully viewed as a means to an end, rather than an end in itself.[10] In this case, multilateralism is a means to legitimize foreign intervention that is being undertaken because it matches what the participants and their domestic audiences want to see happen. Each participating government is subject to differing and fickle approval ratings at home. This means that the participants in complex peacekeeping operations often champion a mutually incompatible variety of liberal democratic ideals. They do not share a common definition of what they hope to accomplish on the ground.

This is largely because no blueprint exists for how to create the perfect liberal democratic society. As several scholars have noted, including Roland Paris, Jack Snyder, and Karen Ballentine, there are elements of seemingly liberal and democratic developments that are self-contradictory. For example, pushing an economy toward market openness—a common liberal goal—can aggravate the class distinctions that motivated ethnic warfare and lead to a hardening of ethnic intolerance in society. To follow one liberal goal can undercut another. Loosening state controls over the media—which sounds good in theory in postautocratic states—can give hard-line nationalists a continuing public voice, by allowing them unfettered access to a free press.[11] If there were one agreed template to follow, about what to do when, the process of change might not be so thorny. But each foreign state and organization has its own ideas about what the direction of political change should be in the society in question and how it should be achieved. Since intervention is made legitimate by gaining wide agreement over its conduct, operations must be designed so as to be acceptable to the full spectrum of foreign participants, and this usually means that authority is parceled out while decisions are negotiated and second-guessed over time. Inconsistency is the inevitable result, even though everyone at base would like to see these societies move in the direction of accepting liberal democracy and its system of humane values.

These operations are further complicated by the need to gain support for the process of change from the people whose mindsets are supposed to be altered. Complex peacekeeping operations are in this sense doubly multilateral, since the agreement of multiple actors matters both in terms of how they are run from the outside, and in terms of how they are structured inside foreign societies. Not only must the international community as a whole, as represented by many different states, give its approval to the intervention process if it is to be considered legitimate. But also, simultaneously, the domestic society of the country where peacekeeping forces are deployed, as represented by many different political interests and actors, must somehow be encouraged to take "ownership" of the process of change. It is this ownership that in the end proves that peacekeeping was being done with the consent of those whose polities are being changed. The goal of the foreign troops has not been really to *force* people to form liberal democracies. Instead it has been to *convince* them that this is the rational thing to do, with force used only to nudge along those who otherwise disrupt this process. In this way, the local community can continue to move forward after the international community goes home.

The need for doubly multilateral legitimacy makes it even harder for complex peacekeeping operations to achieve their goal of controlling political developments abroad than it was for the imperialists of a century ago. The empires of Great Britain, France, and the United States did not try to make their subject colonial societies take ownership of the change they instilled, because they had no intention of withdrawing their occupation forces quickly. They made no effort to foster the widest possible political participation inside their colonies. Instead they tended to select, based on their own self-interests, a particular political group or class to receive most of their attention and resources in each location. They often tried to make that class more like themselves, for example through education, so that this select group would come to believe that their own interests lay in the continuation of the empire. This was believed to reduce the cost of maintaining the colonies. In the end, the imperial powers cooperated only with their favorites in the colonies and left the less fortunate members of those societies to their own fates.

Today, in contrast, political participation by a wide variety of actors is usually a measure that peacekeepers use to define the success of their efforts at achieving local ownership of the peace process. Peace will only be achieved, according to current wisdom, when a broad spectrum of societal groups—including people of differing ethnicities, for example—accepts the idea that the political system they live under is just and fair. Every group's voice must have the chance to have an impact on policy, and every group chased out of their homes by the violence of previous years should be encouraged to return and participate in this new political system. Peacekeeping is fundamentally about establishing justice for all in societies that have been unjust.[12] Some analysts argue that free political participation by the populace is the defining characteristic of true political sovereignty, and that intervening to reestablish such sovereignty justifies international military action.[13] Once that end-state is achieved, the peacekeepers can go home—which is what they most want to do.

The difficulty with making the pursuit of participation and equal justice the basis for peacekeeping strategy is that most of the societies where military peacekeepers are sent today have been torn apart by civil war, usually with roots stretching back into long histories of ethnic or class conflict. In some cases the states imposed on these areas are artificial constructs, not representing true societal affiliation. These societies are by definition deeply politically divided and threatened by internal violence and retribution. Letting all voices be heard can therefore lead to the reestablishment of illiberal policies by democratic means—policies that the international community vehemently opposes. Just because people are democratically elected does not mean that their policies will be just or even-handed. Yet if any voices are prevented from participating in the democratic process—such as the voices of ethnic nationalists or intolerant religious sects who claim they are only seeking the righting of past wrongs—accusations of injustice and imperialism ring out. This aggravates the dilemma of control by increasing the likelihood that liberal democratic ideals will be seen as inconsistent with each other. In Bosnia, for example, to ensure that tolerance is practiced by Serbian and Croatian hardliners who would much rather divide the country into separate ethnic states, the international community regularly ousts democratically elected officials and their appointees from office. This pattern of ousting sends the message to the Bosnian public that it is might, not voting, that makes right, even though the intention of the international community is to promote liberal democratic values. All of this further complicates the effort to coordinate the process of political change.

When there are many voices both within and outside a country, all of whom are trying to influence the direction of political reform during a messy transition period, it is hard to maintain a cohesive vision for the future. This is true of any political transition, but the situation is made more vexing because peacekeeping missions tend to be deployed in order to contain situations that are believed to threaten international security in areas of the world that have strategic value. In other words, they are sent to places that outside countries care passionately about, because they believe that their own interests depend on how the problems in those areas are resolved. Many states want a voice in the process, because many states have a stake in the outcome.

On the other hand, it is this very multilateralism that provides complex peacekeeping operations with international legitimacy. It is what separates them from colonial efforts. If a single country, acting on its own, decides to use military force to change the political configuration of a foreign country for the sake of its own security or economic well-being, the imperialist label will be attached to its actions and it must bear that burden. Everyone has to take on faith the argument that the intervening state has good intentions, because that state alone controls and oversees its policy choices.

By late 2003, U.S. soldiers (along with some closely allied forces) in postwar Afghanistan and Iraq had been engaged for many months (in Afghanistan, almost two years) in what amounted to complex peacekeeping operations outside the multilateral UN framework. In October 2003 NATO finally sought and gained UN authorization to engage in peacekeeping activities throughout Afghanistan, breaking out of the earlier mandate that limited their activities to the capital city of Kabul; and the United States finally sought and gained UN authorization (through Security Council resolution 1511) to lead a multinational peacekeeping force in Iraq, in the face of increasingly violent insurgency there and after a great deal of stalling. But these were de facto continuations of similar missions that the United States and its closest friends did without UN authorization earlier. Military forces had already been directing political, social, and economic developments on the ground with the goal of ensuring security and stability and creating more liberal and democratic societies out of the ashes of authoritarian regimes—in other words, they had been doing peacekeeping in all but the official title. These operations simply lacked the stamp of multilateral legitimacy that had been given to what were otherwise very similar operations in Haiti, Bosnia, Kosovo, and East Timor.

No one from the international community as a whole oversaw what the Americans and their allies were doing on the ground. In that sense, complex peacekeeping may have been coming full circle, as pundits began to talk about a new American empire. As the United States soon learned, unilateral (or small coalition) action may make operations simpler and easier to control, but it also makes maintaining political legitimacy more difficult.

It became easy for domestic opponents of these new regimes to tar those in power with the "imperialist lackey" label, and to gain support for their violent opposition to them. It also became hard for other countries to justify giving much postwar reconstruction assistance to these countries, when they were not permitted to control how their aid was used or to gain economic benefit from their participation. As the United States learned in Iraq, to ignore the call for multilateralism was to be stuck fighting a counterinsurgency war, with its attendant costs in life and treasure. If the United States had done a better job of creating a legitimate peacekeeping operation earlier on in Iraq, with more attention paid to the core tasks of security building, perhaps the ugliness that Iraq has become could have been avoided.

Failures at the Turn of the 21st Century

This intertwined set of problems—the desire by the international community to avoid being tarred with the imperial label while attempting to exert what amounts to political control over foreign societies; and the need to encourage multilateral participation to achieve legitimacy while avoiding inconsistency—sets the context for this book. Complex military peacekeeping operations in the 1990s became entangled in a terrible practical and moral dilemma: liberal democratic change cannot be forced on foreign societies using liberal democratic means.

Nowhere have the liberal democratic military peacekeeping operations of the 1990s created liberal democratic societies. They did not even create much forward momentum in that direction, in any of the countries where they were deployed. The cases will be discussed in more detail in later chapters, but a brief review of their results so far is warranted here.

In Haiti in 1994, the international community employed a series of halfway measures and found itself back at square one after years of intervention that accomplished little. After going into the country with great fanfare in 1994, peacekeepers finally withdrew again in 1999. When left to its own devices, without continuing international oversight, Haiti followed its well-worn historical path of political violence and class warfare, this time around with new players at the helm. Ten years after the military coup of 1991, not much of significance in Haiti had ultimately changed, despite years of international intervention to promote change. In 2004, the U.S. led a multinational peacekeeping operation under UN authority back into Port au Prince again, hoping that this time around it might have more lasting impact.

In the Balkans, in contrast, the international community went in with great political will and became a semi-permanent occupation force. Stability in both Bosnia and Kosovo endures to this day, but does so only because of the continuing presence of foreign military troops, years after the real war-fighting has stopped. International oversight is the only thing that keeps these areas on anything close to a liberal, multiethnic path of development. If foreign troops withdrew, both Bosnia and Kosovo would almost certainly reorganize themselves into ethnically divided territories that practiced illiberal policies toward minority groups.

Finally, the United Nations claims East Timor as a success story. The country attained independence from Indonesia, declaring its sovereign statehood in 2001, and no longer fears out-and-out warfare. Yet the continuing abject poverty of the country, and the violent rioting directed against foreigners in the capital city of Dili in December 2002, belies the notion that intervention created long-term liberal democratic stability. Foreign assistance is still desperately needed, yet the foreign presence is resented by those who lost the battle against independence, as well as by those whose hopes of a better future were raised only to be dashed when the country fell back into a sea of indifference.

In each one of these cases, peacekeeping fatigue eventually set in among the intervening forces. The states leading the operations wished to reduce their forces and save their resources for new problems that arose and appeared more central to their interests with time. The international community did succeed in ending the civil wars being fought on these territories (although in the case of Haiti that success proved fleeting); but occupation did not lead these countries toward a trajectory of liberal democratic development. The idea that peacekeeping operations could accomplish such a thing in torn societies appears to have been a failed experiment.

The administration of U.S. President George W. Bush, and especially the coterie of officials that have been labeled the new empire builders (led by Deputy Defense Secretary Paul Wolfowitz and Douglas Feith, Under-Secretary of Defense for Policy),[14] seemed to ignore this lesson of the 1990s. For many years U.S. defense officials in operations ranging from Haiti to Afghanistan had been eager to avoid the "colonial occupier" label.[15] They sometimes adopted inconsistent policies as a result, since their fear of being called imperialists encouraged them to shy away from commitments that could have cemented political change in areas of the world where U.S. security was at stake. By 2003 that fear evaporated, as many in Washington seemed almost to relish the idea of foregoing multilateralism and creating a new American liberal democratic empire. U.S.

officials seemed to believe that a postwar occupation in Iraq—this time without much of a multilateral component—could achieve liberal democracy through regime change. Looking back to the post–World War II occupation of Germany and Japan, and ignoring the difficulties the United States was already facing in Afghanistan, the administration adopted an optimistic best-case scenario for Iraq's future. It did so even though the population of Iraq was torn by internal ethnic conflicts, steeped in a desire for revenge against the Baath party supporters who had ruled so cruelly for so long, threatened by an upsurge of Islamic militancy among Shiites who were persecuted by the old minority Sunni regime, and surrounded by states with both the desire and the resources to interfere in Iraqi politics in a decidedly anti-liberal direction. Postwar Iraq was destined to end up looking a lot like other peace-kept societies had looked for the previous decade: unstable, violent, and with a population in need of protection by the international community.

The goal of the United States (and of the partners who eventually joined it in the occupation of postwar Iraq) turned out to be the same as the goal of complex peacekeeping missions has been: to win the voluntary support of the local population for outside military occupation that is designed to encourage political change. The aim, once again, was to cajole the society to move in a liberal democratic direction that it would not choose to take on its own. When the United States originally tried to do this without gaining multilateral legitimacy for its actions, the regime it put in place faced increasingly difficult domestic political challenges from those who labeled its supporters colonial puppets. It will be instructive in coming years to see if putting a UN patina on the occupation force truly changed that situation. The occupation will certainly create new winners and losers, and the losers will not give up quietly. And if real multilateral participation in the rule of postwar Iraq eventually occurs, then unless the lessons of the 1990s are learned, this occupation will face exactly the same dilemmas as those complex peacekeeping operations did. It will be plagued by inconsistency and mixed messages that leave the population perplexed, and far from the liberal democratic trajectory that was Washington's original hope when it went in to topple Saddam Hussein.

Plan of the Book

This book takes a deeper look at the comparison between peacekeeping and colonialism, focusing on the key concept that links the two: attempts by outsiders to control foreign societies. Similar political impulses have triggered and then undermined both types of foreign intervention. Powerful states have been the vital players in both eras, and the mistakes they made when they tried to control their colonies have been mirrored in later years (albeit in a better-intentioned, less violent, and more multilaterally sanctioned fashion) in their attempts to shape the future of societies torn by conflict or plagued by tyranny.

As noted above, this book focuses on one particular type of peacekeeping mission—the complex UN-authorized military operations that began to appear in the 1990s in Haiti, Bosnia, Kosovo, and East Timor, and that emerged in Afghanistan and Iraq as time went on—and on one type of colonial imperialism—the kind practiced by the liberal states of Great Britain, France, and the United States at the turn of the twentieth century. These particular forms of peacekeeping and colonialism were chosen for comparison because they have important characteristics in common. As both Boot and Ignatieff have noted, the *military* tasks required of today's peacekeepers in many ways resemble the tasks taken on by the military forces of the imperial era. In fact some of the techniques used by peacekeeping forces today have their doctrinal roots in that earlier time in history. There is an even more notable similarity in the key *political* goals lying behind the two kinds of operations, despite their many differences. Both types of operation have sought to institutionalize political change in societies where change would not happen without outside intervention, and both have required the use of force to achieve their goals.

Both types of operation have also been motivated at least in part by humanitarianism. My choice to study the liberal empires of a century ago is quite intentional. Unlike the colonialism practiced by the brutal King Leopold II of Belgium, for example, the colonialism practiced by London, Washington, and Paris was not simply about grabbing land or exploiting resources or exerting control over subject populations (although it certainly was about all of these things, as well). It was an attempt to remake other societies in the imperialists' own image, and to bring to them what were seen to be the benefits of western civilization. Colonialism as practiced by liberal states at the turn of the twentieth century, like many complex peacekeeping missions today, was designed to move foreign societies in the direction of adopting European and American political and economic values and institutions.[16] This fact sets both kinds of operations apart from the kinds of wars and invasions more typically associated with the use of force, where the goal is simple conquest or victory rather than institutional restructuring.

This book is not intended as a comprehensive history of either turn-of-the-twentieth-century colonialism or of the complex peacekeeping operations of recent times. Plenty of good histories of those events already exist. Instead it is designed as an analytic exercise, to evaluate the usefulness of attempts by outsiders to control political developments in foreign societies with the use of what amounts to military occupation. Both the imperialism practiced by liberal states a century ago and complex peacekeeping operations have been motivated by a desire to restructure weak and impoverished societies for the sake of security in the developed world. It would be a mistake for today's peacekeepers to ignore the lessons of history out of squeamishness about the imperial label. Now that some U.S. leaders seem to have contemplated the establishment of a new liberal democratic empire of their own, the lessons of both the imperial past and recent peacekeeping history have particular relevance, and one can only hope that American policymakers take heed. Empire and peacekeeping have become intertwined as never before.

Three particular findings stand out from the comparison. First, powerful states in both eras have lacked the political will that would be necessary to truly gain control over political developments in foreign societies. Even when apparently strong security motives have underpinned these operations, they have been plagued by inattention from their capitals, resulting in inconsistent actions and ultimately ineffective policies. We should not expect coherence in the goals or methods employed by liberal democratic states; instead, those states should limit the objectives they seek in order to avoid sending the mixed messages that undermine their efforts. Second, and closely related to the first, military organizations then as now are one of the factors contributing to the lack of clear direction we find on the ground. Their natural tendency to reward their members for seeking battlefield glory, combined with the likelihood of either too little or too much oversight from civilian leaders back home, complicates the process of keeping the peace. Yet third, the imperial era makes clear that when properly directed to do so, disciplined soldiers can do a good job of providing public order—something that today's political leaders should be emphasizing as the size of peacekeeping tasks in the world outstrips civilian resources. The tasks performed by imperial soldiers in many ways match what is being asked of today's peacekeepers, and we should therefore not pretend that peacekeeping tasks are unprecedented or out of the realm of military competence. When these three findings are combined, it means that peacekeepers should try to limit their goals but expand their expectations of what military forces can reasonably do. Rather than trying to transform foreign societies, peacekeepers should be directed toward providing security and preventing anarchy in unstable regions of the world.

Chapter 2 provides an overview of how complex peacekeeping operations evolved in the 1990s. This chapter demonstrates that complex peacekeeping today, unlike the UN operations of the past, is centered on the idea of trying to control foreign societies. The goals of the international community underwent a transformation in this period, from the traditional peacekeeping operation's purpose of merely stopping war, to the more intrusive aim of shaping the political development of previously war-torn societies. Liberal democratic societies were thought to be less likely to go to war again in the future, and therefore political transformation came to be seen as the ultimate goal of humanitarian intervention. This is where the dilemmas of control, as well as the resemblance to colonial operations of the past, began to arise.

Chapter 3 explores the motives underlying the colonialism practiced by the liberal great powers a century ago, and juxtaposes them against those impelling the complex peacekeeping operations of the 1990s and today. This chapter demonstrates that despite all of their differences, both types of operation were pursued for a similar combination of reasons that straddled national security interests and humanitarianism. The balance between the two sets of motives in the two eras differed; humanitarianism was more of an afterthought in the colonial period than it is today. Yet the prospect of controlling foreign political developments in both eras served the security interests of the intervening states, even as it furthered their humanitarian purposes as they were defined at the time. It is thus worth considering the difficulties that the colonial powers faced in getting their goals met. In both eras, the international community was divided between the advanced states on the one hand, who had long ago succeeded in creating liberal democratic political institutions for themselves and felt justified in sharing their wisdom in these matters with others, and subject territories on the other, who needed the helping hand of outsiders to move forward into a better future.

Chapter 4 details an additional surprising political similarity between the imperial and complex peacekeeping eras: the absence of sufficient political will on the part of the intervening states, both empires and peacekeepers, to ensure that what their capitals intended was actually possible given the resource constraints they faced. Then as now, attempts to control foreign territory for the sake of external security became mired in inadequate political will to maintain consistent policies and excessive concerns about cost. Within this basic framework of similarity, the two eras were indeed different in important ways. The colonial era witnessed the arbitrary decisions and atrocities of colonial governors who were out of the control of their capitals and publics back home. The peacekeeping era instead witnessed the deployment of security forces who were discouraged for political reasons from doing enough to actually maintain security. Yet the ultimate consequences in the two eras were similar nonetheless, in that the intervening states, a century apart, kept their attention and interest focused elsewhere, and their ability to direct change in foreign societies suffered as a result.

Chapter 5 uses the cases of NATO operations in Bosnia and Kosovo to examine the military tasks performed on complex peacekeeping operations. On the one hand, what is being asked of peacekeepers today is quite similar to the actions performed (often successfully) by imperial soldiers a century ago. On the other hand, the need for multilateral coordination of military activities today makes them much harder to plan well and perform right. Multilateralism is the one thing that removes any hint of individual state gain from what might otherwise appear to be a colonial effort—an element that was missing in earlier times, and was again missing in U.S. policy toward Iraq throughout most of 2003. Yet the need for multilateral cooperation is what often most undermines the effectiveness of such intervention in today's world, as multiple actors pursue differing agendas within the rubric of liberal democratic development. This is true even in the NATO alliance, whose members are presumed to share an underlying political and security vision. The chapter concludes by comparing NATO peacekeeping cases in the Balkans to the Australian-led intervention in East Timor in 1999, where multilateral, UN-authorized participation in the mission was managed by a single lead state, with a greater degree of success than what was seen in the Balkans. Australian actions taken then can serve as a model for future peacekeeping operations now—something of particular relevance as this book was going to press, as the United States began to lead UN authorized multilateral operation in both Iraq and Haiti.

In the final chapter I turn to the question of what a potential solution to these twin dilemmas of control and multilateralism might look like. What this chapter proposes in places such as Afghanistan, Iraq, and Haiti, where international control is necessary to prevent anarchy from overwhelming the security interests of liberal democratic states, is a new form of peacekeeping. Unlike traditional peacekeeping, it recognizes the need for robust military force to be used flexibly by interested state actors. Unlike the complex peacekeeping of the 1990s, however, it recognizes that attempting to control a country's political society through the use of outside intervention is usually both inefficient and unworkable. This new model, which I call "security-keeping," limits intervention by states after a war or humanitarian crisis to the more traditional peacekeeping goals of ending the fighting and restoring basic security, rather than attempting the kind of political and economic control that was tried in Bosnia, Kosovo, and East Timor.

At the same time it encourages outside states to employ military forces flexibly and over the long term, so that new governments have the opportunity to truly gain a foothold in controlling their own territory before the international community withdraws. It requires reconfiguring the reward systems inside military organizations—especially in the United States, which because of its immense relative wealth and power will be called on to play a leading role in most of these operations—to recognize that peacekeeping is a necessary component of the national interest in an era where anarchy abroad is a major threat to the stability of liberal democratic states. This chapter draws out the lessons from the stories told in previous chapters, and presents a set of policy recommendations for those who would attempt to intervene in order to keep the peace abroad today.

TWO

PEACEKEEPING AND CONTROL

Vitina, Kosovo, April 2002

The American platoon, wearing Kevlar helmets and bulky flak jackets over their camouflage gear, left their humvees and moved out on a foot patrol. These patrols happened several times a day in Vitina, now a relatively peaceful town in the American-led military peacekeeping sector of Kosovo. Soldiers armed with large automatic weapons walked at the edges of the main patrol, scanning the surroundings for trouble.

Today was Wednesday, market day. Hundreds of townspeople milled around the soldiers, seemingly without fear. Most of the people were on foot, but some drove trucks or tractors. One tractor pulled an open trailer, on which was perched a calf. Brightly colored stalls sold everything from live, trussed-up chickens to newly made wooden cabinets, and fruit and vegetable sellers lined the streets. Albanian music blared from stalls selling CDs. Small boys slapped high-fives with the soldiers, and groups of teenage girls giggled as they threaded their way, hand in hand, past the troops. Through their local interpreters, the American soldiers chatted occasionally with passers-by, looking in particular for information about either smuggling or ethnic disturbances in town. One man tried to interest the soldiers in some rolled-up posters of local scenery he was selling, but the soldiers were forbidden by U.S. military regulations from buying anything off base. This kept a certain distance between the troops and the populace. Later there would be random vehicle inspection points set

(continued)

Vitina, Kosovo, April 2002 (*continued*)

up, checking for guns, drugs, or illegally shipped cigarettes that circumvented the taxes the internationally led administration of Kosovo imposed on imports.

Before the war in Kosovo, Vitina had had a troubled history. Over the years its population had shifted back and forth between being dominated by ethnic Albanians and Serbs, depending on how political developments favored one group over the other. Now, according to the American forces, it was 91 percent Albanian, and the remaining Serbs were mostly elderly people who were there either because they lacked the money to move back to Serbia proper, or because they wanted to die at home. The rest had fled in fear of revenge attacks from the ethnic Albanians, following NATO's victory over Slobodan Milosevic in June 1999. The Americans had tried to encourage ethnic Serb merchants to come into town on market days to sell their goods, but so far with little success. Those on the ethnic Serb side of the river that cut through town didn't mingle much with the Albanians thronging the market.

At the end of their patrol the soldiers crossed the bridge to the town's Serbian Orthodox church. One wall of gold-embossed icons inside the church dated from the Middle Ages. Guard towers built by the Americans loomed over both entrances to the walled church compound, which also included the residence of a key religious leader, and coils of concertina wire surrounded the rest. The church was guarded 24 hours a day by American soldiers dressed in "full battle rattle," automatic weapons at the ready. The commanders of the American sector would like to remove the guards and use their scarce resources elsewhere, but there is no one else to do the job. The local (primarily ethnic Albanian) police say they will investigate if anyone harms the church, but insist that guarding religious buildings is not their responsibility. Awhile back in the nearby town of Podgorce, the Americans had tried removing a similar set of church guard posts after months of seeming peace. Within hours of the American withdrawal, the Podgorce Serbian church had burned to the ground. It is generally believed that if the Americans were to leave Vitina, the Serb population here would have to leave as well.

Two members of the foot patrol relieved the guards at the Vitina church, and the platoon returned to its humvees for the ride back to base. It was another ordinary day in Kosovo, where ethnic harmony was absent but ethnic peace was preserved by foreign troops. Experts agreed: there was no reasonable prospect that international military forces could leave the territory anytime soon.

As the Vitina example makes clear, international peacekeeping operations have changed drastically in recent years. While some more traditional UN missions are still in place (as in Cyprus), and a few new ones in the old style (as in Ethiopia and Eritrea) have been created, the trend has moved toward operations that blur the distinctions between peacekeeping, postwar societal reconstruction, and forceful intervention. These new operations intrude much more deeply into the domestic political institutions of the societies where they are based, and the use of military force (especially to achieve deterrence, protection, and law enforcement) is intimately connected with their attempts to create political change in foreign societies. If liberal, tolerant political cultures refuse to emerge on their own, then foreign troops will attempt to facilitate them.

Military personnel on peacekeeping missions have taken on the roles of police officers and humanitarian aid decisionmakers in the service of their governments. The governments that send the troops are often the same ones who help direct the path that political developments take in the societies where military operations are deployed. The overall goal of the international community in these cases, led by the states of North America, Western Europe, and Oceania, has been to build liberal democratic political institutions and to foster tolerant and cooperative social orders in societies where these things would not occur naturally on their own.

These goals are decent and progressive. They speak to the desire of good Samaritans throughout the world to stand up for the rights and dignity of the dispossessed and unfortunate. Yet they raise a set of ethical and practical dilemmas. The international community believes itself to be acting on behalf of popular self-determination, in areas of the world where brutal autocracies have silenced democratic expression and have arbitrarily picked political winners and losers. But what should be done when unbridled popular self-determination would lead to an illiberal and intolerant outcome in a foreign country? As Fareed Zakaria has pointed out, democratic states are not necessarily liberal, and attempts to foster democracy may result in policies that the liberal international community finds distasteful.[1] In the example outlined above, independent democratic governance in Kosovo—where many of the dominant ethnic Albanians retained their distrust and hatred of the ethnic Serbs whom they saw as their former persecutors—would likely have led to the expulsion or marginalization of Serbs as a group. This is something that the international community does not want to tolerate, and that is why American troops have been guarding Serbian churches.

A further dilemma arises because the international community is using military force to try to ensure that a favored set of democratic liberal institutions becomes accepted in the country in question. In Kosovo, for example, a majority of both the ethnic Albanian and ethnic Serb populations would probably have favored partition of their territory along ethnic lines, since that would give each of them a sense of security and control over their destiny. But the international community did not want to allow that to happen because ethnic separation would undermine the message of tolerance it wanted to send. There was concern that if ethnic separatism were to be tolerated here, it would encourage nationalists in other states to undertake similar ethnic cleansing campaigns without fear of international reprisal. Yet what message has the peacekeeping regime sent the population of Kosovo about how politics really operates? If foreign troops are used to impose institutions against the will of a domestic majority, it is still might that determines right inside that society. The only question then remaining is whether the good guys or the bad guys are the stronger element. If liberal democratic outcomes are imposed by outsiders rather than truly freely chosen, what will happen when the foreign military forces leave? Finally, if the answer is that those forces can't leave until years or perhaps generations pass and the societal culture changes to accept the validity of the new institutions, how do the powerful states of the world deal with the resulting practical problems of overextension and limited resources that they face, so that halfway, temporary measures don't become the politically expedient alternative?

This chapter describes how these dilemmas arose in the peacekeeping operations of the 1990s. Members of the international community, especially the wealthy liberal western democracies who have typically led complex peacekeeping operations, have a tendency to seesaw back and forth on these questions, either doing so much for a society that their presence is resented as an intrusion, or doing so little that their presence is resented for its half-heartedness. The world casts about for the correct combination of trying to force change on recalcitrant societies, while trying to encourage those societies to "own" the process of change themselves. The question that keeps on returning is how much control outsiders can and should try to exert over societies where western enlightenment values—of individualism, tolerance, and appreciation for the marketplace of both goods and ideas—are absent. At what point does the effort to exert control become self-defeating, and even counterproductive to the international community's goals?

The Evolution of Peacekeeping Operations

The idea that peacekeeping forces can help influence political trajectories in the societies where they are deployed is a new one. Peacekeeping didn't used to be so complex, costly, or dangerous; it didn't used to try to do so much. When "peacekeeping" as a concept was first invented in response to the Suez canal crisis of 1956[2] (the concept does not appear in the UN Charter), the international military forces deployed on such operations were used for a very different purpose from today. Their main mission then was simply to bolster the confidence of each side involved in a ceasefire that the fighting had truly stopped. Traditional peacekeeping forces monitored each side's military activity and reported what they observed. They often provided a buffer against a resumption of fighting, by deploying in border regions so that they would serve as likely victims of any renewed military attacks. This was thought to deter both sides from resuming the battle, as the international community would supposedly be outraged if peacekeepers were killed—although it is questionable whether that proved true, since UN facilities in Lebanon, for example, have repeatedly come under attack. Sometimes traditional peacekeepers also collected the weapons of forces who were voluntarily disarming, and oversaw exchanges of prisoners of war.

International military personnel then went in with the full agreement of all the parties to the conflict. Indeed, they were usually asked in by the parties themselves, who believed that the impartiality of the multinational troops made them trustworthy observers of the situation. They served under United Nations command. The UN Secretary General would appoint the head of each military operation, usually choosing an officer from a neutral country located far from the region where fighting had occurred. Battalions of soldiers were provided to these missions by a wide variety of neutral countries. These countries had varying motives for doing this, but were not particularly interested in the outcome of the conflicts at hand. Some so-called "middle powers" in the international system believed that contributing troops to UN operations would bring them greater respect and authority in international institutions, allowing them to exercise more voice in international security issues than they would otherwise be able to do.[3] Canada and India are examples of countries that frequently participated in UN peacekeeping operations for this apparent reason. Other very poor countries seemed simply to value the money the UN sent them, up to $1,000 per soldier per month,[4] which more than covered their costs and provided a boost to their defense ministry budgets. During the cold war, the great powers almost never donated troops to UN operations, in large part because to do so would appear to violate the impartiality that the UN was supposed to maintain in every operation. At that time, the Soviets and Americans took sides in virtually every conflict anywhere in the world.

The goals of the peacekeepers in previous times were not complicated, and their work was often dull. General Lewis Mackenzie noted that the major problem Canadian officers faced in that first peacekeeping mission in the Gaza strip in 1963 was that their soldiers drank too much because they didn't have enough work to do.[5] A few years later in Cyprus, he recalled that the soldiers sometimes did have shots fired at them from the formerly warring sides, but said that the shots appeared to be designed to miss.[6] Another retired Canadian officer who served in the Cyprus mission jokingly called it "Club Med, in comparison to what these guys do today," since he remembers spending most of his time there at the beach.[7] Traditional peacekeepers used their military training to carry out traditional military activities in ways that provided reassurance after ceasefires had been attained. They did not get involved in trying to create political change. (The one exception was the controversial ONUC mission to Congo in the early 1960s, which was transformed mid-mission into an attempt to put down regional rebel resistance against the authorities in the capital.[8])

Traditional peacekeepers were not assigned to help international aid agencies decide which villages were deserving of assistance, and which were recalcitrant and hence undeserving of help. Nor were they there to control ethnically motivated rioting and mob violence in the absence of honest local police. They did not attempt to oversee the humane treatment of displaced people returning home after a war, to ensure the equitable handling of the concerns of ethnic minorities, or to stop the smuggling of guns and drugs across porous borders. (All of these things are tasks that peacekeepers do perform today.) They were not there, in other words, to control political events on a piece of occupied territory. In fact traditional peacekeeping operations were usually set up in empty strips of land where no civilians were likely to be present. As Erwin A. Schmidl notes, they were most successful when they operated in the desert.[9]

The peacekeeping operations which began to emerge in the early 1990s look quite different from this. Many scholars and policy analysts have written detailed histories of these developments, and it is not necessary to repeat those histories here.[10] The striking change was that the United Nations became willing to get involved in civil conflicts, not just wars between sovereign states, in areas of the world ranging from Cambodia to Somalia and Bosnia to Haiti, where the underlying level of intractable violence and political uncertainty was extraordinarily high. The notion of monitoring simple ceasefires became meaningless in conflicts where the warring parties were not sovereign states but informal rebel groups with factional splits. There was often no way to determine definitively which party had ordered a ceasefire to be broken. The motive for war was often no longer simply to change geographical boundaries but to divide political spoils inside societies; and the conflict was over who would control the wealth and who had the power to allocate it.

This meant, in the eyes of the international community, that peace would now come only through change in domestic political institutions, especially electoral and legal and judicial systems. The international community hoped that if all members of a conflict-ridden society could achieve adequate political representation and the opportunity for economic advancement, then peaceful competition would replace war as the primary means for conflict resolution. Perhaps the best statement of the international community's sentiments on these matters is contained in the August 2000 "Report of the Panel on United Nations Peace Operations," convened by UN Secretary General Kofi Annan and led by Lakhdar Brahimi. Peace operations are thought to encompass the activities of peacemaking, peacekeeping, and peace-building, and the latter category is said to include "reintegrating former combatants into civilian society, strengthening the rule of law . . . , improving respect for human rights . . . ; providing technical assistance for democratic development, and promoting conflict resolution and reconciliation techniques," among other things.[11] The international community wanted political change to last in war-torn societies that had earlier been subject to the whims of corrupt and sadistic leaders, which meant that the United Nations had to change its traditional approach to peacekeeping. The goal was no longer just to stop the fighting, but also to fix the political and societal conditions that had made war seem attractive to those who waged it.

At first the international community struggled to address these new, complex humanitarian crises with minor modifications of traditional peacekeeping tools. These attempts largely failed. Throughout the early 1990s, the United Nations learned again and again that halfway measures were futile. Yet repeatedly, the international community raised high hopes for lasting peace while deploying inadequate resources, with insufficient political will to see the process through to its conclusion. Members of the international community, especially the wealthy western states who had sufficient resources to assume the lead, were reluctant to take on the burden of imposing change on foreign societies. As a result, change did not occur.

The Failures of the Early 1990s

The decade of complex peacekeeping operations began with a partial success, as what was originally designed to be a more traditional operation—

the UNTAC mission deployed under UN command to Cambodia between 1992 and 1993—was able to adapt on the ground to some of the complex circumstances it faced. Following the achievement of a ceasefire between forces fighting a long civil war, the primary goal of the mission was to ensure security in the country so that presidential elections could go safely forward. As would become standard in other missions as time went on, the UNTAC operation was plagued by inadequate resources, especially too few civilian police personnel, and by the inherent difficulties the UN always faces in coordinating troop activities among the different states who donate forces.

The military component of the UNTAC mission was unable to achieve its original mandates of disarming the various factions that had fought Cambodia's bloody civil war, and of establishing a neutral political environment throughout the country in the months leading up to democratic elections. The idea that lightly armed troops under traditional impartial rules of operation could do this was an illusion. Yet UN military troops did succeed in adapting to a different set of needs that they discovered on the ground after they arrived. The police protection that had been envisioned for international poll workers and voters turned out to be inadequate, so military troops, led by their Australian commander Lt. General John Sanderson, stepped in to provide security instead, even though that technically exceeded their mandate. They also succeeded in establishing a successful mine-clearing operation, and educated local Cambodians to take over the process themselves. Sanderson in particular is further credited with convincing the brutal Khmer Rouge faction in Cambodia to cooperate with the international community to a surprising degree,[12] despite its unwillingness to forswear violence. Military officers, in other words, turned out to be good diplomatic negotiators.

Political order was never completely established in the country, and Cambodian civilians never gained a satisfactory level of personal security.[13] Retribution killings and other forms of political violence remained common. Nonetheless, civilian UN officials also claimed some significant successes in the operation. They reworked Cambodia's governmental institutions to make them more compatible with democratic rule. Elections were successfully held, and a new regime was voted in.

Ultimately, however, intervention by the international community failed to accomplish the goal of achieving lasting political change in Cambodia. Political violence continued long after the UNTAC mission went home, and a 1997 military coup heralded the return of autocratic rule in the country.[14] In the absence of continuing oversight by the international community, liberal democratic change did not endure. No one from the outside world had a sufficient stake in the outcome, or was willing to provide sufficient resources, to maintain the trajectory that the 1993 elections set. The international community began to understand that the old model of peace keeping, based on the impartiality of the players rather than any strong state interest in the outcome of the crisis, needed rethinking.

The mixed outcome of the Cambodia operation was followed by the first dramatic failure of the new era, as the international community attempted to grapple with the difficult new circumstances of peacekeeping. This failure occurred in a series of missions to the east African state of Somalia, during the period 1992–1995. The original goal of the first UN–commanded peacekeeping mission there had been simply to feed the starving population, in a country where warlords intercepted all the emergency relief that crossed the border in order to resell it on the black market. With time it became clear that a stronger military presence in Somalia was required to protect humanitarian aid workers; the old model of impartial troop deployments was inadequate for these new circumstances. The strongest Somali warlord, Mohammed Aideed, was a particular thorn in the UN's side as he continued to attack aid convoys even after the UN-commanded troops arrived.

A new and separate U.S.-commanded mission was deployed under UN Security Council authorization to try to deal with this problem, but failed to establish sufficient coordination with the ongoing UN-commanded mission on the ground. At times the political purposes of the two missions seemed at odds with each other. U.S. leaders who saw the UN bureaucracy as inefficient and even corrupt wanted to avoid being tainted by their contribution to the operation. In the words of U.S. Army colonel Kenneth Allard, "What aggravated this situation . . . was a perception problem of avoiding even the appearance of having our forces under UN command."[15] The Pentagon, supported by key Republican congressional leaders, wanted to maintain American control over U.S. troops, and seemingly did not recognize the difficulties that complete independence created in the midst of an ongoing and overlapping UN operation.

One particular sore point was the question of how Aideed should be treated, and whether he should be punished for his actions. Some members of the UN-commanded mission wished to maintain the traditional peacekeeper's neutrality toward all the players in the civil conflict. This was reinforced by the fact that Aideed had been a diplomatic player in years past, serving for awhile as Somalia's ambassador to India, and had friends among those states who were big donors to UN operations. India indeed had a large number of peacekeeping troops in Somalia. The U.S. forces, on the other hand, were specifically tasked by the UN Security Council to go after Aideed, in an attempt to capture him or at least curtail his ability to operate freely. When the poor coordination of missions led by two different authorities was combined with a muddled understanding of the international community's ultimate political purposes in the country, the results were tragic.

The tragedy is chronicled in the popular movie *Black Hawk Down*, drawn from the book of the same title written by Mark Bowden, who interviewed dozens of both Americans and Somalis involved in the events of October 1993. Eighteen American soldiers and more than 1,000 Somalis were killed in a marketplace fire-fight in the capital of Mogadishu, after U.S. forces attempted on their own to capture some of Aideed's top men in an area where Aideed was buoyed by large numbers of civilian supporters with guns.[16] Two of the dead U.S. soldiers' bodies were dragged through the streets by the warlord's armed vehicles afterwards, and graphic footage of these events was broadcast to the U.S. public by CNN and other media sources. The perception arose, especially within the Pentagon and among outspoken Republicans in the U.S. Senate, that American soldiers were being killed far from home for no good reason. The United States military gradually withdrew from the mission, and became reluctant to involve itself in future humanitarian efforts where a clear-cut sense of national interest was not at stake.

No other state stepped in to take the lead after the American withdrawal. As a result, what had been some very successful efforts at refugee relief and local institution-building in the earlier days of the Somali peacekeeping mission were overturned as chaos returned to the country.[17] Without a robust force deployment by a lead state with the will to remain, the warlords managed to drive the UN away. A decade later, Somalia continued to be a leading example of a failed state, with no real central government to provide for the protection and well-being of its citizens.[18]

Immediately on the heels of the Somalia debacle came the Rwandan genocide.[19] This time around, the UN Security Council did not even attempt to grapple with the disconnect between the mandate and resources of the traditional peacekeeping operation already on the ground in the country, and the reality of the events that it faced. In spring 1994 more than 800,000 people in the small central African state of Rwanda, mostly innocent civilians who were ethnic Tutsis, were massacred by their fellow citizens who were ethnic Hutus. The butchering of neighbors by neighbors was fomented by extremist Hutus who had taken charge of the country's government, broadcast ethnic hate messages on the radio, and stockpiled machetes to hand out to their frenzied supporters. These extremists saw themselves as gaining retribution for the humiliations of an earlier era, when ethnic Tutsis had ruled the country and relegated them to the status of an underclass.

A United Nations peacekeeping force of 2,000 troops was deployed in Rwanda at the time, designed to act as a traditional separation and monitoring force between the Hutu-dominated government and an armed, largely Tutsi rebel organization that had been fighting it. But the international community did not take account of the Rwandan government's hatred of all *ethnic* Tutsis. Most Tutsis in the country did not support the rebel force, and in contrast to the simultaneous war going on at that time in the Balkans, the Rwandan civil war did not seem on the surface to be about ethnicity. UN troops were authorized to act only as a traditional buffer force between the government and rebels, and were prohibited from taking any action to stop the violence among civilians. Their commander was in fact repeatedly told to continue to work with the Rwandan government, since the UN was there with that government's permission. The traditional notion that peacekeepers were there with the consent of the host state limited what those in Rwanda could do.

As signs of impending government-instigated mass violence began to appear, the commander of this UN force, Canadian General Romeo Dallaire, made repeated requests to the United Nations to beef up his operation with more troops and a broader, stronger mandate. His requests were denied. Neither the UN Department of Peacekeeping Operations nor the Security Council paid much attention to the warnings, even though we now know that the international diplomatic community received adequate intelligence about what was happening on the ground and should have been aware that genocide was a real possibility. As a result of the international community's failure to act, Dallaire's peacekeepers were forced to watch helplessly as the genocide unfolded. Some Belgian troops on the UN mission were themselves butchered in the massacre.

Dallaire testified afterward that if only he had been given 5,000 adequately armed troops, along with the authorization to use force to seize key points, patrol the streets, and disarm those who were threatening others, the carnage could have been prevented. Many seasoned observers with military and peacekeeping experience second Dallaire's estimation. Even those who disagree with his complete analysis believe that early action by a robust peacekeeping force could have saved many thousands of lives.[20] Instead the international community failed to deploy military personnel in a way that would have changed the political situation in Rwanda, fearing the danger both to their own personnel and to the UN's reputation if another peacekeeping disaster were to happen. Especially following the earlier debacle in Somalia, the United States government was unwilling to become involved in what was seen as yet another doomed humanitarian military mission in Africa. This reluctance to provide leadership to the rest of the international community has been singled out by most observers as the major cause of the UN's failure to act.

The next year, to add to the carnage plaguing the world, the newly independent Balkan country of Bosnia and Herzegovina witnessed the horrors of yet another ethnic massacre, this one in the town of Srebrenica. A UN-commanded peacekeeping mission, UNPROFOR, had been sent to the former Yugoslavia in 1992 after several of its republics were recognized as independent countries. The hope was that UN involvement could dampen what everyone recognized was a tinderbox of ethnic nationalist conflict. Forces were deployed under a traditional peacekeeping mandate to try to stop war in its tracks by acting as a buffer between the parties, but the troops quickly learned that they were inadequately armed to deal with the violence they found on the ground. They also learned that to remain impartial toward the various warring sides didn't make sense in the face of the murderous ethnic cleansing, including death camps, massacres, and mass rapes, that was sweeping the region.[21] As time went on, UNPROFOR operations were further hampered by the kind of coordination problems that had plagued the mission in Somalia. This time, there were disagreements and unclear lines of control between the UN-commanded forces on the ground, and supporting strike aircraft from NATO, which had been authorized by the UN Security Council to lend force to the UN mission after the challenges of ethnic warfare became clear.

These factors together all played a role in the 1995 tragedy. The UN had established a supposed "safe area" in the Bosnian town of Srebrenica, where Bosnian Muslim civilian refugees would be protected from the Bosnian Serb paramilitary groups who were trying to persecute them. But lightly armed Dutch peacekeeping troops on the UN mission were unable to stop the brutal murder of thousands of Muslims after Serbs overran the town. (It turned out that some Muslim forces had illegally retained guns inside the safe area. They were accused of using the town to stage strikes against the Serbs, who felt justified in retaliating against them, even though a later UN investigation found no evidence to support the claim.) Once again there were political disagreements within the international community about the importance of maintaining peacekeeper impartiality. Some advocates of traditional peacekeeping operations feared that if peacekeepers were perceived to be taking sides, they would then become targets of the Bosnian Serb paramilitary soldiers. (This fear turned out to be correct; some Canadian soldiers on the UN mission were taken hostage and used as human shields by Bosnian Serb fighters, and some French troops on the

UN mission were picked off by snipers.) These concerns prevented NATO forces from intervening in Srebrenica in time to stop the massacre.[22] Men and boys were separated from the women and girls in the town, without interference from the UN troops; approximately 7,000 males were systematically executed, with their bodies dumped in mass graves. It was this final failure of the international community to stop suffering and murder, while being forced to take sides in a brutal conflict anyway, that caused the wealthy western states to push for change in how peacekeeping operations would be undertaken in the future. Three tragedies, the last in Europe, were finally enough to cause change.

Complex Military Peacekeeping as a Concept

Led by the West European and North American states in the United Nations, the international community plunged into rethinking the purpose and design of peacekeeping operations. Peacekeepers now encountered not merely more violence among the fighting parties, but also a much greater threat to their own safety and ability to operate. This meant that they needed better armament and better coordination. The very presence of peacekeepers changed the political balance inside countries, since even if state parties to the conflicts accepted the international community's involvement at a technical level, these states did not always control the proxy groups who were actually involved in the fighting (or at least they found it convenient to pretend that they did not control them). Reassurance about the durability of ceasefires and the recognition of geographical boundaries was no longer sufficient to stop the fighting; wars were caught up in the design of domestic political institutions. As peacekeepers encountered incidents of atrocities committed against civilians by the warring parties, doubts grew about the wisdom of the old UN policy of absolute impartiality. To protect civilian populations against harm required the international community to take sides, and to declare that some of those engaged in the war had perpetrated wrongful acts that required punishment.

All of these factors caused the states sending troops on these missions to rethink their priorities. Operations had become very difficult, very expensive, and very dangerous, in a way that traditional peacekeeping didn't used to be. Peacekeeping began to look much more like war-fighting than it used to. After a brief period of euphoria following the end of the cold war about the chances for peacekeeping to change the world—exemplified by then-UN Secretary General Boutros Boutros-Ghali's calls for the United Nations to put political divisions behind it and intervene in the face of virtually any threat to what he called "human security"[23]—what emerged was a rather cynical (if realistic) sense in the international community that everything hinged on "political will."

Such will is something that powerful and wealthy states tend not to display very often in the service of altruism. The states that were the best prepared to deal with complex military situations, and who could most afford to pay for them, did not need to prove themselves in the international system the way the middle powers did. Instead, state self-interest in the outcome of a conflict became a primary motive for complex peacekeeping intervention. Humanitarianism alone was no longer enough to warrant large, expensive and dangerous missions.

When combined with the new kinds of conflict being faced, the need to find peacekeepers with enduring political will also caused the international community to rethink the wisdom of keeping operations under UN command. In the old system, military units were contributed from dozens of countries who had usually never worked together before and lacked the ability to communicate easily with each other. They found it hard to coordinate their operations smoothly and to reach common understandings on key elements of the rules of engagement. The UN commanders themselves were often appointed at the last moment, just before deployment, and had little in the way of intelligence background reports to use in planning their operations. (With its stress on impartiality and its almost universal membership, the UN has not been able either to collect much intelligence on its own, or receive intelligence from states who obtain it for their own security purposes. The UN cannot be seen to be "spying," and states who do spy don't want their information or methods to become known to their potential enemies.) What was needed in these complicated new circumstances was instead well organized, trained and equipped troops who knew in advance what they were going to face and who had the political will to stay the course over the long term. Such troops tended not to come from neutral nations without an interest in the conflict. Instead, they came from powerful countries who had an incentive to see that peace was maintained.

When all of this was added together, it resulted in a new model of peacekeeping operations—what I call complex military peacekeeping. This new model has three basic components.

First, the goal was no longer simply to build confidence among formerly warring parties that the conflict had ended. Instead it was to rebuild domestic institutions from the ground up, to encourage societies to be both politically and culturally more tolerant and inclusive. War was no longer seen to be the result of miscalculation or misperception among states about the other side's intentions. Instead it resulted when deeply divided societies encountered political and economic transition crises, where some groups were winners and others were losers, and resentment between the groups ran high. To stop war from happening again in the future, it was thought, the UN and other international organizations and NGOs had to become extensively involved in designing constitutions and legal and judicial systems, planning and overseeing elections, encouraging the development of political parties and free media, fostering refugee resettlement, economic reconstruction, and educational development, all of which would be directed toward building diverse and tolerant societies where everyone's basic needs were met. The international community intruded much more deeply into domestic societies than it had in the past, influencing and even directing the institutional development of countries where peacekeeping operations took place.[24]

Second, the military forces sent on peacekeeping operations now had to go in prepared for battle. In this new style of peacekeeping there is usually resistance to the international community's intervention. There are always certain parties on the ground who hope to gain something from continuing the war that the peacekeepers are trying to stop, or from undermining the institutions that outsiders are trying to build. Stephen John Stedman has called this the "spoiler problem," where war-enamored parties try to wait out or drive out the peacekeepers, and spoil the peace at a later time.[25] The international community has therefore tried to convince potential spoilers that the peacekeepers mean business. Large numbers of well-armed and well-equipped peacekeeping troops must be deployed for extended periods of time.

Soldiers now are required to be more heavily armed and better trained than before for a wider variety of contingencies. They are sent in under more robust mandates, approved by the UN Security Council, that have allowed them to use force if necessary to protect themselves and the other personnel involved in the broader UN and other international community missions that they are supporting, such as those from the Organization of Security and Cooperation in Europe (OSCE). Sometimes the mandates have also allowed them to use force to protect the civilian populations they encounter on the ground. Earlier peacekeeping missions had been created under Chapter 6 of the UN Charter, which allows the Security Council to "make recommendations to the parties with a view to a pacific settlement of the dispute" (this was the legal justification originally cited for peacekeeping, to make up for the fact that the concept is not in the Charter). Now the need for robust forces meant that mandates were created under Chapter 7 of the Charter instead, which allows the Security Council to "take such action by air, sea, or land forces as may be necessary to maintain or restore international peace and security."[26] The use of force (including the implied threat of its use to deter new outbreaks of conflict) became a constituent component of peacekeeping missions as the 1990s wore on.

Third, because the risks and stakes of the operations were higher, they were most successfully conducted when carried out under a unified command, by states who had a strong interest in seeing peace succeed. As a result, the traditional style of UN command was replaced by the command of single states or state alliances like NATO, whose own troops were expertly trained and equipped to work together and who could lead so-called "coalitions of the willing" into difficult circumstances. State action was still authorized by the Security Council, and peacekeeping mission leaders reported back to the Security Council regularly, but states made their own decisions about how to proceed within the Security Council's mandate. They worked out their own rules of engagement, chose their own deployment locations and strategies, and selected who would be sent where to conduct which activities.

Together these things meant that the international community largely gave up on the notion that the parties involved in war were capable of determining their own futures. Peacekeepers were no longer there with the true and full consent of all parties—often the technical consent of the states involved was coerced under threat of military attack (as in Haiti in 1994 and Bosnia in 1995), or even after full-scale war (as in Kosovo in 1999)—and they were now expected to use force when necessary to achieve their goals. State sovereignty—the norm of mutual respect among states that had earlier kept civil war within states mostly off the UN agenda—would no longer be tolerated as a cover for armed brutality against innocent civilians, according to UN Secretary General Kofi Annan.[27] At least this was true in wars where the Permanent Five members of the UN Security Council were not direct participants. Those five members, who wielded the veto in Security Council resolutions, were spared the intrusiveness that other states faced. The key example here is the Russian war in its breakaway republic of Chechnya, where massive human rights violations on both sides have been well documented, but where the international community's access to the region has been tightly controlled and at times curtailed by the authorities in Moscow.

Elsewhere in the world, the international community, and especially its wealthy western members, declared that there was a preferred direction of domestic institutional development in war-torn societies, one which favored tolerance and liberal democratic values. Force would be used to protect the right of the international community to stay on the ground and oversee these transitions, against those who would use violence to threaten the presence of outsiders. And those who had a national interest in seeing that the international community's preferred outcome was reached would take command, to provide more assurance that progress would be made.

Peacekeeping and Political Change

This combination of shifts in operational design, where societal change is directed by outsiders through the use of force, has led analysts to conclude that peacekeeping might bear some resemblance to colonialism. Obviously the intentions of the international community are benign in these recent cases; unlike the European and American empires of previous centuries, these new operations are not designed to plunder subject societies. But the level of control that outsiders attempt to maintain is very strong and very paternalistic, and it is that relationship of paternalism that has bothered some observers.

A new philosophical understanding of the rights and obligations of the international community has justified this use of force in complex peacekeeping operations since the middle of the 1990s. UN Secretary General Kofi Annan calls this understanding "induced consent,"[28] and Jarat Chopra, an academic who served as a UN administrator in East Timor during its transition to independence and democracy, believes that such induced consent is a necessary component of what he calls "peace maintenance."[29] The argument is as follows. When a society is led by corrupt and sadistic tyrants—whether those tyrants are state leaders or warlords—who practice violence and threaten international security, then the international community has the right to use force to promote peace, justice, and political change in that society even if the tyrants and their followers object. Intervention is not just about stopping wars, but about ensuring that societies move in a direction that the international community favors. In other words, it is about forcing societies to accept political change, even when such acceptance means eradicating patterns of ethnic intolerance or political violence that have been in place for generations.

Chopra bravely states that "Peace-maintenance is not some colonial enterprise. . . . The purpose and behavior of peace-maintenance is the opposite of colonialism."[30] Yet while Chopra's meaning is clear—complex peacekeeping is designed as a means to share the international community's wealth in both resources and experience, not as a means for one country to steal wealth from a weaker group—his statement is not quite right, and his insistence that the two concepts are opposites leaves an analytical gap. Indeed, as Michael W. Doyle points out, John Stuart Mill, one of the classic nineteenth-century philosophers on the subject of state sovereignty and liberalism, argued that benign colonialism by the "civilized" countries in the "uncivilized" areas of the world was justified as a form of humanitarian intervention.[31] Colonialism and complex peacekeeping share the requirement that outsiders use military force to create political change inside a society that would not move in that direction on its own. They also share, as Neta Crawford puts it, "the failure to treat the intervened upon as if they were active agents" who were capable of determining their own futures without help from the outside world.[32]

It is arguable whether protection of *human* security has actually been the motivating idea behind complex peacekeeping. While humanitarianism has certainly been a fundamental goal of this intervention, there are plenty of places in the world where human security has been threatened and peacekeepers have not been deployed. What is clear, though, in the complex peacekeeping operations that have been put in place in Bosnia, Kosovo, and East Timor and that were emerging in Afghanistan and Iraq by 2003 (and that were first undertaken in 1994 with some hesitation in Haiti), is that the international community has acted in the belief that without fundamental societal and political change, threats to *international* security emanating from unstable areas would not go away. Unless societies were remade, the outside world would continue to face danger as a result—from an outflow of refugees or organized crime and drug networks that destabilize foreign economies, from ethnic hatred that threatens to make wars wider, and from divided states whose implosions become chain reactions of retributional violence and humanitarian disaster demanding a response. This means that the goal of peacekeeping in these places has not been just to stop the killing and restore the immediate peace. Instead, it has been to encourage lasting institutional change.

The most successful instances of this new kind of operation have occurred where external authorities from the international community have a high degree of executive control over events in the territory, including political controls that limit the full expression of popular will.[33] The world learned by watching the events in Somalia, Rwanda, and Bosnia in the early 1990s that the free expression of popular will can lead to mayhem, since popular will does not always equate with tolerance and peaceful conflict resolution. When outside control is missing, it becomes too easy for local actors opposed to liberal political change to obstruct the international community's efforts, and to subvert attempts to establish more tolerant and democratic political systems on their territories. Yet at the same time, a high degree of external control breeds both dependency and resentment among the subject population. It entails the danger of creating new examples of the weak and angry postcolonial societies whose poverty and authoritarianism challenged the world in the cold war era.

The Eastern Slavonia Model?

The United Nations likes to have success stories. One example of complex military peacekeeping success that is repeatedly cited as showing the wisdom of firm control by the international community is the relatively short-term mission (known by the acronym of UNTAES) which was deployed in the small section of Croatia called Eastern Slavonia from 1996 through 1998. The goal of the UN-commanded mission was to supervise the return of this territory, which had been seized by ethnic Serb paramilitary forces during the Yugoslavian conflict of the early 1990s, to the control of the Croatian government. UNTAES successfully oversaw the withdrawal of Serbian troops, and the cessation of the ethnic cleansing campaigns that had earlier terrorized the population.

The administrator of UNTAES, Jacques Paul Klein, a civilian appointed by the UN Secretary General who was simultaneously a reserve major general in the U.S. Air Force, attributes his success in large part to the strong degree of control over societal developments that he was granted.[34] He could override the local population on any administrative issue without consulting them first,[35] and even had the power to limit the ability of nongovernmental aid organizations to operate in Eastern Slavonia, "vett[ing] them] to ensure their relevance and capability before letting them into the region."[36] In other words, he played a role similar to that of a colonial governor on the territory, determining the area's political shape on behalf of outsiders who wished to control its destiny.

UNTAES succeeded in stopping the violence in Eastern Slavonia and returning the territory to Croatian state sovereignty. Yet it is not clear how typical the UNTAES mission was, or how useful the example is for the missions that followed. Eastern Slavonia was situated within a unique set of military and diplomatic circumstances. In 1995 the Croatian military had clearly demonstrated its ability to defeat the Serbian forces in the area in battle, using the assistance of United States military advisers. Hence the work of the international community in UNTAES was buoyed by the implicit threat that Serbian noncompliance would lead to direct military action, especially since NATO military aircraft made regular overflights of the territory to bring this point home.[37] In other words, it was not the peacekeepers alone who kept order, but the ethnic Serbians' fear that major war against the NATO coalition could descend upon them if they did not comply. Furthermore, Croatia was a state that had already established relatively well functioning administrative structures, and it had a population well versed in the skills necessary to run a country. This was not really a neophyte state. It was also located on the strategic coastline of the Adriatic, directly across from NATO member Italy, and with a longstanding special relationship to NATO member Germany. (That special relationship was cemented by the fact that large numbers of Croatian guest workers had immigrated to Germany over the years, making ethnic Croats a political force to be reckoned with domestically for the German government.)

For this combination of reasons, the nationalist leaders of both Serbian (rump) Yugoslavia and newly independent Croatia, Slobodan Milosevic and Franjo Tudjman, had strong incentives to cooperate with the international community's dominance of Eastern Slavonia. Neither had much to gain by supporting breakaway paramilitary forces there. This left the local parties on the ground, including paramilitary forces who might otherwise have been spoilers of the peace process, with no one to turn to for support.[38] The political outcome on Eastern Slavonian territory—integration into Croatia, under the diplomatic and military pressure of powerful western liberal democracies—was virtually predetermined, whatever its opponents may have attempted. The peacekeepers merely gave extra support to the Croatian state in reaffirming its own authority in the region.

That kind of peacekeeping—temporary military governorship which quickly leads to peaceful outcomes and integration into relatively stable societies—is not typical of the new situations the international community is facing today, in countries like Afghanistan and Iraq. Nor was it typical of the much more complicated situations that the international community faced in Haiti, Bosnia, Kosovo, and East Timor in the 1990s, where the goal was not integration into a larger stable state, but instead creation of a functioning state out of whole cloth. In these locations, shaky national governments without legitimate or well established military and police forces have been threatened by strong, armed internal dissension. With the partial exceptions of Haiti and East Timor (neighbors of the U.S. and Australia respectively), these countries are surrounded by states with a history of illiberal authoritarianism and weak democratic traditions, not strong western states or NATO members. Not only do most of their neighbors fail to provide good role models for stable governance; but also these neighbors may actually feel threatened by the emergence of strong, western-leaning states nearby, and may try to undermine change from without.

These new governments require more than deterrent fly-overs to boost their new authority. Successful change requires what amounts to long-term international occupation. In spite of this daunting challenge, the notion that outsiders could and should impose control over the political futures of unstable, conflict-ridden societies, using executive fiat backed up by military force, took hold in succeeding years. The idea that the occupations would need to be interminable was downplayed, despite the accumulating evidence.

The following brief summaries of the four major cases of complex military peacekeeping in the 1990s will highlight some of the concerns that have relevance for current and future missions. In each case, the international community approached peacekeeping operations with the idea of achieving political control, in order to move these subject territories in a liberal democratic direction. Yet in no case was this drive a resounding success. Either the international community put too few resources toward the task, leading to temporary solutions that fell apart with time; or the international community put all of its political will into situations that forced it to become a permanent occupation force. All of these cases demonstrate how difficult it is to impose a liberal, democratic, tolerant future on a society where such a direction does not come naturally.

Haiti: The Inadequacy of Halfway Measures

The first effort to create a complex military peacekeeping operation that included the elements outlined above—an attempt at domestic political institutional change, overseen by the international community, backed by the use of force, and led by an interested state—occurred in Haiti beginning in 1994. Yet while U.S. intervention in Haiti was couched in terms of securing lasting change in the country, it lacked the strength of political will that would have been necessary to make change endure in a society beset with overwhelming levels of poverty, violence, and hopelessness. Ten years after the original decision to send in troops, Haiti looked much as it did before forces were deployed—and in late February 2004, the United States and its allies intervened in Haiti with UN Security Council backing once again. The individuals sitting in the top leadership positions in the country had indeed changed, but the basic elements of the political system had not.

In 1994, three years after a military coup ousted Jean-Bertrand Aristide, the first democratically elected president of Haiti, the UN Security Council passed Resolution 940, which authorized the United States to lead a military mission there to restore peace and democratic government to the country. Haiti had a long history of instability and violence, and the attempt to overcome that legacy was daunting. As one group of analysts points out, "Since winning its freedom from the French in 1804, Haiti had

21 constitutions and 41 heads of state, 29 of whom were assassinated or overthrown."[39] Haiti had been occupied by the United States in what had amounted to a colonial effort between 1915 and 1934, and the Haitian army that the U.S. created then became a key player in the authoritarian system that the country adopted afterward.[40] The U.S. military continued to support the combined military and police forces of authoritarian Haiti with technical training throughout the cold war.

Now the United States was trying to help reestablish the constitution that Haiti had optimistically adopted in 1990, under international supervision, in an attempt to create a democracy where none had existed before. The desired end state, according to operational commander U.S. Major General Joseph W. Kinzer, was "a safe and secure environment with a functional and duly elected national government; a professional public security force loyal to the constitution and the national leadership; [and] a growing economy focusing on improving the infrastructure, improving public utilities, and reducing unemployment."[41] In the words of one military officer who served on the mission, "The United States employed its military, under U.N. auspices, as a vehicle to facilitate political change."[42]

Originally it appeared as if the U.S.-led, UN Security Council-authorized Multinational Force (MNF) would have to essentially invade Haiti under hostile conditions. After one false start, followed by tough UN sanctions and a long period of negotiations, Haitian military leaders finally backed down and agreed to rescind their positions and go into exile. U.S. forces went in unopposed. Their primary goal was to work alongside UN-appointed International Police Monitors (IPMs), who for the first time in UN history would be armed, in order to establish safe and secure conditions in the country. At the initial entry phase, when they discovered the disarray that characterized Haitian governmental institutions, U.S. Special Operations Forces—particularly reserve officers employed as civil affairs specialists who worked in administrative roles full-time back home—also took over key positions in governmental bureaucracies, both in the central ministries in Port-au-Prince and in the countryside.[43]

The U.S. military forces were supposed to oversee the voluntary disarming and demobilization of the Haitian military forces, and the IPMs were supposed to oversee Haitian police activities. After this was accomplished they were then to turn over operations to a UN-commanded force, the UNMIH. Realizing that a traditional UN force would be inadequate for Haiti's complicated situation, however, U.S. forces remained in Haiti after the MNF period was finished, and the previous U.S. MNF commander, General Kinzer, was appointed by the UN Secretary General to command what were now labeled the UNMIH military forces.

The operation did not run smoothly. The United Nations IPMs did not arrive in the promised numbers when scheduled, and many of the international police who were sent in to Haiti lacked the training and experience necessary to deter violence and restore public order.[44] Later in the operation, better trained French and Canadian police officers with appropriate skills (as well as the appropriate French language capability for the Haitian population) did arrive in the country, but there was a gap in police deployment at the start of the operation, and there were never a sufficient number of highly motivated francophone IPMs to carry out the training operation as planned. As a result, U.S. military forces had to pick up the slack.

Three days into the MNF operation, many world news organization cameras caught U.S. soldiers standing by as a Haitian mob lynched a member of the old regime on the street. After that instance of bad publicity, the U.S. military was suddenly tasked with taking on police duties. The previous U.S. rules of engagement had not allowed the troops to intervene in Haitian on Haitian violence, but now those rules were reinterpreted to allow American soldiers "to detain and, if necessary shoot, people committing serious criminal acts" such as murder, rape and robbery.[45] Yet U.S. military commanders were reluctant to get bogged down in police work, which they saw as outside their scope of competence. They did not have the resources or training to conduct criminal investigations or provide constant patrol coverage of the whole country. As a result, little direct action was taken to stop the violence the rules were designed to control.[46]

Remnants of the Haitian military who refused to disarm were indeed arrested and detained by U.S. forces, at least temporarily; that was considered a traditional military task,[47] and American troops put great effort into rebuilding jails that had been insecure and inhumane. There were also occasional firefights between U.S. troops and breakaway factions of the Haitian security forces,[48] but U.S. forces were careful to react only after they had been fired upon, so that they could make clear they were acting in self-defense. But these things did not really resolve the security problem faced by the locals. Much of the violence that plagued the ordinary citizens of Haiti was not directed by the ousted forces themselves, who for the most part melted away fairly quickly after the U.S. arrival. Instead, violence was a result of revenge attacks by civilians against suspected members of the old regime, as well as street justice meted out by civilians against other Haitians who were suspected of ordinary crimes. In the old regime, the police forces had been integrated into the brutal Haitian military, and were hence not trusted by the population. The police were known for their corruption and brutality. As a result, Haitian citizens had gotten into the habit of avoiding the authorities as much as possible, and preferred to take the law into their own hands when they felt justice needed to be done.

During the time that U.S. and UN military forces were present in Haiti, regular foot patrols throughout the country helped to deter many violent attacks. Yet there was general agreement that the violence continued wherever the troops were not physically present at the moment, and after outside military forces left, nothing much remained of their efforts. Despite the best attempts of the international community, including repeated training efforts and aid incentive programs, a reliable new Haitian police force that observed international human rights standards never really took hold. Even more important, Haitian judicial institutions remained unreliable, and arrested criminals often ended up right back on the street; after awhile, even the most dedicated Haitian police gave up. The traditional vigilantism practiced by the population continued.[49] No lasting institutions were created to take the place of foreign troops. In the words of John Ballard, who served in the MNF and later became a professor at the National Defense University near Washington, DC, "The operation was not intended to remake Haitian national institutions, but instead to permit Haitians to return themselves to democratic governance. That responsibility still lies with the Haitian people."[50]

As conditions deteriorated in Haiti in the late 1990s, the UN presence was gradually withdrawn. There was agreement among the international community, led by the United States, that it was not worth the continuing expenditure of resources to try to help a country so consumed by intractable social problems, so stubbornly refusing to reform itself.[51] The desired end state was never reached. American military sources call the MNF Uphold Democracy mission in Haiti a success, because it met its original goals: it got rid of the military junta, it restored Aristide to power through new democratic elections, and U.S. forces were able to leave in six months and turn authority over to a UN-commanded mission.[52] Yet the notion of real political change turned out to be illusory. After stepping aside in accordance with Haiti's constitution in 1995, Aristide was reelected to the presidency in 2000; but by that time he and his party were widely seen as corrupt (following parliamentary elections that failed to meet the standards of international observers), and Haiti's opposition movements boycotted the 2000 presidential election. In the following years some of Aristide's supporters took up arms and began terrorizing their opponents, following Haiti's well worn traditions of political violence. Aristide's government paid little attention to human rights despite intense pressure from the Organization of American States, and meanwhile poverty, illiteracy, and HIV/AIDS infection rates remained tragically high.[53] In Haiti in 1994, the international community avoided intensive societal intrusion. They feared that intrusion might have led to dependency, and the United States in particular was wary of getting bogged down in another potential Somalia. In the words of one high-ranking U.S. Army officer who had been stationed in Haiti, complex peacekeeping operations can turn into "tarbabies." He noted, "The military is, and always has rightly been, concerned of being overcommitted."[54] While a complex military peacekeeping operation was attempted, it was not designed to remain in place for the long term. Force was used only to encourage the disappearance of the old regime, not to ensure the consolidation of a new, more liberal democratic one. The peacekeeping operation in Haiti did not, in the end, attempt to control a subject society. While it avoided the dangers of colonial-like occupation, it ultimately proved inadequate to restore security in the country as well.

Ten years later, those who knew Haiti's troubled history hoped that this time around the United States and the international community would stay over the long haul and commit the resources needed to do the job right. Yet once again the U.S. was preoccupied with more pressing peacekeeping needs elsewhere; in the mid-1990s it had been Bosnia that absorbed Washington's attention, and now it was Afghanistan and Iraq. In 2004 Washington would commit to staying in Haiti only 90 days before turning the operation over to the UN, and in early March (as this book was going to press) complaints abounded once again in Port au Prince that the U.S. Marines on the ground were not doing enough to stop political violence and restore order.

Bosnia and Kosovo: Imposing Control over Sovereignty

NATO-led peacekeeping in both Bosnia and Kosovo, supported by other international organizations including the European Union (EU) and the Organization of Security and Cooperation in Europe (OSCE) in addition to the UN, stands in sharp contrast to the case of Haiti. In these two cases in the Balkans, the liberal democratic international community has made a strong effort to control the political destinies of the involved territories. Neither Bosnia nor Kosovo has been allowed to exercise sovereignty. In the case of Kosovo, the international community has not yet even decided who will be granted ownership over eventual sovereignty in the territory, or how a transfer of sovereignty will be accomplished.

The history of the peace accords that followed the ethnic wars and set up these conditions in both cases is well known, and need not be recounted in great detail.[55] A brief summary sketch will be provided here, to set the background for the arguments that follow.

As noted above, when Yugoslavia disintegrated into civil war in the early 1990s, the United Nations attempted to preserve and restore peace in the region through a lightly armed mission (the UN Protection Force, or UNPROFOR) that operated under Chapter 6 of the UN Charter—in other words, via a mission that operated with the permission of the sovereign states where it was deployed (the new state of Bosnia and Herzegovina, often abbreviated BiH, and its new neighbor Croatia) and that recognized these states' political sovereignty. UNPROFOR failed. Its legitimacy was not recognized by the breakaway ethnic groups who were fighting inside each of the newly declared states, and its effectiveness was shredded by paramilitary forces who kidnapped and killed its personnel and massacred civilians in the safe areas it was supposedly guarding. Following paramilitary massacres of thousands of civilians in towns that were supposed to be UN-guarded safe areas, and after a great deal of political discussion and delay both within NATO and within the UN Secretariat and Security Council, NATO forces finally gained UN approval to carry out air strikes against Serbian paramilitary formations. At this point, the international community was intervening on behalf of basic human rights, and no particular agenda for the area's political future was yet in play.

As a result of the NATO air strikes, and bolstered by U.S. military advisory assistance, Croatian forces were able to expel ethnic Serb formations from the ethnic Croatian territory in BiH that they had earlier seized. The Serbs who ruled what remained of Yugoslavia were thereby forced to recognize their own military limits and to come to the negotiating table. Ultimately they had to recognize Bosnia's independence as a state. But the ethnic Serbian entity inside the state of BiH never recognized the legitimacy of the international presence in their part of Bosnia. This created enforcement problems for the international community from the beginning, because it meant that external control was being imposed against the wishes of one of the key actors in the country.[56] Peacekeeping was being done without the full and true consent of the peace-kept.

What emerged from the negotiations between Serbs, Croats, and Bosnian Muslims (or Bosniacs) and the Contact Group of six outside powers who had a self-declared interest in Bosnia (the U.S., Great Britain, France, Germany, Italy, and Russia) were the Dayton Accords of 1995—an imperfect compromise in everyone's minds. The accords reflected the de facto division of territory in BiH that resulted from the fighting, rather than what any group considered "fair," since this was the only way to convince the various parties that they had achieved as much as they could through warfare. It was believed that any other division would cause the fighting to flare up again. The accords were based on the idealistic notion that three separate regions in BiH, each dominated by a particular ethnic group, could manage their own affairs without returning to the nationalist hatred of the past, and could then cooperate at a national level to forge a cohesive government for BiH as a whole. Crucial to the success of the accords was the notion that minority refugee groups would return to their original homes, making each region ethnically integrated. In this respect, the accords reflected the underlying beliefs of the liberal international community that both liberal democracy and ethnic integration were necessary components of Bosnia's future—and that with a little prodding, Bosnian citizens would come to realize this.

The Dayton Accords marked the international community's transition from acting as gut-level humanitarians (protecting the lives of innocents) toward imposing a particular political vision on the future of Bosnian society. This political vision included the idea that ethnic separatism was an evil to be eradicated, that the demographic effects of years of ethnic cleansing had to be undone for the sake of both human rights and stability in the region, and that the international community had an obligation to encourage ethnic integration through refugee returns. The embodiment of these obligations was the creation of a federated government in BiH designed to force the three major ethnic groups to cooperate for the common good. Yet it was necessary, in order to get all the involved parties to sign the peace accords, to divide the country into two separately governed ethnic entities—the Muslim/Croat Federation, and the Republica Srpska for the Serbs—inside that common federal structure.

These accords (officially known as the General Framework Agreement for Peace, or GFAP) gave the international community, or at least parts of the international community, control over both civilian and military affairs in BiH during the transitional period to sovereignty. Annex 10 granted ultimate civilian political authority to the Office of the High Representative (OHR), a newly created international agency not directly affiliated with either the United Nations or NATO. The individual serving as the High Representative is nominated by a steering committee, representing a group of 55 countries and international organizations involved in the peace process, and is then confirmed by the UN Security Council.[57] As the OHR itself declares on its website, the High Representative "is the final authority in theater regarding [the] interpretation [of the civilian aspects of the Dayton Accords], authorized to impose legislation and to dismiss obstructive officials."[58]

The OHR has regularly dismissed freely and fairly elected officials in

Bosnia by fiat. For example, in March 1999 High Representative (HR) Carlos Westendorp fired the freely, fairly, and democratically elected president of Republica Srpska, Nikolai Poplasen, for obstructing refugee returns and the fulfillment of the Dayton Accords.[59] In November 2000, the new HR Wolfgang Petritsch unilaterally fired the freely, fairly, and democratically elected Croatian member of BiH's tripartite presidency, Ante Jelavic, for corruption and for trying to incite separatism among the Croat population.[60] According to one NATO report, "As many as 22 people have been removed from office in a single day for anti-Dayton activities,"[61] even when they have been appointed in accordance with Bosnia's democratic constitution. In other words, the political vision of the (largely western) international community about the future of BiH is inconsistent; ethnic integration often conflicts with democratic institutions, and when it does, integration trumps democracy. Control trumps self-determination.

Laws, too, have sometimes been managed by fiat. For example, in January 2002, six Algerians who had become naturalized Bosnian citizens through marriage were suspected of planning to bomb the U.S. embassy in the capital of Sarajevo in support of the al Qaeda terrorist network. The BiH Interior Ministry detained the suspects, stripped five of their BiH citizenship, and later extradited all of them to U.S. authorities. This occurred with full approval of the BiH Council of Ministers. Yet the BiH Supreme Court had earlier ordered the men released (saying that their citizenship had been revoked without sufficient evidence), and the BiH Human Rights Chamber, a body set up under the Dayton Accords to monitor human rights in the country, had demanded that extradition be delayed for a month and that the BiH authorities try to stop their forcible deportation despite American pressure. In other words, Bosnian actions violated the BiH constitution. The OHR was informed of all of these proceedings and chose not to act in support of the Supreme Court or Human Rights Chamber decision, despite criticism from the UN High Commissioner on Human Rights that the "rule of law was clearly circumvented in this process," and despite the OHR's continuing public statement that "we do call for compliance" with Human Rights Chamber decisions, since such compliance is a part of BiH's planned accession to the Council of Europe.[62] OHR concerns about the security of western states trump OHR concerns about Bosnia's legal process, even though that process was set up by the Dayton Accords and is part of the overall plan for Bosnia's European integration. Americans may all feel safer as a result of these suspected terrorists being extradited to the holding camp at Guantanamo Bay, but the example nonetheless illustrates the degree to which western interests control the sovereignty of Bosnian political institutions, in a direction that looks uncomfortably like colonial intervention. Control trumps liberalism. By late 2003, analysts and policymakers were engaged in a spirited debate about whether the OHR constituted a "European Raj," and about how much weight should be given to the opinion of local Bosnian elites who prefer OHR oversight to untrammeled democracy.[63]

Beyond the civilian powers granted to the international community by the Dayton Accords, Annex 1A gave military authority in the country to a UN Security Council-authorized implementation force (IFOR), which "may be composed of ground, air and maritime units from NATO and non-NATO nations, deployed to Bosnia and Herzegovina to help ensure compliance with the provisions of this Agreement."[64] IFOR was authorized under Chapter 7 of the UN Charter, which meant that it could use force as necessary to fulfill its mandate even without the permission of the involved parties. It could act in the absence of consent. Originally IFOR was intended to focus only on the military aspects of the agreement, overseeing such things as the withdrawal of foreign troops, the disarming and demobilization of ethnic militias, and the creation of a joint BiH military organization. However, it received a great deal of criticism from the international community for not intervening to protect minority ethnic groups in the face of continuing paramilitary threats and violence.[65] In December 1996, IFOR was replaced by SFOR (the stabilization force), again led by NATO, and authorized by the UN Security Council (again under Chapter 7) to contribute to the creation of a safe and secure environment in BiH and to offer selective help to civilian organizations, including the OHR, involved in the peace process.[66]

The international community hoped it was thereby creating a more cohesive framework to shape the political society of BiH. The cohesion of this arrangement often broke down, as various state and international actors with differing visions for Bosnia's future failed to coordinate their policies with each other. The intention, however, was clear. Unlike the earlier case of Haiti, in BiH the liberal democratic international community wished to control the territory's sovereignty so that, backed up by the use or threat of force, Bosnia would move in the direction the international community wanted.

As David Chandler has reported, the officials who have been overseeing the Bosnian transition recognize the philosophical contradiction inherent in their roles. The less democratic they allow BiH to be, the more success they have in achieving ethnic tolerance and the establishment of liberal institutions inside Bosnian society[67]—even if those liberal institutions are sometimes ignored by the OHR. Chandler argues that the international community is trying not merely to create new institutions in BiH, but to instill a new culture, with values and attitudes that would not have arisen on their own.[68] In other words, the international community is engaged in a mission to bring western liberal democratic values to an area of the world where they had not taken root before—even when the means that are used are sometimes neither democratic nor liberal.

Despite the many differences between the cases of Bosnia and Kosovo, the political intentions of the international community have been similar in the two cases, and went through a similar evolution over time. In Kosovo, as in Bosnia, the international community intervened initially largely because of gut-level human rights concerns, but followed this by superseding state sovereignty (in this case, the sovereignty of what remained of the state of Yugoslavia) and attempting to create a society based on ethnic tolerance where one had not existed before. In Kosovo the degree of political control exerted by the peacekeeping operation was even stronger than that in Bosnia.

In the late 1990s, following a long history of ethnic unrest in the Yugoslavian province of Kosovo (whose earlier autonomy within Yugoslavia had been taken away by Serbian nationalists in the mid-1980s), Serbian paramilitary groups began carrying out what they saw as retaliatory strikes against Kosovar Albanian villages which were said to be harboring armed insurgents. Ethnic Albanian guerrilla groups had been attacking the outposts of Serbian government authorities in the region for several years, sometimes killing Serb police officers and other officials in the process. The Serbian paramilitary groups conducting the raids, however, did not distinguish between the armed insurgents and innocent civilians. Their brutal actions created a massive crisis of internally displaced persons as Albanian Kosovars fled their homes for the mountains, raising fears of another round of ethnic cleansing and mass murder in the region. Many humanitarian aid agencies were especially concerned that the Kosovars would starve or freeze to death in the cold winter, and they pressured western governments to take action.

NATO threatened to carry out air strikes unless Serb forces withdrew from Kosovo and reached a negotiated settlement to the crisis in the province. Yugoslavian leader Slobodan Milosevic first stalled, but then agreed to this demand, and the UN Security Council authorized the deployment of an unarmed observer force from the OSCE to oversee the withdrawal. But in late 1998 and early 1999, OSCE observers received credible evidence that a major Serbian military offensive into Kosovo was planned for the spring. Once again the Contact Group of six interested outside nations attempted to convince the parties to sign a peace agreement, this time in Rambouillet. The agreement would give political oversight of the province to the international community and allow NATO peacekeepers to act as enforcers of the accord. Kosovar Albanian paramilitary representatives signed the agreement in hopes of getting NATO support for Kosovo's eventual break from Serbia, but Milosevic refused to do so, seeing the language of the agreement (probably rightly) as the first step toward independent statehood for Kosovo. Serbian paramilitary forces then began impeding and attacking the OSCE mission.

Shortly afterward the NATO military offensive against Yugoslavia began, involving progressively more intensive air strikes. As the Serbian position weakened over a period of many weeks, and as Russia intervened as a mediator, Milosevic was reluctantly brought back to the negotiating table. A Military-Technical Agreement was signed between Yugoslavia and NATO, under which Milosevic agreed to the deployment of KFOR, an "international security force" of NATO-led troops which would be sent under a UN Security Council Chapter 7 mandate "with the authority to take all necessary action to establish and maintain a secure environment for all citizens of Kosovo and otherwise carry out its mission."[69] The KFOR commander was given final authority in the interpretation of the agreement and in overseeing the security situation in Kosovo. Shortly afterward, in June 1999, the UN Security Council both authorized KFOR and created a new UN mission, UNMIK, to oversee the civilian reconstruction and political transition period in Kosovo.

UNMIK operates through four "pillars," which are together mandated (among other things) to "perform basic civilian administrative functions, promote the establishment of substantial autonomy and self-government in Kosovo . . . , maintain civil law and order, promote human rights, and assure the safe and unimpeded return of all refugees and displaced persons to their homes in Kosovo."[70] UN agencies are responsible for the first two pillars (police and justice, and the civil administration of the province), while the OSCE is responsible for the third (democratization and institution building) and the European Union is responsible for the fourth (reconstruction and economic development).[71] This time the international community congratulated itself for successfully consolidating its attempts to control the sovereignty of political society from the start. UNMIK encompassed a much broader array of functions than what the OHR in Bosnia supervised alone, and KFOR, unlike the IFOR mission in Bosnia, was authorized from the beginning to use force on behalf of the UNMIK mission. In other words, civilian and military functions were integrated under international control. The international community approached Kosovo as if it were a protectorate—a territory unable to function on its own and in need of foreign assistance, since it had not yet reached political maturity.

Outside political control would be cemented with the support of outside military force.

Kosovo's status as an international protectorate has taken on a life of its own, because the international community has been unable or unwilling to decide how and when the territory's future status should be settled. As Simon Chesterman notes, UNMIK's mandate "avoids taking a position on the key political question of Kosovo's relationship to Serbia," and as time has gone by the issue has remained unresolved.[72] It was decreed that for the period of the complex peacekeeping operation, however long it lasted, political institutions should be built in Kosovo that gave the territory "substantial autonomy." Beyond that, however, the next step remains uncertain. The notion of declaring independent statehood for the territory, or of giving it the status of an autonomous province within the state of Serbia, or of partitioning Kosovo to reflect the ethnic divisions between Kosovar Albanians and Serbs, are all proposals that have been put on the table. But each of them seems fraught with danger.

On one hand the territorial losers in any division of the territory might be so dissatisfied that they would restart the armed conflict, should international forces be withdrawn. On the other hand, after years of effort, the international community's intervention might in the end accomplish nothing in terms of its goals of ethnic integration and tolerance, perhaps even serving as a precedent to encourage ethnic cleansing elsewhere.[73] No solution seems able to answer both of these objections. As a result, the UN and NATO are shackled with the responsibility for keeping the peace, and running the country, in Kosovo for the foreseeable future. The international community believes that popular will in Kosovo cannot be safely allowed to determine the territory's sovereignty. Once again, control trumps self-determination.

The intentions of the international community in both Bosnia and Kosovo have been righteous: the creation of peaceful, ethnically integrated, liberal democratic societies with free markets. Their peacekeeping methods are strictly restrained by both international law and (in the case of military contingents and national aid agencies) by the national laws of their donor states. Outside forces cannot do whatever they please. Yet there is no question that outsiders have attempted to control the political destiny of Bosnia and Kosovo by force, and to move their societies in directions they would not go on their own. They cannot withdraw if that trajectory is to have any chance of being maintained; otherwise the Balkans may suffer a similar fate to Haiti. This, then, is where the comparison to colonialism has been made.

East Timor: A Brief Infatuation with Trusteeship

A bloodbath enveloped East Timor following its referendum on autonomy in September 1999, and the world failed to prevent it, even though many international observers had predicted that chaos would erupt if no one intervened. Militia groups supported by the Indonesian military launched a furious attack against civilians suspected of supporting independence from Jakarta, and razed as much of the infrastructure of East Timor as they could after the vote went against them. Australian government officials had expected violence if the referendum went as it did—with the East Timorese population voting against autonomy within Indonesia, and hence implicitly supporting independence—and the government in Canberra had prepared long in advance for its defense forces to evacuate Australian nationals from the island.[74] The United Nations had even obtained copies before September of the orders sent to the Timorese militia commanders who were paid by the Indonesian army to oppose independence, which described the campaign of violence that was to be waged if the population voted "no" on autonomy within Indonesia.[75]

But the Indonesian government refused to give permission for the United Nations to send an armed mission to East Timor to preserve order during the referendum, and the international community did not yet push to intervene. Instead, an unarmed UN observer mission (UNAMET) was in place, which was itself attacked in the melee. It would have required an act of war—or at least of strong diplomatic coercion—for anyone to intervene militarily in advance of the vote. UNAMET did, however, gain permission from Indonesia to have Australia send in an evacuation mission for its own workers, as well as for foreign diplomatic personnel.[76]

Within two weeks of the territory's eruption, which was astonishing in its level of fury and destruction, Indonesia was convinced under pressure from its international financial benefactors and trade partners to permit a Chapter 7 mission led by Australia to enter East Timor and restore order. What this INTERFET mission discovered was a wasteland. The East Timorese capital of Dili was relatively empty of people, outside of the remaining militia forces and their armed opponents on the other side, because everyone who could leave had either fled to the countryside or been forced across the border into Indonesian West Timor by the militias. Buildings had been looted and torched, food stores and electricity generators had been destroyed, garbage and human waste covered everything and vermin were everywhere, and several large massacre sites were found.

INTERFET did a remarkable job of restoring order, first inside Dili within a few weeks, and then in East Timor as a whole over the next several months. Food and humanitarian assistance got through to where it was needed, the leaders of the militia violence were convinced to leave the territory, and the militias themselves were disbanded and more or less reintegrated into society. But the international community did not stop there. Ending the violence was not considered sufficient. Instead it deployed the UNTAET mission, whose goal was to create a functioning independent government in East Timor where none had been before.

The East Timor case illustrates the dilemma the international community faces when it tries to do so much for a society. The UNTAET operation was in place from 1999 through 2002, and it effectively ran a country where both preexisting infrastructure and a trained professional local population were nonexistent. Non-Timorese Indonesians had run the territory before, and the Timorese population lacked both education and experience, so the UN came in to give the new country a jump-start. UNTAET, like the UNTAES case in Eastern Slavonia described above, is lauded by the United Nations as a complex peacekeeping success story. It was indeed successful, in the sense that the brutal killing and destruction that brought the UN in to the country was stopped; but that was largely accomplished by INTERFET very quickly, before the more massive UN presence arrived.

UNTAET was also successful in that it did indeed largely rebuild the country's government institutions, and East Timor (now officially known as Timor Leste) gained its sovereignty and independence from Indonesia. Yet the UN was criticized for ignoring the views of local Timorese leaders, including the pro-independence guerilla leader who was later overwhelming elected president, Xanana Gusmao, and the man who had been the international voice for Timorese human rights throughout the Indonesian occupation era and then became Foreign Minister, José Ramos-Horta. East Timorese leaders had submitted a proposal to the earlier UNAMET mission in the country about how locals after the referendum might be integrated into a transition government, but the UN ignored the proposal. The follow-on UNTAET mission was widely perceived to have failed even to explain the policies it chose to the East Timorese population.[77] After almost a year of foreign control the UN did appoint a new cabinet of ministers that put locals in charge of infrastructure and administration, but foreigners retained control over the key portfolios of finance, the police, and justice, and largely ran the local district governments.[78] In the words of Jarat Chopra, who headed UNTAET's Office of District Administration until he resigned in protest over the UN's actions there, "Rather than trying to render itself obsolete as swiftly as possible . . . UNTAET resisted

Timorese participation in order to safeguard the UN's influence."[79] Once again, control trumped self-determination.

Believing that it was more important to establish a competent administration in the country quickly than to give control to the East Timorese, the UN kept foreigners in key positions and paid them according to international standards while the native population remained largely unemployed. (The one exception to this was the judicial system, where UNTAET "Timorized" institutions as quickly as possible by appointing local officials to a system whose characteristics were borrowed from external models.[80]) One consequence of this two-tiered social system, something that made world headlines, was the fact that UN employees routinely ordered cappuccinos from the cafés that sprang up to service their needs, which cost more than the average Timorese daily wage.

In 2001 and 2002 East Timor held a successful election for a new Constituent Assembly, adopted a new constitution by popular referendum, and elected its first president. At this point East Timor was granted recognition by the United Nations as a sovereign state. UNTAET closed up shop, being replaced by the smaller and much less intrusive UNMISET mission. UNMISET is still authorized under Chapter 7 and includes both a UN military and police component (with heavily armed Australians and New Zealanders continuing to guard the border with Indonesian West Timor) in addition to a civilian one. But its role is to support the East Timorese administration, not to administer East Timor.[81]

East Timor thus underwent an odd combination of situations: it was first administered by foreigners who did not pay much attention to local Timorese views, and was then almost precipitously given over to Timorese control without much time for on-the-job learning by local administrators. In addition, the UN mission was not allowed to use any money to build anything that would be left in East Timor when it was withdrawn, or to finance healthcare or education; it could only finance its own mission, and it took all of its equipment with it, including communication lines and power generators, when it left.[82] Individual state foreign donors fund the East Timorese government budget, which faced difficulties in the aftermath of the UN withdrawal. The business climate in the country has dried up because there is no local wealth to support the cappuccino cafés and the other facilities that foreigners patronized. By early 2003, the average per capita income of the population was less than $100 per month and the unemployment rate stood at 70 percent, in a country with few indigenous resources, a population that remained largely uneducated, and many trained guerrilla fighters who now found themselves with nothing to do.[83]

While the sea between East Timor and Australia has a wealth of oil and natural gas reserves, the UN did not do much to help East Timor with this resource, either. The country found itself stuck in prolonged negotiations with Australia about how access to the petroleum would be divvied up between them, without an experienced legal staff to help its side.[84] Economic hardship in the country was exacerbated by a drought that cut East Timor's agricultural export earnings, especially the coffee that was traditionally sold abroad. Perhaps as a result of all of these things, a December 2002 popular protest in Dili against police brutality turned into violent rioting that attacked foreign businesses. Meanwhile cross-border raids continued into 2003 from dispossessed former militia members in West Timor, as well, and it was not yet clear that domestic police and military forces would be up to the task of dealing with any of these things in the absence of UN forces.

Granting total administrative control over the country to foreigners, who then quickly withdrew as peace was achieved and their political will to remain declined, left East Timor a potential powder keg of economic resentment. It is not clear that all the effort at liberal democratic institution-building there will amount to much in the long run, because the will to rule in the short run was not backed up by adequate resources or long-term planning. It is too early to tell for sure what will happen in Timor Leste, but that means it is also too early to call the progression of peacekeeping missions there successful.

The Horns of the Dilemma

What these examples show is that the international community in the 1990s faced two dangers as it attempted to control foreign territory for humanitarian purposes. Either it went in to these countries saying it was going to remake society, and then exhibited inadequate political will to do the job completely, as happened in Haiti; or it tried to do too much, creating political systems that depended on forceful outside supervision in Bosnia and Kosovo, and an economic system that depended on foreign occupation in East Timor. In all four cases, the international community had good intentions. But in all four cases, the gratitude felt by the local community for the foreign assistance it received has been tempered by resentment at foreigners who either don't seem to care enough, or who want to control too much. The initial presence of the peacekeepers may have been welcomed by many ordinary people on the ground, but in the end the international community's lasting benevolence has been questioned.

It is too early to know what the ultimate political results of all of these interventions of the 1990s will be, since peacekeepers remain on the ground in all four countries as this book goes to press. It is perhaps too early to declare that failure is the certain end result. In Bosnia, Kosovo, and Timor Leste, new political institutions have been built under international oversight. It is impossible to know for sure what will happen to those institutions once foreign troops withdraw, although the continuation of nationalist political party strength in Bosnia and Kosovo and of abject poverty among the vast majority of East Timorese puts the notion of long-term success in doubt.

In thinking about future interventions, however, it may be useful for the international community to draw out the lessons from these cases, while recalling the experiences of most postcolonial societies. The examples outlined above demonstrate that despite the differences between colonialism and complex peacekeeping operations, the efforts in the latter cases to control political developments in particular countries do to some extent resemble colonial governorship. Institutions are structured to match the goals of outsiders, and political winners and losers are chosen based on their responsiveness to outside pressure. The resemblance between complex peacekeeping operations and colonialism will be explored more in the next chapter. Meanwhile, what might the experience of post-colonial societies portend for the future of peace-kept societies?

In the words of historian A. E. Afigbo, the political choices and styles adopted by colonial governors in Africa at the turn of the twentieth century were "emulated by their successors"[85] in the postcolonial era. Those colonial rulers were often brutal, arbitrary, and illiberal, and so were many of the indigenous African leaders who emerged to take their places after the colonial yoke was thrown off by independence movements. There are, of course, examples where at least relatively strong democracies have emerged out of a colonial past. India is a favored case of historians like Niall Ferguson, who argue that British colonialism helped rationalize disorderly and conflict-prone societies.[86] But while India proper may have a functioning (if imperfect) democracy, autocratic Pakistan and parts of unstable Afghanistan were territories of British India, too, areas particularly subject to the brutal whims of rogue imperial officers. And while the Indian Army today is renowned for its professionalism and its adherence to British regimental values, the citizens of the Indian province of Jammu and Kashmir rightly fear the arbitrary violence used by state security forces trying to flush out terrorists. While British colonialism may sometimes have been less nasty than its French counterpart, it is hard to sustain the argument that its overall legacy was positive.

The peacekeepers of the 1990s certainly did not mimic colonial governors in their political choices, so we have no reason to suspect that the presence of peacekeepers will make these countries any more brutal or authoritarian in the future than they would have been in the absence of intervention. But would the international community nonetheless be content to see the future leaders of the peace-kept countries emulate the decisions that the peacekeeping states did make? Should the leaders of Haiti follow the example of the international community and give up on the idea of police and judicial reform because the problems are just too recalcitrant in the face of ingrained social norms of violence? (This does seem to be the choice they have made.) Should the leaders of Bosnia (and whatever Kosovo becomes in the future) intercede, as the international community has done, to overturn democratically made decisions when those decisions do not square with their own ideal visions of what the country should become? (Certainly, for nationalists that choice will be tempting.) Should the future leaders of East Timor do as the international community did and ignore the ideas of their own population about institutional reform, and then withdraw into foreign investments the resources that are necessary for the institutions to continue to function well? (The experiences of other new democracies in the world indicate that such a result would not be unprecedented.)

If the international community (and especially the liberal democratic western states who dominate its decisions) wants to have a lasting impact on stability and security in these kinds of cases, it must come up with a better model of how to intervene. One such model will be proposed in the final chapter—a model that focuses on providing immediate security to the population, rather than attempting to control long-term political developments in foreign societies. In the meantime, it is time to make the comparison to colonialism explicit.

THREE

STATE INTERESTS, HUMANITARIANISM, AND CONTROL

A country torn apart by war, and ruled by an oppressive regime for many years, is now beginning political reform under foreign supervision. The ultimate goal is for the country to be a self-sufficient and independent democracy. Meanwhile, foreign administrators are helping locals to set up the basic building blocks of a parliamentary and judicial rule-of-law system. The country's social institutions, ranging from primary education to health care, are all being overhauled, so that they can be brought closer to developed world standards.

This foreign effort is supported by a large deployment of military personnel. In part the soldiers are there to provide safety and security for the authorities, who are challenged by armed rebels who do not recognize the legitimacy of the new system. In part, however, the soldiers are being employed in very nontraditional duties. In the absence of reliable local institutions, soldiers are serving as policemen, judges, jailers, and customs officers. They are also training a new national military force for the country, which will concentrate on internal security problems. Foreign soldiers are meanwhile engaged in a great deal of humanitarian activity, building roads and schools, distributing food in outlying areas, reorganizing garbage collection services, and serving as medics.

Military personnel are instructed to use the minimum amount of force necessary in order to avoid civilian casualties. They are also told to respect local customs and to treat people humanely. Officers are encouraged, in fact, to try to win the rebels over to their side by offering them preferred

(continued)

> *(continued)*
>
> access to foreign aid and trade opportunities. One overarching military goal is to win popular support for the foreigners' presence, in the hopes that this will make security in the country easier to maintain.

These paragraphs could depict an idealized version of the international peacekeeping going on in Kabul in the aftermath of the war in Afghanistan in 2002. With a few changes in detail, they could just as well describe the situation of international peacekeeping forces throughout many areas of the world in the mid- to late 1990s. But those cases are not the source for these paragraphs. Instead this description is drawn from the history of the U.S. colonial occupation of the Philippines in the early twentieth century.[1] Large parts of this vignette could also describe the policies followed by Great Britain and France in many of the colonial areas they occupied in the same era.

It may grate on liberal Western sensitivities to think that international peacekeeping operations have something in common with colonialism, but they do, despite all of their differences. The United States, Great Britain, and France were all relatively liberal (if flawed) democracies a century ago. Each nonetheless took colonies, and attempted to reshape them to a greater or lesser extent to look more like themselves, using military force to back up their attempts at persuasion. Leaders in each imperial country believed they were doing good for humanity even as they were doing well for themselves, contributing not only to their country's own wealth and security but also to the betterment of those living in unfortunate circumstances. It is probably not a coincidence that each of these three countries have been dominant actors in recent complex peacekeeping operations, nor is it a coincidence that it is their leadership as permanent members of the United Nations Security Council that has shaped the evolution of peacekeeping since the end of the cold war. Peacekeeping has a colonial heritage.

In the last chapter I defined what I meant by complex military peacekeeping operations, and examined how and why those operations evolved as they did in the 1990s to become efforts to control political and economic developments in particular societies. In this chapter, I will continue to explore the comparison between complex peacekeeping and the colonialism practiced by liberal states at the turn of the last century by examining the political goals that motivated each type of operation. They were similar in many important ways. Both were characterized by a desire to control foreign societies, and both were driven by a combination of state security and humanistic goals.

There are obvious differences between the two types of operation. I do not mean to imply, as some more radical analysts today do, that the peacekeepers of today have old-fashioned colonial intentions. The imperialism practiced by London, Paris, and Washington a hundred years ago was, at base, about securing profit for their own nations, and this is certainly not what peacekeeping is about. In fact peacekeeping is an expensive business that saps state treasuries without providing many investment opportunities for international business. Imperialism was also about gaining possession of territory for competitive reasons; Great Britain, France, and the United States at that time were engaged in a form of balance of power politics where the amount of land controlled by individual states was seen to matter. Peacekeeping is not that, either. Peacekeeping is usually done cooperatively, and the chief difficulty lies in convincing countries to agree to contribute to operations, not in trying to keep them out of territory claimed by someone else.

Complex peacekeeping operations are largely centered on humanitarian activity and liberal political development, and while these things were components of the era of colonialism that I am considering, they did not define colonialism the way they define peacekeeping today. The balance of humanitarian and self-interested goals shifted significantly to favor humanitarianism in the peacekeeping era. In fact the imperial states that are considered here at one time or another all had military personnel or civilian governors who committed what would now be considered atrocities against civilian populations. All three colonial states also behaved far differently in outlying areas where they had not yet established full control—the interior of Africa, the island of Mindanao in the Philippines, and the northwest frontier of the Indian empire (what is now Pakistan and Afghanistan), for example—from how they behaved in the more stable regions of their colonies. In those outlying areas, the empires were focused on fighting rebels who opposed colonial rule, using any means necessary to win. The imperial pacification campaigns that Rudyard Kipling termed "the savage wars of peace" do not bear much resemblance to complex peacekeeping operations today.[2]

Yet if we stop at the list of differences, we miss the striking similarities in motives that have compelled states to be leaders of imperialism and of complex peacekeeping operations. I begin, therefore, with a list of caveats to make clear that I am not equating peacekeeping with colonialism. I then turn to some of the important similarities between the two types of operation, and draw out why those similarities should matter to today's policymakers.

The Caveats: How Colonialism Differs from Peacekeeping

A deeper look at the American occupation of the Philippines makes clear by example that colonialism was in many ways far different from today's peacekeeping operations. The American use of military force in the outlying areas of the Philippines was much harsher than it was in the scenes described above from Manila. In those outlying areas, intentional human cruelty was a defining aspect of the Filipino experience with the American occupation, in a way that would be unacceptable on today's peacekeeping missions. Despite instructions from home to use minimal force and to respect the local population, the "men on the spot" in colonial operations could violate human rights arbitrarily with a great deal of impunity.

The worst example of a brutal American commander in the Philippines occupation was Major General Leonard Wood (who in spite of his viciousness has been eulogized since 1940 in the name of the basic training camp for the U.S. Army in Missouri). While the United States in Wood's era easily controlled the more urban parts of the Philippine islands, rebels in some outlying areas remained violently opposed to foreign rule. On the island of Mindanao in 1905, Wood's counterinsurgency troops were ambushed by a group of Muslim Moro fighters, whose compatriots had a long history of armed resistance to foreign occupation. After the ambush the Moro fighters withdrew into a closed-off volcanic crater, where hundreds of Moro families (including unarmed women and children) were holding a traditional political meeting. Seeing his opportunity to rid the area of rebels, Wood ordered his 800 troops to deploy secretly around the rim of the crater and use their machine guns to mow down everyone inside. Many hundreds of Moros were left dead. When the American press got word of what had happened, there was a heated congressional inquiry and a great deal of public outrage and editorial criticism. Wood was clearly not serving U.S. interests in the Philippines, as the broad American public understood them, and was not following doctrinal protocol for treatment of the Filipino population. U.S. President Theodore Roosevelt nonetheless bucked popular opinion and commended Wood for his bravery, promoting him to the command of the entire Philippines Division.[3] Similar incidents happened regularly in the British and French colonies, too.

The harshness of colonial military actions is not the only thing separating colonialism from peacekeeping. Some of the fundamental goals of empire also differed significantly from the goals of today's peacekeeping operations. The Philippines, for example, were part of the booty won by American forces after fighting a war against Spain over spheres of geographical influence in the western hemisphere. The United States did not go into the Philippines because of any preexisting sympathy for the Filipino population or its humanitarian situation. Instead, American leaders hoped to use Manila as a base to gain a competitive foothold against other imperial powers in Asia. The fundamental purpose of the American occupation was territorial competition, not humanitarian assistance. The notion that the United States was in the Philippines to help the Filipino population became the official explanation for the occupation, but this occurred mostly because it was what was most acceptable to the American public. A large number of American interest groups could all agree to publicly support such a policy, whatever their real underlying motives for occupation may have been.[4]

Over time the United States did establish some democratic institutions in the Philippines, and scholar Tony Smith argues that this historical experience provided a reference point that encouraged the emergence of real democracy in the country in the 1980s.[5] Washington heavily criticized the despotism of the earlier Spanish colonial rulers on the islands, and attempted to distinguish its own colonial administration from what the Spaniards did. At first, democratic development in the Philippines was limited to the community level. But as the decades progressed, a national legislature was formed under American tutelage, which was elected by universal male suffrage and made decisions about most non-defense related domestic economic and social policies. Washington still kept control over the foreign and defense policy of the Philippines, nonetheless, from the turn of the last century until the Japanese invasion of the islands during World War II. Ultimate sovereignty over the territory was ceded to the Philippine people by the Americans only in 1946.

Despite the autonomy on some issues that Washington granted to the Philippines legislature, true political reform in the country was circumscribed by the existing class structure of Philippine society. While the United States did establish universal male suffrage in the Philippines, this was not a real indicator of political equality. Rather than seeking to establish a more equitable socioeconomic system in the country as part of its political reform package, the United States used the existing land-holding class in the Philippines to cement its own imperial control, rewarding local elites who put down dissent with political appointments.[6] This system encouraged political corruption and office buying, and ensured that a few prominent families actually controlled what appeared on the surface to be a functioning democracy. In all three empires considered here—the British and French as well as the American—it was common for the occupiers to work with a chosen set of political favorites in their colonies, since that way the imperialists' own political control would be cemented by support from within.

This more jaundiced view of American colonialism in the Philippines points out the important differences between colonialism and peace-keeping. In today's peacekeeping operations, individual soldiers may still take actions on the ground that violate human rights. But they do so in spite of immense training efforts to the contrary, and they often face court-martial by their own countries when they are caught. In today's operations, foreign military organizations usually have no desire to dominate foreign societies; instead they want to go home as soon as possible to concentrate on more pressing defense needs. Leaders of peacekeeping operations believe that the way to accomplish this is to convince the local populations to take "ownership" of the processes of peace and change in their countries, turning over control to locals as soon as it is feasible. And in contrast to the state competition motivating the occupations of the colonial era, today's UN-authorized peacekeeping missions represent the multilateral, cooperative efforts of people from a wide variety of countries, including both states and NGOs.

Today's actions are supported by universal international law. Accompanying foreign aid programs are designed so that powerful states give to the weak, rather than profiting off of them. Political goals often focus on class transformation, attempting to replace the economic power of the old system's corrupt elites with that of new owners of small businesses. International political advisors seek to establish independent functioning democracies quickly, not over a period of decades, and they encourage the broadest possible political participation by all members of the target society.

Given these significant differences between the two eras, it may seem as though they are not worth comparing. But they are. Both constitute attempts by strong liberal democracies to control foreign political societies. And there are crucial similarities in motives and means between the two eras as well.

Common Characteristics of Colonialism and Peacekeeping

It has to be noted up front that the characteristics of colonialism, both good and bad, varied across time and place. In some ways it is hard to say with any precision what "colonialism" entailed, even when the concept is limited to these three countries in this particular era. Different governments over the years, as well as different individual colonial administrators, held varying philosophies about the design of colonial policy. The policies actually implemented by colonial officials in the field often deviated from the official directives issued by the capitals, leading to further variations in intention and effect.[7] Yet despite these variations, the three imperial states examined here made a common set of key political choices that shaped much of their colonial policy. In turn, these commonalities are reflected in today's peacekeeping operations.

All three states who engaged in colonialism in this era, like the leaders of peacekeeping operations more recently, took on new missions in order to further their national interests as defined by the domestic coalitions who kept their governments in power. In both types of cases, this primarily involved concerns about national security as it was defined at the time. (As we will see below, profit had become less of a motivating factor for territorial control by the late 1800s than it had been earlier in the colonial era.) All three states, just as the leaders of peacekeeping operations do today, simultaneously tried to serve what they considered humanitarian ends in the countries where they intervened. Often state self-interest and humanitarian goals were intertwined with each other, so that motives falling into one or the other category could not easily be distinguished from each other. The same holds true of peacekeeping operations today.

It is sometimes tempting to treat states as if they have unambiguous motives, and to say that they act, for example, on behalf of power and profit. It is also commonplace in the academic political science literature to try to separate out state interests from normative or ethical ideas, and to argue that as global understandings of ethics and appropriateness change, states redefine their interests to align them in accordance with those understandings.[8] The dying out of colonialism in the twentieth century is one example often cited of how changing international norms about self-determination led states to believe that colonialism was no longer in their interests.

Yet in the colonial era, as in peacekeeping operations today, interests and ethics reinforced each other. Control over foreign territory was justified by the great powers as a way for the civilized nations of the world to bring economic development and political enlightenment to those who would otherwise be without them. As we will see below, both the leaders and the publics of the great powers seemed genuinely to believe that colonial occupation was a kind of charitable act. At the same time, bringing Euro-American values, institutions, and assistance to new territories was a means to enhance the security of the colonial powers, because it served as a mechanism of political control in territories whose economic and geographic resources were believed to be important for great power competition. Despite the differences in how security has been defined in the two eras, concerns that are to some extent similar motivate the great powers today, who believe that anarchy and instability in regions near their own borders threaten their well being (often including their economic well-being). The growth of liberal democratic values and institutions in territories that have undergone peacekeeping operations is something that the great powers believe would benefit everyone, themselves as well as the local inhabitants. Self-interest cannot be juxtaposed against a sense of morality as the motivating factor of either colonial actions or peacekeeping operations, because both have been important sources of policy choices.

Interests and norms have been intertwined; the states who are primarily responsible for creating international law have been concerned to legitimate their policy choices through international agreements. The colonial powers considered here wanted to be seen as following common norms of behavior in their colonies; since they were among the lead designers of those international laws, they could ensure that it was the pursuit of their own interests and their own definitions of humanitarianism that were legitimated. The same thing is true of the leaders of most peacekeeping operations today, who have championed the legitimacy of their own intervention, based on a universal obligation to uphold individual human rights, against the arguments of those who would instead privilege the importance of state sovereignty as a legal precept of the United Nations Charter.

National Self-Interest and Control Over Colonies

As in any era, it is difficult to define exactly what the state interests were of the liberal colonizers at the turn of the twentieth century, and where those interests came from. Yet as Philip D. Curtin notes in his sweeping history of Western empires, while some territory may have been acquired "in a fit of absence of mind" (according to an old saw about British imperialism in particular), there is no question that from about 1870 to 1910 the European powers were "out for conquest."[9] A complex mixture of military and economic motives was at work in defining imperial state interests, buttressed in the cases of Britain and France by ideologies of empire that seemed to transcend any interest that could be measured with cold, hard facts. All the great powers of Europe (as well as the United States) were competing against each other for control over new territory, and this meant that empire was a tool to use in the European balance of power game. Colonial occupation helped maintain national security, as it was then defined.

The great powers by this point were not occupying colonies primarily for profit. In fact, they perceived that having colonies was in their interest even though the expense of controlling imperial territory probably out-weighed the competitive benefits that empire provided. Some *private* inter-national trading companies got rich off of the colonial ties that their gov-ernments provided for them, but as time went on the imperial states them-selves were probably spending more on the maintenance of colonies than they received in return from their possessions. The pursuit of empire was difficult to justify on a rational basis, given its expense.[10]

For example, Lance E. Davis and Robert A. Huttenback performed an exhaustive economic analysis of the British Empire in this era, using a cost/benefit perspective to examine the impact of everything from taxes to defense expenditures, and from business development expenses to investor returns. They determined that while some individual investors benefited from the colonies, the British state as a whole did not. (The one exception was the colony of British India, which was self-sufficient in providing for its own expenses and required little financing from London; it did turn a profit for the British state.[11]) Davis and Huttenback discovered that after 1880, even business interests taken as a whole did not profit much from the colonies. While certainly there were individual companies that did well, most businesses based in the British Isles had higher rates of return on their investments than most businesses based in the colonies.[12] According to Davis and Huttenback, "For the general investor in the years after 1880, the Empire was probably a snare and a delusion—a flame not worth the candle."[13] As theorist Michael Doyle and others have argued, colonialism may have been mostly an exercise in national prestige, supported by the particular domestic interest groups who benefited from it.[14]

Yet crucial state interests *appeared* to be at stake in the colonies in spite of their expense, because of how states defined their national security goals. By the turn of the last century, leaders in all three imperial states came to believe that maintaining colonies abroad was in their long-term security interests—something that had not been true in previous times. Earlier, states had been content to claim ownership over land without keeping much of an ongoing personnel presence there. Maintaining func-tioning colonies was expensive and difficult; it required occupying terri-tory, which in turn required the planning of complex political and military actions on the part of the imperialists. Earlier, the European states had not been so interested in the notion of territorial control.[15]

Now, though, the imperial states considered each other competitors, believing that great power warfare at some future point was likely and that the wealthiest and most powerful states would win. National wealth revolved around access to raw materials, including agricultural products, even if maintaining access to them was costly; and many of the colonies were rich in these resources. (Indeed, Davis and Huttenback found that agricultural and extractive industries like mining were the most profitable type of colonial businesses.[16]) When states possessed a colony, they could prevent their competitors from having equal access to those resources. What had earlier been a desire to open up new areas for free trade became, in this era, a drive for exclusive control over territory. State competition, not surprisingly, also included control of the seas that led from the capitals to the colonies and allowed access to the resources in question. A big part of what provided control over the seas was the ownership of ports far from home, even ports in areas which were not rich in raw materials themselves. States' ability to hold territory in distant areas helped them define their relative standing in relationship to each other, and commercial and military interests were mutually reinforcing.[17]

In earlier times, state leaders had often delegated control over their colonial territories to the same private trading companies who were now trying to grow rich off of them. These private companies would field their own armies and fight wars without a great deal of interference from their patrons.[18] Some of these chartered companies continued to operate in central Africa as late as the 1920s.[19] But for the most part, imperial governments by the late nineteenth century cared more about their colonies' long-term upkeep than they had earlier, and sent their own representatives out to occupy and govern these spaces rather than entrusting them to private interests who were hard to oversee without government officials being stationed there. It became ownership and control of the space that mattered for great power competition, not merely the planting of a flag.

These changes in how states viewed their colonial territories, and hence in how they viewed their security interests more generally, were enabled by structural changes in the environment, specifically changes in technology. Occupation of the colonies was possible now, in a way that it had not been earlier, because of new inventions and scientific discoveries.[20] The invention of the repeating rifle and the machine gun gave a huge military advantage to the Europeans and Americans who owned them. Large groups of angry people could now be more easily cowed by a small number of foreign troops. (One of the reasons why colonialism declined as the twentieth century wore on was the proliferation of weapons to the colonized, who could begin to fight back.[21]) The discovery of quinine and other prophylactic drugs also allowed European officials who had grown up in northern climates (and who therefore lacked any natural resistance to tropical diseases) to live in the tropics more comfortably. Steam ships and railroads made navigating immense distances easier, and along with the telegraph improved communication between the capitals and their colonies. These technological changes meant that states were able to invest their own scarce resources into their colonies to an extent that hadn't been prudent earlier, because European and American officials could now live in the colonies in relative safety and security. Structural changes enabled states to take on new definitions of their own security interests.

Since international security concerns appeared to be at stake in the colonies, and since structural changes allowed occupation by state officials to occur, the imperial actions taken by the great powers came to have components that resembled modern-day complex peacekeeping operations. The imperial capitals now had reasons to care about the long-term viability and stability of these territories. Earlier, the British and French private companies and plantations who were sent abroad had been allowed to plunder the colonial territory that they were granted. The political support that the capitals received from these small but wealthy groups of traders was so great, in comparison to the relatively insignificant state interest that the imperialists had previously believed they held in their colonies, that the consequences of short-term thinking in the colonies seemed unimportant. Now, on the other hand, states became interested in preserving and husbanding colonial resources for the future.[22] These resources included not only the obvious ones of land and raw materials, but also the more abstract good will of those who were subjected to imperial control. Without that good will, colonial governance would have been more difficult to accomplish, because people who hate those who occupy them tend to carry out violence against the occupiers and thwart them economically.

The need to establish good will meant that the imperial capitals believed they had an interest in encouraging economic development in their colonies. Development would relieve poverty, and make the subject population more appreciative of the benefits of being in the empire. Simultaneously, development would expand the trading opportunities for home-state companies, and improve the climate for potential investors. This would broaden the spectrum of industries at home who benefited from colonial possession, and in turn would help cement political support for the continuation of colonial control. It would also create a tax base to help make the colonies self-financing, minimizing imperial expenditure on their upkeep while silencing critics at home who doubted the colonies' real utility.[23] In other words, the imperialists encouraged economic development and improvement in their colonies, or what the French called *mise en valeur*,[24] at least in part because it served their self-interests to do so. The better the colonies were doing, the easier it would be politically to maintain them.

Colonial occupation hence became self-perpetuating and self-reinforcing: once it was in place, it created the economic and political momentum to propel itself forward. The burgeoning interests of imperialist states in the long-term health of their colonies motivated them to make life in their colonies more secure. That way their own officials and traders could live in the colonies without fear of internal instability. If the environment were made secure, imperial possessions could also be more easily defended from predatory moves by state competitors in the race for territorial control. Permanent colonies, in other words, required what amounted to peacekeeping operations for the sake of imperial national interests.

The Humanitarian Impulse and Colonial Control

Today's international community may not like to hear it, but humanitarian concerns were also a component of the colonialism practiced a century ago by Great Britain, France, and the United States, even though the form of those concerns was very paternalistic and even though they came second to the desire for conquest. The liberal leaders of empire wanted to share European and American values, institutions, and achievements with areas of the world that were less fortunate, and each of them believed that the superior attributes of their own civilizations were a gift to bestow on others.

There is an irresolvable scholarly debate about how *genuine* the humanitarian impulse was among imperial leaders. Some scholars argue that while the imperialists said they were acting out of a desire to be moral and generous, their humanitarianism was in fact just window-dressing for naked self-interest.[25] There is no way to determine the truth about this question, since one can't probe the minds of dead leaders and people's psychological motives are usually mixed. Yet certainly their writings indicate that they believed themselves to be sincere.

More important, there is no question that Great Britain, France, and the United States all *justified* imperialism to their domestic populations through its purported humanitarian benefits, and in turn this justification influenced how their policies toward their colonies had to be designed. All three of these countries were relatively liberal democracies a hundred years ago; even if none of them had universal suffrage, all of them had elected legislatures that were subject to criticism by the opposition and the press. Public opinion mattered. That means that however false the original claims about humanitarian motives may have been, humanitarianism became a necessary element of colonial practice, at least in part because home publics demanded it. Daniel Philpott has argued that "civic liberalism," or a public moral sense, is one of the major factors propelling recent peacekeeping operations.[26] Civic liberalism mattered in the colonial era, too.

Colonialism could not have been sustainable without the tacit support of the voters. The creation and direction of colonial policy was answerable to the people at home who read the papers, and hence it had to be seen as ethical. Most of the good citizens of these imperial states believed themselves to be morally upright. The vast majority of the population in all three countries was Christian, and it wanted to fulfill what it saw as the Christian obligation to show benevolence to others, especially those who were weaker. People did not want to see themselves as exploiting others for the sake of economic gain, but instead as missionaries on behalf of progress. The voters expressed outrage and conducted legislative investigations when word leaked out about atrocities that were committed by their representatives in the colonies.[27] Governments therefore had an incentive to try to ensure that colonial rule appeared benign. Voters also felt a sense of responsibility to the disadvantaged of the world, and wanted their officials in the colonies to act on behalf of justice and with noblesse oblige.[28]

Imperial leaders provided a variety of moral justifications for their colonial actions. For the U.S. in the Philippines, the legitimating principle of occupation was to bring democratization to a country steeped in Spanish despotism. For France, the legitimating principle of actions in Africa was the *mission civilisatrice*—the belief that the superior achievements of French language, culture, philosophy, and science could be transmitted to foster cleaner, more efficient, more prosperous and more rational societies in the non-European world, which would eventually become part of greater France.[29] For Great Britain, the term "trusteeship" was used to indicate that, each at its own pace, the colonies and their indigenous leaders would sooner or later be guided along the path toward good self-government.[30] For all three colonial powers, these moral goals led to certain common policy choices. The abolition of slavery abroad, along with other practices that were considered barbaric (such as polygamy), was a common justifying theme—even though in practice some French officers traded in slaves themselves.[31]

Beyond the need to justify their actions, imperial leaders also had a second straightforward incentive to follow relatively humane practices in the colonies. The capitals tried to minimize the cost of maintaining their empires,[32] and caring for the well being of the colonial population was one means to lower the costs of occupation. Humanitarianism, in other words, was a cheap way to gain control. Fighting wars is a very costly business, especially against rebel insurgents who are willing to die for their opposition to colonial rule. To win without fighting was better, as the classic military theorist Sun Tzu would say; the imperialists needed to find a way to control their colonial populations short of constant violence.

Direct rule by multiple layers of colonial officials, who arrived in the field after having had comfortable, relatively easy lives in the imperial capitals, was not a cost-effective solution. Those officials had to be paid handsomely to convince them to move halfway across the world and live in relative deprivation, isolated from their families and communities (at a time when communication was slow and unreliable), and beset by the threat of violent unrest and disease. The fewer officials that had to be sent out from the capitals, the cheaper the occupation. A means for political control had to be found that involved neither the expense of traditional military operations, nor a great deal of oversight by foreign bureaucrats.

The ideal mechanism, used to a greater or lesser degree by all three powers, was psychological: it was to try to make the people of the colonies *want* to be connected to the empire. Life inside the empire had to seem better than the alternative. As Michael Doyle has argued, subjects needed to be persuaded that foreign rule was to their benefit, with force used only as a last resort.[33] As Jeffrey Herbst has pointed out, the use of violence was a sign of the weakness of the occupiers, and their inability to maintain control using other means.[34]

Sometimes control was accomplished using indirect rule, allowing existing political structures in the colonies to continue to function under imperial oversight. As Curtin notes, "actual rule over the conquered societies was far more in local hands than in those of European administrators."[35] Members of the local population who cooperated with the empire would be paid off for their support. This might mean granting particular local figures public office, as was the case in the Philippines. It might mean giving weapons and other provisions to those on the right side of rebel insurgencies,[36] or protecting particular local markets from both taxes and attack.[37] It sometimes even meant turning a blind eye to the practice of slavery by one's friends, while condemning it in one's enemies.[38] In all three empires, it was often imperial military officers who made or helped make the judgment about whom to reward. Like today's peacekeepers, their village patrols gave them good intelligence about who among the locals was doing what.

Other times, political control was furthered by providing direct humanitarian aid to the population. While there is no question that much of colonial practice was violent and inhumane,[39] there is also no question that rule by brute force alone was not in the interest of the imperial states—it was simply too expensive. In the words of Louis Faidherbe, founder of the

French colonial administration in Senegal, the imperial powers had to "maintain tranquility so that the natives may work and produce in all security to feed our posts with their products, and so that they may recognize the advantage of our domination."[40] All three of these imperial states therefore pursued some form of a "hearts and minds" campaign, designed to convince the population at both an emotional and intellectual level that imperialism was a good thing.

Hearts and minds considerations permeated the doctrine given to military forces on the ground, who were regularly involved in humanitarian aid and civil construction projects. Such benevolent acts were combined with highly structured educational systems,[41] designed to inculcate the lesson that imperial administration served local interests. The imperialists believed that education was one of the major fruits of civilization they could share with their colonies, even as it privileged one vision of civilization in comparison to any other. Gerrit Gong argues that colonial expansion was in fact a clash of civilizations, where the Europeans and Americans would set the rules about what was civilized and what was not, and would convince those in the colonies to accept their views.[42]

Some aspects of these hearts and minds campaigns were blatantly racist and classist. For example, one of the goals of the French Empire in Africa was to discourage the use of local languages and replace them with French (in some Muslim areas, Arabic was a tolerated alternative). French was seen both as the language of unity across cultures, and as culturally superior to other languages because of the legacy of French literature.[43] Free public schools were therefore established in France's colonies to improve the natives by teaching them French. The best opportunities for educational advancement were provided to urban students, who were seen as more capable of cultural assimilation than their rural counterparts. Yet in spite of the arrogance of these policies, there appeared to be a genuine belief in Paris that to learn French and to receive a European-style education provided an opportunity for those in the colonies to lift themselves out of a life of misery. The same can be said for efforts to provide the colonies with basic French-model hygiene and sound architectural planning.

Simultaneously, the provision of these services to the locals was a mechanism for institutionalizing imperial control at a relatively low cost. As Timothy Mitchell notes, when locals are trained to follow carefully constructed imperial procedures—in education, in social policy, in building construction, and so forth—eventually the structures and practices of colonialism become so embedded in society that they seem natural and are much less likely to be questioned.[44] At that point most of the colonizers can stay home in their capitals, because the colonies will run themselves peacefully.

Beyond the need to justify colonialism to their home populations and the interest that the empires had in maintaining control at minimal cost, humanitarian aid also furthered imperialist interests for a third reason: it fostered investment and trade. Development assistance worked hand in hand with commercial interests, and the two were philosophically intertwined. One indicator of this was the fact that Christian missionaries in the colonies, such as British explorer David Livingstone, cooperated with home-state traders and investors in the belief that the spread of Western values, culture, and trade links were part and parcel of their main mission of religious proselytizing.[45] All things European, both Christianity and commerce, were seen as moral.

The economic development that occurred in the colonies in fact tended to benefit the citizens of Europe and America more than it helped the locals. Colonial administrators, for example, used conscripted local labor to build pieces of infrastructure and to transport goods to port cities from rural areas, tending to undermine the moral imperative of ending slavery. Health programs concentrated on wiping out the diseases that bothered the European occupiers rather than those that killed the native population. Nonetheless, in spite of these hypocrisies, part of the civilizing mission included the desire to lessen the ills of poverty, and it was widely believed that international trade integration would help achieve this goal.[46] Peace was seen as a necessary background condition for trade to flourish, which meant that deploying military troops in what would now be called peacekeeping roles was also part of the developmental philosophy.[47]

These three requirements—the need to justify colonialism in the public eye at home, the need for cheap security in the colonies and local acceptance of outside rule, and the need to foster trade and investment through development—meant that colonialism in this era was not simply about economic exploitation of one group by another, nor was it simply about the unthinking use of force. It was constrained by principles that could be seen as a means for improving the lives of the colonized,[48] even as they served the interests of empire. Humanitarianism was part and parcel of state self-interest, even as some idealists pursued it in the colonies for its own sake.

National Self-Interest and Complex Peacekeeping

Clearly the particular set of national interests that supported imperialism, defined by great power competition to control and exploit foreign territory, is not what motivates peacekeeping today. The kind of complex peacekeeping operations talked about in this book are mostly multilateral, necessitating the cooperation of many states, and done under the authorization of the United Nations. Yet, as in the colonial era, powerful states today tend to become involved in complex peacekeeping operations largely when they perceive that their national interests are involved. They act out of strong humanitarian impulses as well. But peacekeeping forces are not sent everywhere that violent human suffering exists. Once again, self-interest and humanitarianism are intertwined.

Perhaps the most searing example of state self-interest overcoming the humanitarian impulse is the tragedy of Rwanda, outlined in the previous chapter. Both Al Gore and George W. Bush, the major candidates for the U.S. presidency in 2000, agreed that the United States did the right thing by not intervening to stop the genocide.[49] Gore was Vice President when the United States made its decision not to intervene, and Bush's campaign included a pledge to lower the U.S. commitment to peacekeeping, so it is understandable that these two would affirm the choice that was made. Yet it is unlikely that this affirmation is shared by the larger liberal democratic international community. In most corners, including the UN Secretariat itself, the failure to act in Rwanda is viewed with shame. Humanitarianism in response to terrible suffering did not prove a strong enough impulse to overcome the desire by states to save their political capital, their economic resources, and the safety of their troops for areas of the world that were more central to their national security interests.

Humanitarian concerns were involved in all of the complex peacekeeping missions of the 1990s, and humanitarianism cannot be discounted as a motive in any of the cases. But that does not change the fact that the humanitarian impulse is insufficient to explain why peacekeeping happens sometimes and not others. National self-interest almost always motivates those who lead complex operations, at least in part.[50] A return to the examples of complex military peacekeeping outlined in the previous chapter helps illustrate some of the self-interested motives behind the missions.

Haiti

It took three years for the United States to take strong action in response to humanitarian concerns about the situation in Haiti after the 1991 coup, and the delay in this case is perhaps the best illustration that humanitarian concerns alone are not sufficient motivation for complex military peacekeeping operations to be deployed even in areas that border the great powers—even when the decision is eventually taken to intervene.

In 1991, Haiti's brutal and corrupted military forces ousted the newly democratically elected president Jean-Bertrand Aristide, after he had been in office for only seven months. What had seemed like a possible new beginning for a country steeped in centuries of poverty and political violence was cut short. Coup leaders and the militia who supported them— the Front for Haitian Advancement and Progress (FRAPH)—killed more than a thousand of Aristide's supporters. The new regime, led by General Raoul Cédras, was harsh in its smashing of dissent. Its security forces, the Force Armée d'Haiti (FADH), meanwhile ignored street crime and encouraged Haiti's tradition of deadly popular vigilantism, leading to even more chaos and death.[51]

While the international community, represented both by the United Nations and by the Organization of American States, publicly deplored these events, it was not until 1993—following two years of misery—that the United Nations Security Council authorized the United States to lead a complex peacekeeping mission to help restore Aristide to power. An initial attempt by U.S. and Canadian forces to land in the capital of Port-au-Prince in 1993 was aborted when angry crowds appeared on the shore, deterring the ships from docking. Under the threat that a full-scale invasion would be launched if they met further resistance, Cédras finally ceded to the Americans and peacekeepers arrived on the island in September 1994.

A violent humanitarian emergency near American shores did eventually lead Washington to intervene, but it took three years to galvanize sufficient political will for it to happen. Humanitarian concerns in this case were voiced most loudly by African-American political pressure groups who argued that an American failure to act to restore democracy to Haiti would amount to racism. But humanitarianism failed to lead to immediate action. Washington's primary interest was instead to stop the influx of tens of thousands of Haitian refugees who had set out by boat for U.S. territory as the dictatorship became more oppressive. What convinced U.S. leaders that some kind of direct military action on their part was finally necessary was that a caucus of African-American legislators began loudly protesting the U.S. policy of turning away Haitian boat people, and of imprisoning those who would not turn back at Guantanamo Bay, Cuba.[52]

Beyond the domestic political furor involved, American national security concerns were associated with this refugee question. The need to rescue, intercept, and process Haitian refugees approaching U.S. territory by sea was tying up U.S. military and Coast Guard resources that might otherwise be used for counter-narcotics activity or for monitoring the actions of Cuba's Communist leader, Fidel Castro.[53] In other words, pressure from particular domestic interest groups coupled with strong national security interests was required for intervention to take place; humanitarianism alone did not lead to strong action in the first three years of the Cédras regime. In part, the humanitarian impulse was tempered both by the recent seeming failure of American troops in Somalia, and by the fact that major security crises were simultaneously underway in the Balkans and Rwanda. There were limits to the military actions that U.S. leaders were willing to take.

In 2004, in contrast, U.S.-led multilateral intervention into the newly resurgent chaos in Haiti was quicker than it had been a decade before. While many liberal commentators criticized the Bush administration for its reluctance to provide more *economic* assistance to Aristide before the crisis point was reached, it took only a few weeks for Washington to send in the Marines once political violence broke out in Haiti in mid-January 2004. A close reading of events reveals once again, however, that humanitarian motives on their own were insufficient to motivate intervention. As late as mid-February, senior Bush administration officials were announcing that no military intervention was likely, especially since the Pentagon was so focused on Iraq, Afghanistan, and the potential for serious crises elsewhere (ranging from North Korea to Iran).[54]

What apparently caused Washington to call for an emergency meeting of the UN Security Council on February 29, 2004 to authorize the dispatch of troops to Port-au-Prince—and to use the offer of safe passage to urge Aristide out of office—was once again the threat of a refugee exodus spinning out of control. This time around, the idea of keeping intercepted Haitian asylum seekers for processing at the U.S. military installation in Guantanamo Bay, Cuba—the policy followed in the early 1990s—would have been difficult, given that the United States had set up a major military prison camp there to house accused terrorists captured in Afghanistan and elsewhere. Washington's policy in 2004 was instead to return all Haitian boat people back to the Port-au-Prince harbor. When armed Aristide supporters seized the Haitian Coast Guard facilities at Port-au-Prince, leaving Haitian Coast Guard personnel "fleeing for their lives," Washington decided it had had enough.[55] This time around, it was not domestic interest-group pressure that motivated U.S. actions, since the Congressional Black Caucus voiced its support for keeping Aristide in place as the democratically elected leader of Haiti. Instead, it was national security interests plain and simple that led Washington to call for a UN-authorized peace mission.

The Balkans

The motivations underlying NATO intervention in the Balkans remain hotly contested, with cynics arguing that NATO's major goal in both cases was to increase NATO's own sense of purpose and strength, and others responding that humanitarianism was the primary impetus behind the efforts. As was noted in the previous chapter, NATO military intervention in the form of air strikes in both Bosnia and Kosovo was undertaken largely for humanitarian reasons. Intervention in Bosnia was championed (among others) by Jewish-American lobbying groups, who argued that genocide should never be allowed to happen again.[56] Intervention in Kosovo was supported, again among others, by humanitarian NGOs who feared that the Albanians being driven from their homes by Serbian paramilitary groups would face mass starvation and death from exposure if the raids were not stopped.[57]

In both cases it was clear that the international military representatives on the ground—lightly armed in the case of UN peacekeepers in Bosnia, unarmed in the case of OSCE observers in Kosovo—were incapable by themselves of stopping the ethnic cleansing that was either underway or threatened. UNPROFOR was unable to hold the safe areas inside Bosnia or stop the ongoing military onslaughts in Bosnia and Croatia. OSCE monitors in Kosovo were unable either to protect themselves against growing Serb paramilitary harassment, or to stop what appeared to be plans for a major Serbian anti-Albanian campaign in Kosovo in spring 1999. Shocking news about death camps and mass rapes in Bosnia, and about massacre sites and village attacks in Kosovo, mobilized popular support for the interventions. Yet similar conditions in Rwanda had not prompted intervention. Something besides pure humanitarianism must have separated out the two sets of cases from each other.

The self-interested motives for intervention and peacekeeping in both Bosnia and Kosovo are easy to enumerate. As in the case of Haiti, in both Balkans cases a major motivation for NATO intervention was that NATO member states feared refugee crises. Balkan refugees who had fled their home countries were consuming state welfare resources and competing for low-wage jobs to an extent that was perceived to threaten the economic stability of Western Europe, especially in Germany and Italy.[58] Just as was the case in Haiti, refugee movements, especially in the case of Kosovo, carried with them broader security threats. When the start of the NATO bombing campaign caused Serbian forces to expel the Muslim population from Kosovo, the presence of large numbers of Kosovar Muslim refugees in Macedonia began to empower hard-line anti-Albanian politicians in Skopje. Macedonia had been a country which seemed up until that point capable of avoiding the ethnic violence that plagued so much of the rest of the former Yugoslavia. The refugee crisis in Macedonia spawned real fear that European stability was threatened once again, in an era when Europe was supposed to be drawing together as never before in the European Union. This meant that a stabilizing presence was required in the region once the bombing campaign was over.

At least part of the motivation for NATO involvement in both of these cases was also to demonstrate allied (and especially American) resolve to maintain the credibility of the alliance as a European security institution after the cold war was over.[59] Humanitarianism in the Balkans was buttressed by clear self-interest. The relative ranking of the two motivations in NATO's hierarchy of goals may never be firmly established; they were intertwined.

East Timor

When Australia led the initial UN-authorized mission to restore peace following East Timor's popular vote for independence from Indonesia in 1999, Canberra was motivated at least in part by the national guilt felt for its 20-year recognition of Indonesian sovereignty over the island. Most of the rest of the world had condemned Indonesia's 1975 invasion of East Timor, while Australia had opted for cooperation with the Indonesian authorities instead.[60] The Australian population now demanded humanitarian action by the government when Indonesia did nothing to stop the massacres following the independence vote. A sizeable Timorese émigré population in Australia was particularly vocal about this issue.

But Australia's concern for East Timor was not based solely on emotion. As noted in the previous chapter, Australia was not willing to challenge Indonesia militarily over the question of protecting the East Timorese; it did not sacrifice its national security interests for the sake of humanitarianism. Instead the intervention was delayed pending Indonesia's permission—even though there was good intelligence available about the chaos that would result after the referendum, and the referendum results themselves technically ended Indonesian claims to the territory.

Australia did react very quickly once Indonesia's permission for intervention was gained, and there is no question that humanitarianism was a major part of Canberra's motivation; indeed Australia pushed hard to ensure that Indonesia would support a UN intervention sooner rather than later. But Canberra's interests were also caught up with East Timor's territorial proximity to Australia. The island is located around 650 km (or around 350 mi.) from the key northern naval base at Darwin, and the major factor shaping Australia's defense policy since the end of the cold war has been the perceived need to protect itself from potential instability in the areas surrounding its territory.[61] The crisis in East Timor gave the Australian Defense Forces an opportunity to demonstrate their continuing value to the state after the cold war ended, since one of the scenarios that had motivated defense planning had come to pass.

While not mentioned publicly, concerns about a refugee influx were probably part of Australian decisionmakers' concern as well.[62] Canberra has struggled in recent years to erect barricades against an influx of economic refugees from Southeast Asia, amidst great public outcry about unfair treatment of these beleaguered groups. If a large number of real humanitarian refugees were to join the hordes seeking entrance, Australia's immigration system might have been overwhelmed. Australia also hoped that a peaceful resolution in East Timor might encourage Indonesia to pursue cooperative solutions in other parts of its territory that were suffused with ethnic violence, leaving the sea lanes around Australia more stable in the future.

Furthermore, Australia also has a large potential economic interest in the development of the oil and gas fields that lie in the seabed between itself and East Timor, the so-called Timor Gap. While Australia's earlier support for Indonesia had ensured that Canberra would get favorable treatment in the Timor Gap oil agreements signed in previous years, instability in East Timor threatened the potential return on Australia's state investments. While the final disposition of the contracts on these fields remains unclear—despite a treaty signed in 2002, both a border dispute and a commercial lawsuit continue to stall progress—one argument that Australia can make to the government in Dili for favorable treatment on this issue is that it provided peacekeeping help when East Timor most needed it.

While humanitarianism certainly played a crucial role in all of the complex military peacekeeping operations of the 1990s, in each case state self-interests were also clearly involved. In each case, bringing stability to a war-torn region served the security interests of militarily powerful states. While the purpose was not at all the territorial competition that had motivated the great powers during the colonial era, it did involve territorial pacification abroad for the sake of security at home. Military intervention was once again followed by at least short-term occupation, in order to ensure that state self-interests in territorial stability were met.

Philpott argues that the security issues involved in these cases did not involve a "direct and significant stake" for the states involved. He believes that concerns about refugees, or about a vague definition of future European stability, "were hardly the direct challenges to security that realists expect as occasions for intervention."[63] Instead, he sees the humanitarian concerns of domestic actors inside liberal democracies, and the convergence of these concerns across countries, as the primary engine for complex peacekeeping operations. Certainly, in each case discussed above, political pressure from domestic groups concerned about humanitarianism was a major contributing factor explaining the decision to intervene. Yet that factor alone does not explain why intervention happens in some cases and not others, nor does it explain the reluctance of states to intervene and what is often a long delay in the timing of intervention. Philpott's "civic liberalism" in democracies is balanced by the concerns of hard-headed realists, who demand that clear national interest direct both budgetary expenditures and the use of military force. As in the colonial era, intervention occurs because national security interests and humanitarian goals reinforce each other, and the two motives cannot be teased apart.

As in the late colonial era, structural changes made the expansion of intrusive peacekeeping possible. Humanitarianism and state security interest were buttressed by enabling factors. In part, superior technology again played a role; this time around, the key military advantages held by those who led the complex peacekeeping operations included advanced night-vision and reconnaissance equipment that allowed the tracking of rebel formations and gun smugglers, as well as stand-off precision-strike aircraft that permitted the international community to easily enforce its will on those who might otherwise be recalcitrant—all technologies that underwent massive improvement in the 1980s and 1990s in the service of other military goals of the United States in particular (directed first against the Soviet Union, and later against other enemies like Iraq).

Change in the structure of the international political system also played a crucial role. The end of the cold war meant that Russia could be persuaded to allow the Euro-American states to lead peacekeeping interventions without interfering, giving the United Nations Security Council the ability to authorize humanitarian action in a way that would have been unthinkable in the earlier era of frequent vetoes. Russia could even be persuaded, in the cases of Bosnia and Kosovo, to contribute significant military resources to joint peacekeeping efforts, enhancing the multilateral legitimacy of the actions taken. Structural change made the idea of occupying territory for the sake of liberal democratic development possible, in a way that it earlier would not have been.

Humanitarianism and Complex Peacekeeping

The intertwining of humanitarian and self-interested motives has an interesting twist in today's operations. In contrast to the imperial era, when colonialism was accepted as a normal component of state policy by a broad spectrum of political actors, today there is no agreement that complex peacekeeping missions serve the national interest. As a result, the

United States government has felt that it must convince the domestic public (and especially the U.S. Congress) that its goals are *not* purely humanitarian when American troops are sent abroad, and that national interests are truly at stake.[64] Rather than using humanitarianism to publicly justify policies that are pursued for underlying state security reasons, state security interests are sometimes used to justify policies that may truly be motivated by more idealistic humanitarian impulses.[65]

The need to demonstrate that self-interest lay behind peacekeeping decisions was one of the requirements laid out by President Bill Clinton's Presidential Decision Directive (PDD) 25, "U.S. Policy on Reforming Multilateral Peace Operations," promulgated in Spring 1994.[66] One of the reasons that the Clinton administration did not take action to stop the Rwandan genocide was because such action could not be justified on the narrow grounds of self-interest that this policy laid out—a choice that received harsh criticism from NGOs and liberal commentators.[67] Yet from the other side, PDD-25 was lambasted by conservative Republicans for its failure to go far enough. It would not prevent peacekeeping overextension, in their view, because "self-interest" was too ambiguously construed.[68] A somewhat similar debate about humanitarian overreach, and whether the national interest was served by peacekeeping deployments, unfolded in Great Britain in late 2001.[69] Humanitarian motives do not serve the same justificatory purpose that they did in the colonial era.

Yet self-interest and humanitarianism remain intertwined in today's complex peacekeeping operations. Not only is this because peacekeeping operations are undertaken for both interest-based and humanitarian reasons. It is also because humanitarian actions have rational, objective benefits for the countries leading these operations, and help to motivate the choices that are made. At some level, all humanitarian efforts undertaken by peacekeeping forces have a self-interested component, since they help to demonstrate the good will of those who have intervened (especially military troops who might otherwise look intimidating).[70] In turn this can serve an intelligence function for the peacekeepers, since the citizenry who believe that the military presence is benign are more likely to be forthcoming with useful information.

Beyond this, though, examples from Haiti and Bosnia help to demonstrate the range of state political motives lying behind the design of humanitarian actions. These examples illustrate once again the twin dangers of complex peacekeeping operations: either doing too little because of the lack of political will to see an operation through to its conclusion, or trying to do so much that it becomes impossible to leave while still maintaining control over developments.

In Haiti in 1994, the primary goal of the U.S. government was to get out quickly and hand over operations to the United Nations. Despite the managerial role that U.S. forces initially adopted inside Haitian governmental institutions (outlined in the previous chapter), American troops were specifically instructed not to engage in humanitarian activities that could be classified as economic development. Those tasks were to be left to nongovernmental aid organizations,[71] while the troops were to focus only on humanitarian tasks related to their immediate mission goals of overseeing secure elections and then leaving. In the words of one of the officers deployed to Haiti, "The MNF had to walk a fine line between restoring critical services and infrastructure and supplanting the very institutions they were trying to resurrect."[72] As a result humanitarian assistance was limited to fulfilling the immediate, pressing needs of the population, rather than anything that might be considered "nation-building."[73]

The United States wanted to ensure that it did not create a situation where the Haitian population became dependent on its presence in the country.[74] Military engineers rebuilt electrical and water supply systems in Haiti to get them functioning again, and put major effort into reconstructing prisons to make them both secure and humane. These things were consistent with the goal of restoring immediate order so that elections could be held. But the troops in Haiti did not get involved in village reconstruction or business development aid, the way they later would in the Balkans.

It turned out that the nongovernmental aid organizations arrived on the scene later than expected, and there was a sense that they lacked good coordination of their activities. This meant that while the strategy of limited aid allowed the United States to leave the country in quick order (serving Washington's primary interest in conserving its national resources for other tasks), it also contributed to a sense among the Haitian population that the United States was half-hearted in its intervention.[75] This may explain why the fundamental tenor of life in Haiti did not change very much in the ensuing years despite the change in government that the U.S. helped oversee. Serving immediate interests in state aid policy may have detracted from the longer-term interest in Haitian stability. This was reinforced by press reports in 2004, where Haitians on the ground were quoted as saying things like, "Last time around they didn't do much."

Bosnia presents a very different picture. Paddy Ashdown, the High Representative appointed to oversee the transition process in BiH in 2002, wrote that "Bosnia will be seen as a new model for international intervention—one designed not to pursue narrow national interests but to prevent conflict, to promote human rights and to rebuild war-torn societies."[76] Ashdown is correct that narrow national interests have been, at least for the most part, subsumed under the interests of the international community as a whole in BiH.[77] It is nonetheless the case that the primary focus of humanitarian action there—reconstruction designed to foster the return of people displaced by the war—has been in tune with the national interests of the surrounding West European countries. Their goal has been to send their Balkan refugee populations home.

Germany's humanitarian policy in the Balkans stands out in this regard. German military construction units that are earmarked for humanitarian assistance work were deployed alongside other NATO troops in Bosnia, but not under NATO command; instead they were "co-located for national purposes." Their goal was specifically to encourage refugee returns, rather than other possible humanitarian goals, because Germany felt economically burdened by the presence of Balkan refugees on its soil.[78] This caused some officials at NATO headquarters to believe that the German troops were there primarily to serve German national interests.[79]

Yet Germany is not unique. While NATO troops as a whole have engaged in more immediate, purely humanitarian aid (such as flood relief and clothing donations), a major goal of all military humanitarian assistance work in Bosnia has been to encourage refugees to return. Civilian Military Cooperation (CIMIC) units have engaged in everything from road and bridge reconstruction around targeted villages,[80] to demining operations in destroyed housing sites,[81] to the rebuilding of electrical infrastructure,[82] for one major purpose: to facilitate the return of minority groups to their original homes. Even when the immediate relocation of displaced people has been merely from one area in BiH to another, the process had positive feedback on the overall refugee situation, since the internally displaced were themselves often occupying homes left by others because of the war.[83] When one group left, the other could return. Analysts for the U.S. Naval War College have called SFOR's policy in Bosnia "a policy of deliberate politicization of assistance."[84]

These military efforts have complemented the strategies of civilian aid agencies working in BiH. The European Commission, for example, has funded small-scale projects to encourage refugee returns, often disbursing this money through SFOR military civil affairs projects.[85] The European Union and the UN High Commissioner for Refugees together created what was called an "Open Cities" program, which targeted international reconstruction assistance to villages whose mayors expressed a willingness to allow and encourage refugee returns, and denied financial aid to those whose mayors opposed this goal.[86] National aid agencies supporting the peacekeeping efforts, including both the British Department for International Development (DFID) and the Canadian International Development

Agency (CIDA), have similarly focused their efforts on the return and reintegration of displaced persons to their original homes. Their conditional aid has gone, for example, to small business owners who employ multiethnic returnees, and who donate a significant share of their profits to multiethnic community rebuilding efforts.[87]

All of these efforts at encouraging returns in BiH have been designed to control political developments in the country, to ensure that an ethnically mixed polity emerges in the future. But their results have been indeterminate. On one hand, the overall number of returnees seems large. As of late 2002, UN High Commissioner on Refugees data indicated that 367,000 "minority returns" had occurred in BiH—in other words, cases where people chose to reclaim or rebuild homes in locales where they are members of ethnic minority populations, surrounded by members of the ethnic groups who had engaged in ethnic cleansing against them during the war. There are many examples where individual towns have regained the mixed ethnic balance levels they enjoyed before the war broke out.[88] This has happened under strong pressure from the international community for local officials to enforce the property reclamation laws that were put into effect under the Dayton process. It often required the international community to intrude into the details of local contracts and land survey assessments.[89]

Yet many of those who have taken repossession of their homes have done so merely to sell or exchange them, because they believed that as ethnic minorities they lacked good opportunities for education and employment in hostile ethnic areas.[90] When home-owners have returned, it is often older members of the family who have gone back, since working-age people have found better jobs in other locations. The schooling available to ethnic minority children is also often inferior to that available elsewhere.[91] Perhaps the greatest indicator that ethnic reintegration has moved more slowly in BiH than the international community had hoped is that in the October 2002 general elections, held seven years after the Dayton accords had been signed, the same nationalist parties responsible for waging the war still did quite well. Even durable and well-funded humanitarian efforts that are directed at political change are difficult to make succeed.

International Law and the Justification of Foreign Control

One key indicator of the importance that countries place on justifying their actions in the public eye, whatever their true underlying motives, is their decision to turn to international law to support their choices. Great Britain, France, and the United States all actively participated in the drawing up of a series of international agreements about colonialism in Africa in the late nineteenth and early twentieth centuries. They wanted to legitimate their actions in the eyes of international law as it existed at that time. They also saw international law as a means for furthering their control over territory, by limiting what their competitors could do in response to their own actions.

The diplomatic agreements of that era reflected the obligation these states believed themselves to have to work toward humanitarian goals in their colonies. The most prominent example was the Berlin Conference General Act of 1885, an international agreement signed by the major European and American powers at a conference convened by Otto von Bismarck, Chancellor of the German Empire. The primary purpose of the act was to draw up borders and divide the African continent into distinct colonial jurisdictions, to prevent unnecessary war and protectionist trade competition among the imperial states. This contributed to the imperialists' overall goal of saving money; when geographical areas were recognized as belonging to particular empires, there was less need to defend them from the predatory ambitions of other states.[92]

But this agreement also contained a humanitarian plank. It said that:

> All the powers exercising sovereign rights or influence in the aforementioned [African] territories bind themselves to watch over the preservation of native tribes, and to care for the improvement of the conditions of their moral and material well-being and to help in suppressing slavery, and especially the Slave Trade. They shall, without distinction of creed or nation, protect and favor all religious, scientific, or charitable institutions and undertakings created and organized for the above ends, or which aim at instructing the natives and bringing home to them the blessings of civilization.[93]

A later conference convened in Brussels in 1889–90 continued to focus the attention of the imperial states on the need to abolish the slave trade, as well as to control the trade in small arms, in their African colonies.[94]

The *legal* components of these agreements have been criticized for their frailty. There were no binding treaties passed, merely agreements that did not require ratification in parliament. Boundaries between imperial holdings in Africa were recognized primarily because it was in the imperialists' self-interest to do so, and not because of the existence of the accords themselves.[95] And as far as humanitarianism is concerned, some analysts claim that the good intentions reflected in the documents remained only on paper.[96] The references to moral obligations were vague, and may have been inserted primarily to satisfy the missionaries who attended the proceedings. Tellingly in this regard, the Berlin Conference did not recognize the principle of self-determination. Africans themselves were not invited to participate in the meetings.[97] The American representative to the Berlin Conference raised this as an issue for discussion, suggesting that local consent and self-determination were important humanitarian issues, but he was rebuffed. The European imperialists wanted to preserve their freedom to make ad hoc arrangements with individual local chieftains whom they might buy off from time to time, and to avoid overarching legal recognition of any specific model of local African authority.[98]

The neglect of self-determination was seen to be legitimate because the international legal principles of that time did not apply universally to all international actors. Instead, as Robert H. Jackson eloquently notes, sovereignty, or the right (and responsibility) to control one's own territorial destiny, was assumed to belong only to states who accepted the norms of Western civilization. States were recognized as legitimate holders of "positive sovereignty" when their existence was based on some kind of constitutional order, and when they were considered to be responsible actors by other holders of sovereignty.[99] This meant that the legal principle of sovereignty divided the world into two categories: those who were members of the club because of their high moral standing, and those who were fated to be dependencies because of their continuing threat of unruliness. In effect, there was the world of the settled and acceptable West, and the backward, disordered rest.[100] Africa was considered *terra nullius* (land without prior ownership), even though it was populated, because no "civilized" state had owned the land before.[101]

The effort to legitimate colonialism through the use of international law reflected the paternalism of the entire humanitarian impulse at that time. The imperialists had to take care of their colonies because the colonies were incapable of taking care of themselves. The colonies were like children, needing guidance from states who were more mature. International law, in the words of Ethan A. Nadelman, had its roots "in the notions and patterns of acceptable behavior established by the more powerful Western European states," reflecting European dominance.[102]

It would be easy to stop there and say that there is only a surface resemblance between the colonial use of international law to justify empire, and the modern use of international law by the United Nations system in its peacekeeping operations. Today's international law, after all, is universal, not imposed by the great powers. But the two-tiered legal system of paternalistic oversight continued throughout the era of decolonization, first with the League of Nations mandate system, and then through the UN Trusteeship Council. It began to unravel only when Third World states started to be granted independent voices in the UN General Assembly in the late 1960s.[103]

Some might suggest that it would be better to compare complex peace-keeping operations, and the way that the international community uses them to control political developments in particular territories, to the UN trusteeship system than to colonialism. Trusteeship is a less politically charged term, and its oversight by the UN implies a multilateralist benefi-cence that colonialism lacks. Conceptually, however, trusteeship was based on the same legitimating principles of inequality and paternalism that colo-nialism used, and was no more palatable to its subjects. When it was devised as a system, shortly after the UN was founded at the close of World War II, the UN was dominated by the same three powers whose imperial-ism is discussed here: the United States, Great Britain, and France.

International law plays a much more important role today in legitimat-ing state action on complex peacekeeping missions that it did in the impe-rial era. Resolutions passed by the United Nations Security Council are binding on all UN members, and the mandates they set for peacekeeping missions genuinely direct and limit the actions that are taken in the field. States tend to accept the norms behind these international laws because they wish to maintain reputations for being good international actors. This means that international discussions about who will administer a war-torn territory under which sets of laws, about who will command a peace-keeping mission and which rules will limit the use of force, and about who is responsible for which kinds of political and economic development assis-tance, have practical implications and are not just paper agreements.

Yet a similarly tiered system of international authority is still in place, even though it no longer divides sovereign from nonsovereign states. The most crucial tier is based on the fact that the United States, the Soviet Union, and Great Britain were the victors in World War II. Together they set up an international legal system, the UN Charter, which they hoped would guarantee their continued cooperation after the war and would reward their allies while ensuring that neither Germany nor Japan could threaten international security in the future. They made themselves, their ally France, and (what was then nationalist) China the permanent five (P-5) members of the UN Security Council, thereby giving themselves and their friends the authority to create and enforce binding resolutions on the international community.[104] The veto power that they maintain to this day helps to determine what is considered legitimate and illegitimate in inter-national intervention (even though it does not determine whether such intervention takes place). It helps to ensure that UN authorized peace operations remain under the control of the great powers.

All UN member states must abide by the resolutions passed by the Security Council, including resolutions that set up peacekeeping operations. Only the P-5 may veto a resolution, and this means that their tacit support is achieved through private negotiation before any realistic peacekeeping resolution is brought to the table.[105] This makes them an exclusive club for important negotiations. Ten additional states sit on the Security Council as rotating members, and nine affirmative votes from the 15-member Council are required for a measure to pass, so the P-5 cannot rule without the support of other UN members. They nonetheless effectively control the mandates behind the creation of peacekeeping missions, because nothing can be implemented in the Security Council without their approval. In the words of Barry O'Neill, the rotating members of the Security Council have "tiny power," since "it is rare that a nonveto player will be in a position to make a difference."[106]

This same P-5 has an overwhelming level of influence over who gets appointed to the position of UN Secretary General, since each of them can veto potential candidates. While the Secretary General's office has little direct authority, its holder can set the agenda of discussion through public pronouncements and quiet diplomacy. As a result the Secretary General helps influence where and how peacekeepers are sent on missions.

Together these things mean that the viewpoints of the P-5 end up dominating current discussions in the international community about what limits should be placed on complex peacekeeping activity. P-5 member China (which was granted the seat previously occupied by Taiwan in the early 1970s) sends very few peacekeepers abroad. Unless the question of recognition of Taiwan is somehow involved in a peacekeeping mandate, Beijing tends to remain relatively quiet about how peacekeeping missions are carried out. It may abstain on a key vote, rather than supporting a resolution, but its vetoes are rare.[107] Russia, the fifth member of the club (which inherited the seat occupied by the USSR when the Soviet Union ended in 1991), can sometimes stand in the way of peacekeeping mission approval. But in practice in recent years, Russian support for complex peacekeeping missions is usually obtained by the United States and Europe either through including Russian troops on missions near Russian territory (as was the case in Bosnia and Kosovo), or by making it clear that consensus is part of the overall package of Russian entry into the community of developed democracies.

Effectively what this means is that it is still the United States, Great Britain, and France who are the decisive voices in making complex peacekeeping policy. While most complex peacekeeping decisions now are multilateral, requiring support from other states in a way that colonial policy did not, the same three states remain dominant players when it comes to decisions about intervening into the political systems of other countries. The same set of players still have the ability to make sure that international legal norms meet their own state self-interests. Universalism is not as strong a norm as it might first appear.

This was seen as recently as spring 2003 in the wrangling over intervention in Iraq: the crucial actors were the United States and Great Britain on one side, and France on the other, supported by Russia. One of the fundamental reasons that agreement could not be reached between them on authorizing an invasion of Iraq was that France and Russia came to loggerheads with the United States over their conflicting state interests. France and Russia wanted to maintain the oil contracts their state-supported companies had signed under the regime of Saddam Hussein, and also to limit Washington's ability in general to use its unprecedented military power unilaterally in ways that might be opposed to the interests of Paris and Moscow. The United States wanted the freedom to use its military resources as it saw fit for the sake of increasing its own ability to influence political developments in the region, and perhaps its own control of economic resources in the long run. All of the players used legal terminology in their debates in the United Nations, but it was fundamentally state interest that set the boundaries of international legal interpretation.

The fact that state interest underlies international law matters a great deal, now in particular, because peacekeeping operations have changed so much in recent years and are much more intrusive than they used to be. As the previous chapter makes clear, over the past decade complex peacekeeping operations have infringed more and more on the sovereignty of the areas where they are deployed. This has been done largely on the initiative of the liberal democratic great powers, who see intervention to safeguard human rights as a legitimate activity. The practice has been strongly endorsed by UN Secretary General Kofi A. Annan—again reflecting the importance of the power to choose the Secretary General—who argued in 1999 that individuals have sovereignty as well as states, and that state sovereignty should not be a shield for human rights violations.[108] Many non-Western states, who are less powerful and who have contested human rights records themselves, objected to Annan's statements.[109] They pointed out that the UN Charter is based on the fundamental principle of defense of state sovereignty against aggression. The controversy was reflected in Annan's Millennium Report a year later, which spoke of the dilemma the UN faced between defending humanity and defending sovereignty.[110]

But the liberal democratic mindset is clearly winning the struggle. With time, peacekeeping operations in practice are becoming more and more associated with the ceding of territorial sovereignty to the international community. The 1995 Dayton Accords set up the intrusive Office of the High Representative for BiH, which has the right to fire democratically elected officials and mandate laws by fiat in order to move the country in the direction the international community wants it to go. The interim administration for Kosovo was appointed by UN officials in 1999 to oversee everything from the creation of new police and judiciary systems to education and health policy. While a Kosovo-wide assembly was democratically elected in November 2001, and a president chosen the following February, UNMIK refused to accept a framework text that said "the express will of the people" would determine Kosovo's future, because the Security Council has not yet reached agreement about whether Kosovo should become an independent state or remain a province of Serbia.[111] And in East Timor, the United Nations effectively ran the country for more than two years, amidst complaints that outsiders were not taking sufficient measures either to encourage or to train members of the local population to take over government duties.

In other words, even though the international legal framework that guides peacekeeping operations is much more robust than the one which justified (at least in the minds of the occupiers) colonial occupation, and even though there is no question that peacekeeping operations have a strong humanitarian component, the same basic power structure (with its attendant set of state interests) continues to function today. Despite many statements that peacekeeping is designed to assist self-determination, the great powers (with the exception of the 1994 Haiti mission) have not been overly eager to relinquish sovereignty to the people living in the areas where peacekeepers are sent. Instead, as the previous chapter emphasizes, their goal has been to maintain international dominance in these regions until the trajectory of events demonstrates that liberal democratic values have taken hold. The goal is to control political developments in territories not yet ready for independent statehood.

It appears that the United States in 2003 began to take this trend a step further. It acted unilaterally in Iraq with a few well-chosen friends, not truly multilaterally, and its policies thus flew in the face of international law. Yet it appears that one major goal of the Bush administration's invasion of Iraq was to forcibly establish a more liberal democratic regime in Baghdad, which would then spread its influence to the entire Middle East region.[112] In other words, the conjunction of interests and humanitarianism in empire may have come full circle, in ways that set the course of peacekeeping operations in the future.

Why the Similarities Matter

When all of these comparisons are drawn together, the fundamental message that comes through is that states leading complex peacekeeping operations, like states leading colonial occupations, will make choices that they perceive as being in accordance with their security interests. They will intervene in ugly humanitarian crises, as they earlier intervened in their colonial possessions, only when they can do so at limited cost, and only when they can justify their actions as preserving important national goals. On these peacekeeping missions, they will pursue liberal democratic assistance policies that are designed to further their ultimate ends of establishing a secure international environment, much as the humanitarian actions of a century ago furthered the desire to expand the boundaries of the "civilized" world. In both cases, these ultimate ends are associated with a desire to control the direction of political developments in the countries where intervention is occurring.

This means that the designers of complex peacekeeping operations may be able to learn something from the colonial experience about what happens when outsiders try to control the political events in foreign societies. In the earlier imperial era, these attempts often backfired because concern about costs, coupled with insufficient political will, meant that the grand humanitarian goals of the capitals were not realized in practice. For different reasons and through different trajectories, a similar disconnect between goals and means is evident today. It is this topic that the next chapter addresses.

FOUR

POLITICAL WILL AND SECURITY

Afghanistan, Summer 2002[1]

Throughout the summer of 2002, fighting between rival warlords continued as it had for almost thirty years. The private armies of the warlords sometimes numbered in the tens of thousands, and huge caches of arms were found throughout the countryside. In an effort to stop these clashes, the United States began to train a new national army, hoping that it would be able to reestablish the peace. But the largely illiterate soldiers of this new army were not well paid and had a tendency to desert their posts. The warlords refused to let their best men join the national force, fearing that the new army would be used against them if it ever became strong enough.

Organized violence permeated the country. Dozens of civilians were killed in the eastern city of Gardez when a warlord attacked it with rockets. On the western border, the town of Zaranj was considered so dangerous that the United Nations would not allow refugees to return to it. In the northern city of Mazar-e-Sharif, a member of the local population who worked for the UN Food and Agricultural Agency was dragged out of bed in the middle of the night and shot; another UN worker in the same city had his home attacked by an armed gang who raped all of the women living there. The newly appointed governor of the southern province of Khost could not take up his duties because a local warlord would not let him. The warlord's brother occupied the governor's offices with a large group of armed men; after promising to vacate the premises so that the government

(continued)

Afghanistan, Summer 2002 (*continued*)

could establish itself, he returned later the same night to sleep in the building with his militia. Meanwhile, the markets in this provincial capital were shuttered because of the violence, and protective sandbags lined the street corners and rooftops to try to stop the passage of bullets.

A small peacekeeping force (known by the acronym ISAF), led first by Great Britain and then by Turkey, worked under UN authorization in the capital of Kabul. Its presence probably dampened local street violence, but it was forbidden from going beyond the territory of the city. In Kabul, five policemen were arrested in uniform for firing on this peacekeeping force. It turned out that their intended target was not the peacekeepers, but a local police chief. 160 people were arrested by the central government because of what the authorities said was an attempt to destabilize the new regime. An assassination attempt against the Minister of Defense failed, but the bomb that was used killed five innocent bystanders. A couple of months later, an assassination attempt against one of Afghanistan's three vice presidents succeeded.

Beyond the small official peacekeeping force, American and allied special forces troops also provided aid to the local population in strategically important regions where Taliban and al Qaeda forces might still be hiding, aid that sometimes resembled complex peacekeeping operations in other places in the world. The Americans attempted to stop fighting between warlords in areas where ongoing U.S. military operations were at stake, and sent soldiers to guard the presidential palace, but made clear in their press conferences that those efforts were secondary to their main military mission.

A drought plagued the country, and local health officials reported that disease and malnutrition levels were increasing. Western governments and international aid agencies did provide food and agricultural assistance, medicine and health care, clothing and educational materials to the local population, but their efforts were concentrated in the larger towns and cities, which were actually less needy than rural areas. Anyone who traveled away from large population centers was likely to be attacked by bandits, so aid simply could not get through elsewhere. Much more money was promised to the country than was actually delivered. This was at least in part because international donors believed lawlessness and instability in the country were so great that any additional money would simply disappear.

As the U.S.-led war against al Qaeda and the Taliban wound down, the liberal democratic international community vacillated about how to approach Afghanistan's future. On the one hand, the international community wanted a strong, stable, westward-leaning central government

Afghanistan, Summer 2002 (*continued*)

to emerge in Kabul. The United States and its allies pressured various Afghan leaders to ensure that the *loya jirga*, the grand council of political representatives that met in June 2002, elected Hamid Karzai as the country's transitional leader. Karzai practiced tolerance toward Afghanistan's competing ethnic groups and factions, and was seen by the West as someone who could forge a cooperative government to overcome the legacy of the long civil war.

On the other hand, the United States—and every other capable country as well—was reluctant to create the large and robust international peacekeeping operation that Karzai wanted to have deployed on Afghan territory. The situation in Afghanistan was allowed to crumble back into the same anarchy that it saw in the 1990s after the withdrawal of Soviet occupation forces. Even while U.S.-led forces were battling the remnants of the Taliban and al Qaeda in one area of the country, the groundwork was being laid elsewhere in Afghanistan for the resurgence of anti-Western militancy and terrorism in years to come.

While the security situation in Afghanistan quickly fell off the front-page headlines of major U.S. newspapers as the war wound down in 2002, conditions there did not improve greatly with time. The Taliban regrouped and staged raids from Pakistani territory. Warlords continued to fight the battles they had waged against each other for the past two decades. Both the remnant coalition forces throughout the country and the peacekeepers in Kabul endured ongoing attacks. Amidst all this, the civilian population suffered, and their trust in the good will of the international community declined as their hopes for a peaceful new life were not realized. Afghanistan was a country crying out for a robust, large-scale UN-authorized peacekeeping force to restore order, but the United States refused to lead such a force itself, and no one else volunteered for the job.[2] Finally in mid-October 2003, NATO forces (who had taken over the peacekeeping mission a few months before) were authorized to spread out to other selected regions of the country, cooperating with the U.S. occupation forces under an expanded UN Security Council mandate.[3]

Unfortunately this set of circumstances, where powerful states are slow to send robust forces into dangerous and difficult situations, and solid peacekeeping operations are delayed as a result, is all too typical. Sometimes pundits chastise the United States for being the world's policeman, but in fact the opposite is true: Washington is reluctant to use its resources for police operations, and in the absence of American leadership there is often no one else willing to take on the responsibility.

In recent times we have seen this lack of American follow-through even in circumstances where U.S. military action has contributed to the instability in a society. The scenario of postwar Afghanistan was immediately repeated in Iraq, where the Pentagon appeared to have no cohesive plans in place for what would happen after the spring 2003 war. Weeks after the active war ended, armed gangs roamed not only the countryside but also the capital of Baghdad itself, looting everything from books off university shelves to the city's electrical power grid cables. No one stopped them.[4] Kurds and Arabs in the north of Iraq resumed the armed clashes that many experts had predicted as soon as the Baath regime security forces were out of the way. American troops were initially flummoxed.[5] The failure of American troops to even guard the arsenals of the old regime soon had tragic consequences, as moderate local leaders, the American occupiers, and even the broader international aid community in Iraq found themselves subject to deadly terrorist bombings. Insurgents targeted everything from the mosques of anti-extremist Muslim clerics to the Baghdad headquarters of both the United Nations and the International Committee for the Red Cross—not to mention the hotel where the U.S. occupation regime was based and the daily patrols by American troops.

It was obvious that something like this was likely to happen in Afghanistan and Iraq without the presence of robust outside policing before either war started. The failure of the United States to learn the lessons of the past decade of its involvement in complex peacekeeping operations was in some sense shocking. Yet the lack of political will to deploy forces for effective security keeping isn't a new phenomenon among great powers who intervene abroad. This chapter explores how insufficient political will hobbled the effectiveness of attempts to achieve security in foreign societies in both the imperial and complex peacekeeping eras.

In both eras, intervention in the periphery was a relatively low priority for the great powers. This meant that the security policies followed by the occupying forces in both the colonies and the peace-kept territories were not always well matched to the supposed political goals of the states who sent them there. Stable political development isn't possible if people are afraid for their lives and possessions. The absence of real security in the target countries undermined the ability of the intervening states to gain the kind of political control they sought.

In the imperial era, the problem was that military forces on the ground were allowed to do too much, without sufficient oversight from their capitals. Despite their strong interest in establishing territorial mastery of their colonies, each of the three liberal imperial powers wanted to keep their costs in running the colonies as low as possible. As a result, they directed many fewer bureaucratic resources to their colonies than toward other aspects of their foreign and defense policy. The resulting lack of policy attention meant that colonialism suffered from inconsistency, and that those ruled by outsiders suffered from the arbitrary and sometimes cruel decisions made by administrators who were unchecked by their client states back home. The message that the empires hoped to instill in the colonies, that all good things come from cooperation with liberal great powers, was not conveyed in practice.

In recent times, the problem has been that military forces on the ground have often been prevented for political reasons from doing enough to ensure their control over the security situation in target countries. Like the colonial operations that preceded them, complex peacekeeping operations have also tended to be a relatively low priority for the states that have led them. As a result, especially in the cases where the United States has played a significant role in leading the operations, the primary concern has been to preserve the future war-fighting capabilities of the troops, rather than to do the best possible job of securing the societies whose welfare is at stake. Further concerns about cost have led Washington to rely increasingly on reservists rather than active-duty soldiers for what amount to long-term and dangerous hardship tours abroad. The domestic political costs of this choice have further sapped the will of the United States to lead robust peacekeeping operations with confidence.

Then there is the issue of casualties. The United States goes to war with the expectation that it will suffer casualties in combat. But at least part of the problem faced in these supposedly non-combat situations is that U.S. troops sent on peacekeeping operations—as well as occupation duty— along with those of some of the NATO ally states, have often been instructed to privilege their own safety over the achievement of mission goals. This has meant they have to limit their participation in activities that resemble policing—things ranging from guard duty to riot control— because police work in unstable societies is inherently dangerous. Since adequate civilian police forces have not been available to fill the gap, security has suffered, as has the local population's trust in the intentions of the international community. It is hard to convince people to follow a partic- ular model of government when doing so doesn't bring them personal security.

We saw the consequences of these combined problems most starkly in both Afghanistan and Iraq. As soon as the war in Afghanistan was won, war against Iraq topped the U.S. defense agenda and the Pentagon wanted

to focus its personnel requirements on the Gulf. As soon as the open warfare period in Iraq was won, attention shifted again, to the possibility of
war in Korea and to instability in Liberia and Colombia, and the Pentagon
appeared surprised and dismayed to learn that a minimum of 100,000 U.S.
troops would be required for the secure occupation of Iraq.[6]

It might appear that the colonial era and the peacekeeping era are at
opposite ends of the spectrum. Imperial militaries were often too brutal in
the actions they took, and peacekeepers are often too reluctant to take
action. Yet there has been a key common factor explaining these situations—both have been low priority and underfunded activities—and a key
common result: the chosen methods of using military forces on the ground
have subverted the ability of outsiders to achieve security in target societies. And in turn, insecurity has made the idea of achieving control over
the political agenda in those societies difficult to achieve.

The Costs of Inattention in Colonialism

Since the imperial powers had a strong interest in the occupation and welfare of their colonies (as chapter 3 argued), it would seem logical to conclude that colonial policy should have received a great deal of attention in
the capitals. Yet it did not. Even though Great Britain, France and the
United States all believed at the turn of the twentieth century that their
colonies were important to their security interests, their foreign policy
attention was focused elsewhere. The primary concern for each of them—
and indeed the reason for their occupation of colonies in the first place—
was the competition they faced from the other great powers and their fears
of future great-power war in Europe. The details of how their empires were
run were much less interesting and important to the overall scheme of their
security strategies than was the European theater, as long as their ability to
occupy colonial territory was maintained. In practice, this meant that the
actions taken by imperial representatives in the colonies received little
attention or oversight, either from the imperial governments at home or
from the public at large.

The national military command hierarchy in each of the three imperial
capitals wanted to ensure that precious defense resources would not be
wasted on the colonies. The focus of military planning at the turn of the
twentieth century was on the great power skirmishes that occurred in
Europe as the Ottoman and Hapsburg empires declined, and on the war
between the great powers that everyone thought would arrive soon (and
indeed did arrive in 1914 with the outbreak of World War I). Those at the

top believed that the tactics used against poorly armed native uprisings in the colonial frontiers were irrelevant for these more important upcoming wars, and the generals feared that troops too accustomed to colonial actions might be left badly prepared for real battle.[7] The idea that what the troops did in the colonies was unimportant for real military planning certainly contributed to the capitals' relative neglect of colonial administration, which in practice was often conducted by military governors.

Neglect meant that there was no sustained bureaucratic effort to create consistent, long-term strategies of colonial development. Few central state resources were directed toward supervising what went on in the field. As a result, colonial polices varied significantly over time as newly elected governments came and went, and the directives handed down by ministerial officials were often not actually implemented.[8] Even the standard truism that the French practiced an assimilationist policy in their colonies, trying to make the occupied people second-class Frenchmen, while the British practiced a policy of indirect rule, allowing the occupied to be themselves as long as they gave allegiance to the crown, turns out to be more a convenient fiction of the capitals than an accurate description of imperial reality. Administrators in the field tried whatever they thought might work to keep the subject populations in check, whether or not it fit with the goals of their capitals.

Neglect was exacerbated by the technical shortcomings that made communicating across long distances difficult at that time in history. Detailed oversight from the capitals was not feasible, certainly not in anything resembling real-time. As a result, colonial populations found themselves subject to the judgments and whims of individual administrators on the ground. All three imperial capitals largely allowed the "man on the spot" in the colonies to decide what to do in any given circumstance, because he was seen as the expert who had the most knowledge about what the real situation on the ground was. A new term, "man-on-the-spotism," was even coined to describe the lack of clear planning that went into colonial developments.[9]

Neglect from the capitals allowed the military officers who often served in colonial governorship roles to ignore their orders to show restraint, and instead to brutalize the locals with impunity. While many colonial officials were well intentioned, not all of them were. Some scholars have even argued that colonial service attracted sadistic and violent misfits from mainstream society, who knew they could torture and kill people without consequence, and who faced little competition for jobs that were considered by most people in the capitals to be unpleasant because of their health risks and inconvenient locations and facilities.[10]

The instances of abuse tended to be concentrated in the dangerous areas where counterinsurgency campaigns were being waged. Many officers resented the force restrictions they officially faced, believing that colonial populations could only be tamed through violence that would show them who was boss. Especially when the colonial occupation forces were targeted for vicious attack by guerrilla fighters whom they considered barbarians, the desire for revenge could easily lead enraged soldiers to lose sight of the broader imperial goals of carrying out a low-cost and peaceful occupation of the colonies. Even British officers, who are the most famous (and often self-congratulatory) advocates of waging hearts and minds campaigns, regularly stooped to the temptation to carry out indiscriminate retaliatory violence against villages and crowds when individuals attacked or thwarted them.[11] Crops were burned, homes were destroyed, and guns were shot into peaceful political gatherings. Obviously, the knowledge that these events had happened filtered out to people living in the stable areas of the colonies, and the cruel and deadly actions taken in the counterinsurgency campaigns tended to undermine the efficacy of the hearts and minds campaigns waged elsewhere.

In both Britain and France, officers sent to the colonies were widely viewed as being socially inferior to their counterparts who remained in the capitals.[12] Often they were people who were unable to buy their way into a more desirable posting in a comfortable location. This meant they had something to prove, and prove themselves they did. After serving in the colonies these officers often had an even harder time fitting back into the metropolitan armies in the capitals, because their comrades resented the medals they had won through their exploits.[13] Colonial officers often rose to the top ranks because of their battle achievements. In France, most of the high command who fought in World War I had colonial experience,[14] despite the previous suspicion that those who fought in the colonies were unprepared for real war; and in Britain, almost every regiment cycled some units through service in India at the least.[15]

Military medals and promotion at this time were largely earned through conquest[16]—which of course gave the "man on the spot" in the colonies an incentive to provoke skirmishes and engage in territorial expansion even when it went against the orders he had received from his capital. In the words of one British colonial veteran who came from a military family himself, growing up in Pashtun territory at the fringes of the Indian colony, "The [Northwest Frontier] was a wonderful training ground. . . . Enough people got killed and wounded to keep everybody on their toes. There was always the chance of winning a decoration and the certainty of a campaign medal. Many a military reputation had been built on a Frontier war."[17]

This meant that colonial commanders would sometimes provoke warfare in order to have an excuse to expand their areas of control, without the knowledge of their capitals.[18] Given inadequate communication capabilities and the general lack of public interest in the colonies, officers on the ground were assumed to be the most knowledgeable people about local conditions and were respected for their expertise. Especially when those officers said that security was deteriorating and that going to battle was necessary in order to maintain existing colonial possessions, their capitals tended not to doubt them or to investigate too deeply.[19]

In imperial times, then, even when seemingly liberal states were in the lead, neglect and inattention meant that the humanitarian intentions of the capitals were often not realized in the field. The messages that the empires wished to send about political and social reform were not adequately communicated, and instead the subject populations rightly associated colonialism with arbitrary violence. The imperial capitals lacked the political will to put adequate resources toward solving the complex problems that surrounded the governing of their colonies, and as a result they lost a tool to help them in their quest for political control. Even though, as chapter 3 has argued, they had an incentive to win over the colonial populations for the sake of low-cost rule, they squandered the good will of their subjects by failing to put sufficient effort into overseeing their agents in the field.

The Costs of Not Prioritizing Peacekeeping

In contrast, military activities on complex peacekeeping operations have not lacked oversight. If anything, they have been constrained too tightly by governments at home who are eager to conserve resources for more important activities. The actions of peacekeepers are often second-guessed in their capitals for the sake of domestic political battles being waged at home. Despite this difference in the political management of operations, a similar underlying factor often impeded the effectiveness of both kinds of operation: in both eras, the capitals have focused their foreign and defense policy attention elsewhere. Complex peacekeeping missions often end up being less successful than they could have been because the noble goals that originally inspired the intervention are not adequately connected to the means that are actually available to use in them. Political officials do not want peacekeeping troops to enter into danger that could lead to casualties—and hence political costs—especially when those costs could affect other, more important, war-fighting missions.

In the 1990s it was thought that the problem of low political will that often plagued peacekeeping operations might be resolved by having single strong states or "coalitions of the willing" lead these operations. Having lead states with strong interests in the operations' outcome was also identified as a way to overcome the inadequacies in training, intelligence, and coordination that so often bedevil traditional Chapter Six peacekeeping missions. All the same, the states involved in Chapter Seven operations are still often unwilling to provide the resources that would be truly necessary to fully perform the tasks at hand. It is especially instructive to focus on the example of the United States, because U.S. military forces were usually key players in the complex peacekeeping missions of the 1990s.

U.S. leadership in the UN Security Council (and in NATO) has often been necessary for the missions to get off the ground, even in cases such as Interfet in East Timor where U.S. forces played a relatively small role in the overall operation. (While the small number of U.S. troops there primarily provided logistics and communication support and advice, Australian forces maintain that the American presence was absolutely crucial to Interfet's success.) Military budgets and personnel levels were drastically cut throughout Western Europe and North America just as the number and complexity of peacekeeping operations was growing in the 1990s, because the publics in these countries wanted a peace divided in the aftermath of the cold war. This meant that states were not eager to take on the responsibilities and expense involved in leading complex peace operations. With few exceptions, a common pattern emerged: political leadership by the wealthiest and most powerful state, the United States, was necessary for a complex peacekeeping mission to come into being.[20]

Yet the U.S. was reluctant to lead if the risk of casualties was too high. Throughout the presidential administrations of both Bill Clinton and George W. Bush, the idea of sending U.S. forces on peacekeeping missions engendered a great deal of domestic political controversy. Often the debate followed party lines, with Democrats arguing on behalf of a major peacekeeping role for U.S. military forces, and conservative Republican legislators and administration officials responding that American defense resources—including the lives of troops and the willingness of the public to support the military—should be conserved for more important missions. In 2002, for example, when talking about events in Afghanistan, numerous Republican White House and Defense Department officials called peacekeeping activities "nonmilitary" operations, referring to them as tasks that anyone could do, whereas no one else could take on the warfighting responsibilities of U.S. soldiers.[21]

But in cases where a strong U.S. national interest in having a military presence in a peacekeeping operation has been clearly at stake, American troops have not stayed home. Instead they are sent on missions even when they lack the range of resources to actually accomplish mission goals. Often, too few troops with the wrong kind of training are sent on missions that are too large in scope. Washington has engaged in numerous military peacekeeping operations without paying adequate attention to their advance planning and coordination, leaving beleaguered soldiers on the ground to pick up the pieces as best they can. We saw this clearly in Haiti in 1994, and yet the problem still existed by the time the hot-war phase ended in Iraq nine years later. Even the most powerful liberal democratic state can have a hard time establishing coherent policy when it comes to peacekeeping.

This problem first came to public light in the late 1990s. A 1996 Joint Chiefs of Staff (JCS) study revealed that a major problem faced by U.S. military commanders in peacekeeping and other nontraditional operations was inadequate coordination with American civilian authorities, including the aid officials who might be involved in humanitarian assistance policy.[22] Military planners lacked a clear sense of what they would be expected to do, and often found themselves scrambling, in the absence of clear civilian directives, to find appropriate personnel for nontraditional duties. Most of the burden of these new peacekeeping activities fell on the so-called civil affairs officers, people who were trained in the areas of administration, engineering, and construction, or other services such as medicine. What made the problem worse was that 97 percent of civil affairs personnel were drawn from the reserves.[23] In other words, they were people (usually older and hence more established in civilian life than active-duty personnel) who did not expect to be called up during peacetime for long stints away from their families and regular jobs, and their deployment was therefore accompanied by a host of new social and political difficulties.[24]

In 1997, at least in part in response to the JCS study on coordination problems, Clinton issued a national security directive, PDD-56, which was supposed to lead to more integrated planning across U.S. agencies for future peacekeeping operations. While the actual directive remains classified, a publicly released version calls for more training to be given to both military and civilian peacekeeping officials based on lessons learned from previous operations, and requires the Deputies Committee of the U.S. National Security Council (an interagency group representing various cabinet departments) to establish working groups to prepare interagency implementation plans for future contingencies.[25] Yet a follow-up study conducted by an outside consulting group in 1999 concluded that "the spirit and intent of PDD 56 directed-training is not being followed" and that "no one has stepped forward in the leadership role."[26] According to the presidential directive, peacekeeping was supposed to be an important component of how the United States defined its role in international security. Yet it was not important enough for a concerted planning effort to be made. Several years later, in both Afghanistan and Iraq, successful and highly professional U.S.-led military actions were followed by ad hoc, piecemeal efforts at establishing security in war's aftermath. Waging war, not building peace, was where the Pentagon put its resources—and reservists, called up for long stints away from their normal lives, were still left to pick up the pieces. By September 2003, there were 20,000 American Army Reserve and National Guard troops serving in Iraq and neighboring Kuwait, and their tours were being extended to a year.[27] This trend of relying on reservists began in the peacekeeping operations of the 1990s; by 2000, for example, over 20 percent of American forces who had been deployed in Bosnia were reservists.[28]

The United States and Policing

There is a related set of sensitive political issues that arises when the United States is a key player in the operations—as the lead state in the Haiti mission, for example, or as a sector commander and behind-the-scenes propellant in the NATO missions in Bosnia and Kosovo. The United States military tries to avoid taking on police-like functions as much as possible, at least in part to avoid casualties on missions like peacekeeping that are considered less central to U.S. security concerns than war-fighting. Policing is considered too risky for soldiers to do, and not within their core competencies. The goal is to conserve the lives and preserve the essential war-fighting skills of troops who may be needed in future wars, while maintaining public support for military action by limiting the perception that troops are being put in harm's way for no good reason.

There are certainly other countries whose military organizations resist, or are even constitutionally forbidden, from taking on police duties. (The next chapter will look at the example of Spain, which is constitutionally prevented from having its military forces engage in police actions, including on NATO peace operations.) Peter Viggo Jakobsen notes that a variety of KFOR leaders, including commanders from Great Britain and Germany, not just the United States, have been reluctant to have military troops perform police duties.[29] There are also countries whose military organizations have resisted multinational political directives to engage in particular policing activities, even though as organizations they are perfectly willing and capable of engaging in police activities in general. (The next chapter will look at the case of French troops in Kosovo.) But as in colonial times, the French and (especially) the British military organizations, as well as strong British allies like Australia who had some experience in late colonial warfare, are in general quite willing to employ their troops flexibly for policing activities. All of these countries' military organizations, alongside such stalwart traditional peacekeepers as Canada, have also been quite accepting of the notion that peacekeeping operations might cause casualties among their troops, and that the possible death of soldiers is an acceptable risk to take. The United States has been an outlier in its reluctance to take on policing duties and to risk casualties on peacekeeping missions, and this has meant that Washington's goals for these complex missions are not well matched with the means available to fulfill them.

A peculiar political handicap that the United States has faced in participating in peacekeeping missions in recent years is the legacy of the operation in Somalia, described earlier in this book.[30] The American experience on that mission gave U.S. policymakers a very different understanding of the dangers involved in peacekeeping operations from that held by most Western countries. Most of the U.S. military operation in Somalia was in fact well run and successful. The strong American military presence helped get food to the population, and frequent shows of force for the most part kept the warlords cowed. But what the word "Somalia" will always conjure up in the minds of U.S. policymakers is the disastrous October 1993 raid in Mogadishu.

In retrospect the tactical mission to try to get Aideed's supporters in a crowded marketplace was poorly planned, even though the capture technically succeeded. Its designers did not consider the contingencies that any commander should know might arise in the fog of war, and the troops were left with an insufficient tool kit of alternative plans. Yet U.S. congressional leaders reacted strongly to the apparent principle behind the event, rather than to its particulars; they rallied against the idea that U.S. troops should be put in danger for something that was not clearly in the U.S. national interest. Washington had no particular stake in Somalia in 1993, beyond humanitarianism. The lesson that many Americans, probably wrongly, took away from Somalia was that it was a mistake to become involved in peacekeeping missions when the United States didn't have a direct interest at stake, because peacekeeping was a dangerous business doomed to failure. American lives and resources should be preserved for the wars that needed to be fought.

This one, relatively minor (except for its ultimate consequences) tactical operation in the whole scheme of American involvement in Somalia in fact bore little resemblance to most activities carried out on peacekeeping operations in most places in the world. Instead it resembled the kind of counterinsurgency warfare waged by U.S. forces in Vietnam—preparing and waging a battle against an armed enemy who is surrounded by civilian supporters. It also resembles the raids carried out in Bosnia today by NATO forces against indicted war criminals. But it is important to keep in mind that those raids are usually not led by normal peacekeeping units under the command of the SFOR mission, even though the press often reports them as if they were. Instead they are mostly carried out by special combat forces acting under purely national command. SFOR is informed of their actions and coordinates its activities with them, but they are not part of the peacekeeping mission per se.[31]

What happened in Somalia had virtually nothing to do with the kind of civilian-oriented policing operations that are more commonly part of complex peacekeeping missions today. Indeed what is particularly sad is that earlier in the Somalia operation U.S. soldiers had worked hard to create and train a local Somali police force, and had successfully detained local criminals themselves when it was necessary as part of their mission to restore security in the country.[32] Policing in the Somalia peacekeeping operation worked. It was instead a counterinsurgency effort that led to the casualties which provoked withdrawal.

The message that the public has taken away from Somalia has had an unfortunate side-effect for future U.S. participation in peacekeeping missions of all kinds, and especially for the U.S. ability to adapt to doing police work on those missions. Force protection—the act of ensuring the safety of one's own troops—became more important in the United States than meeting any of the actual mission goals.[33] Commanders were told that the American public would tolerate zero casualties on peacekeeping missions, and understood this to mean that their own career advancement depended on them keeping their troops out of harm's way. As a result, U.S. policy on peacekeeping missions has often been to keep troops safe by insulating them from the local population as much as possible.

Previously we saw what this meant for U.S. operations in Haiti in 1994: American troops were often unable to intervene directly to restore civil order in the frenzied situation they found on the ground, because they were discouraged from taking police action in response to civilian disputes. In the Balkans, this approach meant that U.S. troops were prohibited from patronizing shops or cafés off-base, because mingling with the locals was seen as being too dangerous, and all village patrols by American soldiers had to be conducted by soldiers carrying M-16 automatic rifles and wearing Kevlar helmets and flak jackets.[34] Early on in Bosnia, U.S. patrols had to move out with a minimum of four vehicles[35]—emphasizing their status as military occupiers. This made it difficult for U.S. soldiers to establish the kinds of personal relationships with local inhabitants that are required for policing duties to be carried out successfully. U.S. troops look both frightened and frightening.[36] American officials sometimes denigrate the NATO troops who do fraternize with the locals, claiming that those who get too friendly aren't respected, and talking about the instances where the forces of other countries have "gotten in trouble"—as when a Spanish security unit got drunk at a pub in the Bosnian Croat city of Mostar and was disarmed by the locals.[37] But other NATO military officers refer dismissively to the American troops with their bulky protective gear as "Ninja turtles."

In practice, U.S. troops in the Balkans do engage in police activities alongside their NATO partners. They are especially proud of the border patrol duties they perform, for example to interdict smuggling between Kosovo and Macedonia.[38] Yet because of the American stress on force protection and strictly military methods, some of the other police-type actions that U.S. troops have been involved with seem to have veered back and forth between startled retreat and aggressive ham-handedness. American forces have an uncomfortable relationship with the idea of doing police work on peacekeeping missions.

On the one hand, American troops have learned that they are not supposed to put themselves in danger in police-type operations. Several times U.S. army peacekeepers deployed on NATO operations in Kosovo have been called back mid-mission by their commanders for force protection reasons.[39] For example, U.S. troops were involved in a NATO response to ethnic rioting and murder in the city of Mitrovica, located in the French area of peacekeeping operations in Kosovo in February 2000. In an effort to regain control of the Serbian side of the city, NATO launched an intensive search operation to look for weapons inside ethnic Serb houses. The NATO command called American troops in to be involved in the search. In retrospect, American forces believe that they were to some extent set up by the French, because they had expected French troop support for their action which did not materialize.[40] Be that as it may, the Americans made a truly careless tactical error, given the violence they should have known they were likely to encounter during a forceful search in a hostile sector: the civilian interpreter they used for their part of the search was an ethnic Albanian, whose presence provoked outrage from the ethnic Serbs who were being subject to the search.

While the interpreter was withdrawn, mobs later began stoning, punching, and kicking the American soldiers, who withdrew rather than use violence in response.[41] What was particularly surprising is that the Americans had not expected the level of violence they encountered; they had apparently

not gone in with the riot gear necessary to protect themselves from the protestors, such as face masks and rubber bullets.[42] According to a report by
Jeffrey Smith in the *Washington Post*, one laughing Serb said to another at
the demonstration, "I told you that they are going to leave."[43] It had become
common knowledge that the United States withdrew from Somalia after its
soldiers were killed in Mogadishu, and as a result Washington gained the
reputation for withdrawing from peacekeeping operations under the threat
of casualties, rather than sticking out the difficulties of violent situations
where civilians were involved.

On the opposite extreme is an example that stands out for its echoes of
another era: the way that U.S. forces have sometimes handled raids on
Kosovar villages that are suspected of hiding illegal weapons or of harboring hate-crime perpetrators. *Washington Post* reporter Dana Priest has
reported in some detail about the general level of rough treatment, including slapping, death threats, and other forms of brutality, that were often
used (at least early on in the mission) by U.S. troops trying to track down
criminals.[44] Those actions, however, were later subject to internal investigations, and several soldiers and officers were punished for their failure to
follow the rules. What is surprising about the case that follows is that its
outline is provided by the American troops themselves, who apparently
saw nothing amiss in the actions they took.

American forces officially state that they have been careful on such
"cordon and search" missions in Kosovar villages to strictly observe
proper human rights procedures. Yet a report about a helicopter raid in the
newsletter that is produced by American forces on the ground in Kosovo
has an uncomfortable resemblance to a scene in Francis Ford Coppola's
movie *Apocalypse Now*. The movie, set during the American war in Vietnam, is based on Joseph Conrad's novel about nineteenth-century colonial
governorship in Africa gone wrong, *Heart of Darkness*. The 2001 article
describes a 5:00 a.m. surprise mission, where an unnamed ethnic Albanian
border town in Kosovo was surrounded and house-to-house searches were
conducted for weapons, contraband, and ethnic rebel identification documents. U.S. forces went into the mission both by helicopter and by
armored vehicle. The article states, "As the sun dawns over the horizon,
the morning silence . . . is broken by [Wagner's] music 'Flight of the
Valkyrie [sic—the standard title is "Ride of the Valkyries"].' Several helicopters, tanks, and personnel carriers then accompanied the music."[45] In
the 1979 movie, American attack helicopters broadcast that same tri-
umphal music as they begin strafing and napalming a Vietnamese village
at sunrise, and their commander (played by Robert Duvall) says, "Yeah, I
use Wagner—scares the hell out of [them]."

Since the movie was very popular—it won two Academy Awards and was re-issued in a new version in 2001—it is likely that at least some of the Kosovars undergoing the cordon and search caught the reference. U.S. forces have defended the surprise element in the cordon and searches as necessary in a fundamentally uncooperative environment. One officer I spoke to explained that they had to broadcast some kind of alarm to wake up the sleeping villagers and let them know that the forces mean business. An American civilian official at NATO headquarters said that the situation was so bad at that time in those Kosovar villages that "no one" would object to the style of the raids done there.[46] Nonetheless, it is hard to think of an alarm that would put further psychological distance between the military occupation forces, and the villagers whose safety they were ostensibly there to protect. If the ultimate goal is to have Kosovars "own" the process of political change so that it continues after the military presence is withdrawn, it is probably not a good idea to associate that change with being shocked out of bed by helicopter loudspeakers playing Wagner at 5 a.m., as they descend on a village and surround it with tanks. (According to Priest, they rarely found much of any value in these searches anyway.)

Military Professionalism and Policing

American officials and analysts often state that military and police officers are trained for different things, and that this means their activities should be kept separate from each other. The apparent errors noted in the preceding examples in dealing with the psychological vulnerabilities of the involved populations might serve to confirm that assessment. Military forces are trained to fight and win wars, the argument goes, while police are trained to go out on patrols and perform investigations. Military troops work best in large, well organized groups and are skilled at using violence or the threat of violence to deter and kill enemies. Police officers work best as individuals or in pairs and use the law to deter and detain criminals.[47]

But these observations alone about the existing strengths and skills of military versus police personnel don't explain the fervency of the arguments made on this issue. In the imperial era, military personnel did police work as a matter of course. Despite the many striking examples that have come down in history where their actions went wrong, British troops in particular were known for their ability to exercise disciplined restraint and effectiveness in their colonies, when dealing with situations like riots.[48] Many Western countries today—including the United States—have a track record of using military personnel in policing roles with no ill effects. Active duty American military personnel have sometimes been called in to deal with domestic civil disorder that has left local police overburdened, as in the unrest in Los Angeles following the Rodney King police brutality crisis in April 1992.[49] Canadian troops have helped Canadian police deal with potentially violent situations, including a 1990 armed standoff with native Mohawks over land rights that brought the soldiers acclaim for their professionalism and fairness.[50] British military personnel have done a lot of police work, called "aid to the civil authorities," in Northern Ireland. While some of their actions have provoked heated controversy (especially the activities of military intelligence units, who are widely accused of having practiced torture in detention centers), British forces often express pride in their own political objectivity and restraint, again in dealing with riots, for example, and say that their skills in this area reflect the lessons they learned from empire.[51] Christopher Bellamy notes that "some of the hardest, toughest fighting soldiers in the world excel in peace-support operations," and adds that his survey data indicate that "local populations have most respect for peacekeepers who are also unmistakably professional soldiers, robust in their manner and well equipped."[52]

Yet many hawks in the United States believe that for soldiers to do police work—and peacekeeping in general—will lead to a loss of military professionalism. Military resources are scarce, the argument goes, and as noted above, many argue that the United States should not be wasting its well-trained warriors on missions that anyone can do.[53] Asking military officers to perform tasks not directly tied to fighting and winning the nation's wars is said to degrade their war-fighting capabilities. Many senior American officers who have been involved in peacekeeping operations, however, do not agree with this argument. They admit that unit performance in highly specialized war-fighting skills, such as the use of heavy weapons, declines after a peacekeeping stint and needs remedial work to be brought back up to speed.[54] But at the same time, soldiers gain more unit cohesion because of the need to work together in difficult environments, and junior officers come back from peacekeeping operations with better decisionmaking skills, a greater ability to take individual initiative with confidence, and a greater understanding of what combat conditions are really like in the midst of uncertainty.[55] These are all things that are valued in today's complex battlefield, where small units are dispersed among an innocent civilian population that has enemy elements hidden within.

Nonetheless, the argument that peacekeeping leads to a decline in military professionalism continues to be heard frequently inside the Pentagon. It probably dates from the classic 1957 book by Samuel P. Huntington on

American civil-military relations, *The Soldier and the State*. Huntington argued that "a distinct sphere of military competence" sets officers apart from the rest of society, namely "the direction, operation, and control of a human organization whose primary function is the application of violence."[56] He believed that the military governorships carried out by U.S. forces in Germany and Japan following World War II were especially damaging to the military mindset, and that this in turn caused civilians to neglect "the postulates of professional military thinking."[57]

Almost immediately after Huntington's book was published its major points were challenged by sociologist Morris Janowitz, who argued that the combination of nuclear deterrence (which would prevent major war from breaking out) and an expanding defense bureaucracy (which demanded new military administrative skills) had permanently changed what military professionalism meant in the United States.[58] No longer would military officers be primarily engaged in fighting major wars. Professional officers instead should be thought of as people who had specialized skills, a strong group identity and a set of governing ethics and standards of performance. The particular set of skills considered important within their profession would change with time, and would inevitably become more diverse as technology and society became more complex. Janowitz recognized even in 1960 that the military organization preferred not to take on what he called the "constabulary outlook" associated with policing, but it was not for reasons of professional competence and training. Instead, military officers tended to feel that those duties were less prestigious than war-fighting.[59] It is not surprising that this institutional tendency continues, but this insight suggests that it is a result of the political reward structure practiced in the United States, rather than any innate characteristic of the military mindset or training. The imperial armies gave medals to those who waged war in the periphery, and thereby discouraged officers from practicing the calm diplomacy that would actually have made their empires easier and less costly to manage. It is ironic that the United States may be in some way following in their footsteps today.

Some might argue that policing by regular troops isn't necessary. There are specially trained military forces—U.S. military police (MPs), for example, and the special hybrid forces that some countries have, like the French *gendarmerie* or the Italian *carabinieri*—who have at the ready the necessary tools to do such work.[60] Large numbers of U.S. MPs were in fact scheduled to be sent into Iraq in May 2003, as order deteriorated there in the postwar environment. These troops are experts in riot control techniques, in the proper handling of evidence and prisoners, and in obtaining and analyzing intelligence data from their interactions with the local population and local police forces.⁶¹ Likewise, the U.S. constabulary forces in postwar Germany (whom Huntington found so inappropriate) were, after the initial war termination period, volunteers who reenlisted after their combat tours were over, and then given special training in police duties.⁶² But there simply aren't enough of these specially trained forces to be at the ready in every situation where a police presence is demanded on peacekeeping operations—especially in an era when the military budgets of many European states have been drastically cut, and these hybrid forces may be needed for ethnically motivated civil unrest at home.

There is no doubt that it would be better to have well trained *civilian* police officers—experienced in conducting investigations, in collecting evidence, and in detaining prisoners, and less intimidating to the local population—do the bulk of police work on peacekeeping operations if it were possible. But often, as in the case of mid-1990s Haiti discussed in the previous chapter, they simply are not available in time. In virtually any peacekeeping operation it takes police forces a long time to gear up for entry, since there is no standing reserve of police units trained and ready to go. This is what Michael Dziedzic calls "the deployment gap."⁶³ When military troops arrive in the theater first, someone has to keep order, and it falls on the soldiers to do so. Often those being asked to take on these duties are not the military police or trained constabulary forces; they are instead whoever happens to be present in the field when the need for their help arises.

Beyond this timing issue, there are simply not enough highly qualified civilian police officers to be sent on the multitude of complex peacekeeping missions that require them. Some countries, like Canada and Australia, do have national police forces (the Royal Canadian Mounted Police and the Australian Federal Police, respectively) who are regularly assigned to peacekeeping missions by their governments. But most of the slots for international police personnel on peacekeeping missions must be filled by individual volunteers, and it is very difficult to recruit highly qualified people for these jobs. Most urban police forces throughout the world already feel that they are understaffed, and it is not surprising that they discourage their personnel from volunteering for foreign duty. Individuals who take leaves of absence to serve abroad are often warned that their chances for promotion at home will evaporate. Retirees can be sent as the commanders on police missions, but it is hard to get enough cops to walk the beat. As a result, many of the personnel slots on international police missions in places like Kosovo are filled by people who are not trained in police departments, but instead as park rangers or security guards. They lack the skills necessary to investigate violent crimes or control riots.⁶⁴ And according to

Priest, in places like Kosovo they are often there for the money, and reluctant to risk life and limb to get out among the local population and investigate crime.[65]

This means that often there is no one except regular military forces available to take on policing duties. When they do so either half-heartedly, or with excessive zeal, their capitals' desires to have a safe and secure environment left in their wake cannot be well fulfilled. Like the empires of the last century who rewarded their officers for war-fighting, not pacific colonial duty, the leaders of peacekeeping operations today find that their ability to get their goals met is hampered by a narrow definition of military professionalism. Once again, ends and means don't match, and the intentions of the capitals fail to be fulfilled by the actions taken.

Recognizing the Problem

Calls for something to be done about the dearth of good police forces on peacekeeping operations are not new. They have emanated from the UN community, from the United States Army, and from think tank analysts.[66] What the comparison to the colonial experience highlights, however, is two key lessons involved in the politics of building security in foreign countries.

First, military personnel will do what they are rewarded for doing in terms of advancement and recognition in their organization. If military personnel are not rewarded for taking actions that contribute to the security of occupied territory, then it will be impossible for the international community to establish political control in those areas. Unless directed otherwise, military officers will probably gravitate to what they do best, and what they joined the military to do: to plan, fight, and win wars. In the imperial era, that won them medals; in today's era, it is usually the path to promotion. It is not coincidental that civil affairs work on peacekeeping operations is assigned to reservists; the more "important" work of warfighting is left to those who will advance in the organization. Insufficient political attention is paid to the problem of policing.

Political scientist Deborah Avant argues, "We should expect that military organizations will be responsive to civilian goals when military leaders believe that they will be rewarded for that responsiveness."[67] She cites promotion policy as a key mechanism for rewarding the behavior of officers—a point which is reinforced by the imperial experiences of Great Britain, France, and the United States. Peter Feaver agrees that "assertive control" by civilians is necessary to ensure that those with professional military knowledge and expertise are truly fulfilling the demands of the democratic polity, and agrees with Janowitz that professional militaries in modern societies are capable of many functions other than war-fighting.[68] Most recently, Eliot Cohen has urged American civilian leaders to be less hesitant in exerting control over the military officers whose job it is to serve them, noting that the emergence of what amounts to a new imperial army in the United States demands rethinking of the traditional concerns associated with mass armies of the twentieth century.[69]

Yet the second key lesson that the colonial experience highlights and the peacekeeping era confirms is that none of this urging will make a difference if the civilian leaders of liberal democracies do not recognize the importance of these missions to their own national interests. If their attention is focused on war-fighting, police actions will not matter to the public, and the design of military operations in these areas will not be subject to the kind of political pressure that is necessary for anything to be adequately planned or funded in a democracy. The experts can talk all they like about the need for reform, but the talk will have no effect if the issue remains a low priority in leaders' minds.

While the argument continues to be heard that the public will not tolerate casualties on peacekeeping missions, several studies have demonstrated that this was false even in the immediate aftermath of Somalia.[70] Instead, the evidence shows that the public will rally around military missions, even dangerous humanitarian missions, when the political chiefs in Washington take the lead in explaining why those missions are important. It is not that liberal democratic states are incapable of being good peacekeepers; it is instead that leaders must make peacekeeping missions a priority if they are to maintain the political will to do them well.

Aracinovo: Politicization Avoided

It is difficult to demonstrate with hard facts that American political sensibilities have gotten in the way of on-the-ground peacekeeping effectiveness. This is because it is hard to tease out exactly who is responsible for particular decisions on peacekeeping operations—whether it is civilian Pentagon appointees who represent the political interests of the presidential leadership, or instead senior military commanders who wish to preserve their resources, and who represent the accumulated wisdom of the officer corps. But an example where civilian political interests in casualty avoidance were sidelined, and where mission effectiveness appears to have been enhanced as a result, occurred in the Macedonian town of Aracinovo, just outside the capital of Skopje, in June 2001.

U.S. troops have been based in Macedonia as part of the extended mission of the KFOR peacekeeping operation in neighboring Kosovo. Skopje is very near the Kosovo border, and a portion of the Skopje international airport, known as Camp Able Sentry, has been used as the major rear area for resupplying the American forces headquartered at Camp Bondsteel in Kosovo. Macedonia therefore has special strategic significance for the United States. The tensions between the country's ethnic Macedonians and ethnic Albanians have to some extent mirrored the tensions in neighboring Kosovo, and they were worsened by the influx of huge numbers of ethnic Albanian refugees during the height of the Kosovo war in spring 1999. Yet despite some violent incidents, Macedonia had initially remained relatively peaceful in the initial KFOR era. It also remained relatively pro-American because of earlier U.S. participation in the UN Preventative Deployment Force (UNPREDEP) that had protected the Macedonian border from the Yugoslavian civil wars of the mid-1990s. This made Macedonia an attractive ally for Washington when the KFOR peacekeeping operation began in 1999, especially since it was hoped that an ongoing U.S. military presence in the country might keep ethnic violence quelled.

But by mid-2001, there had been months of skirmishing between Macedonian government forces (who were primarily ethnic Slavs) on the one side, and ethnic Albanian irregular forces on the other (many of whom were at least technically Muslim). The Albanian rebel forces were reportedly flowing back and forth across the border from Kosovo, receiving supplies and funding from the commanders of the Kosovo Liberation Army (KLA). In June, a contingent of 150 Albanian rebel fighters who had been challenging government forces was pinned down by government troops in the town of Aracinovo. Ethnic Albanians and Macedonians had lived together peacefully in Aracinovo in the past. But now the Macedonian government forces destroyed the town's mosque, arguing that it was being used by the rebels as a staging base for mortars that could hit both the airport and a major oil refinery. Ethnic resentment skyrocketed as the town became a flashpoint, leaving the country on the brink of out-and-out civil war.[71]

NATO and EU officials, hoping to avoid the outbreak of a larger conflict that could once again send the entire Balkans region spiraling into ethnic chaos, brokered a ceasefire between the rebels and the Macedonian government. The Macedonian government agreed, by some reports under heavy NATO and EU pressure, to allow the rebels to leave the town under NATO guard (and using NATO transportation), in exchange for the rebels laying down their weapons.[72] The NATO Secretary General's personal representative, Pieter Feith (a civilian), ordered an American officer (whom he technically outranked) to use his troops for this purpose, since no one else was available in the region. The American commander complied, and American civilian contractors acted as the bus drivers for the withdrawal. The Albanian rebels left under American protection, and the tension in Aracinovo was broken. The next night, though, a nationalist Macedonian mob attacked the parliament building in Skopje, angry at what they saw as a government sell-out. They accused the American civilian contractors of secretly training KLA fighters.

While Macedonian leaders feared that civil war would result, it did not; and in retrospect the successful withdrawal and disarmament of rebels in Aracinovo probably helped prevent civil war. Indeed American actions on the ground contributed to NATO's credibility as an impartial go-between in the Macedonian conflict. Two months later, NATO forces were asked to come in on a new peacekeeping mission in the country, with the support of both the government and the rebels. NATO troops on that new mission collected rebel weapons in what was known as Operation Essential Harvest—an action that helped reassure both sides that their ceasefire would hold. While this latter operation certainly did not convince the rebels to turn in their best weapons, it did provide a mechanism for outside European forces to maintain a presence in the country, helping to prolong a stable peace that would otherwise have been shakier.

But American participation in the Aracinovo withdrawal was a fluke that almost didn't happen. If Bush administration officials had been aware of what was going on, the notion of an escort reportedly would have been overruled because of the danger involved. It turns out that the whole set of events transpired on a summer weekend. No one in Washington had been expecting it in advance, and that reportedly meant that there was no one in the White House who knew about the events at the time.[73] The rumor is that when the whole story was revealed the next day, U.S. Defense Secretary Donald Rumsfeld was both embarrassed and angry at having been kept out of the loop. According to one U.S. official, while the troops have the "right of immediate response" to save lives and protect property when they are deployed on peacekeeping missions, there must be a clear understanding of the limits of what this means, so that "junior" commanders in particular do not make "subjective decisions" about the situation and embroil U.S. forces in actions that exceed their mandate.[74]

The officer leading the American convoy was Colonel Anthony J. Tata—not a junior rank of commander at all. While it is not clear from public sources exactly what communication transpired on the ground, it appears from news reports that Brigadier General William C. David, the commander of the American presence in Kosovo, was well enough

informed of the events that he was able to watch them via camera trans-
missions from an unarmed aerial drone flying overhead. Both the Pentagon and the Macedonian defense ministry also received this real-time
footage.[75] The problem, from the U.S. perspective, was therefore not that
the U.S. military organization was brought into a set of events against its
commanders' best judgment. Instead, it was that the Secretary of Defense
was not given the opportunity to pre-approve a tactical action that put
American troops in harm's way.

As the Americans were trying to return to their base at the Skopje airport after the successful escort was completed, their way was blocked by
an angry and armed Macedonian mob that was probably incited by disaf-
fected government security forces. Working with advice provided by General David (who was using the real-time drone footage), Col. Tata decided
to retreat and have the now-empty bus convoy take a series of detours back
to base in order to avoid confrontation. Other NATO troops helped out
by ensuring that the roads used by the Americans were cleared of mines.[76]
The troops arrived back at base safely, if later than expected. But the possibility of danger was very real, and it is understandable why an attack on
U.S. forces would have been a political nightmare, since the whole relationship between peacekeeping in Kosovo and Macedonia would have
been difficult to explain to the public.

This was a case where the NATO command of a UN-authorized peacekeeping operation approved an action with full American military command knowledge and support. The action was probably necessary for the
ongoing success of the U.S. effort in Kosovo, since instability surrounding
Camp Able Sentry in Macedonia would have been very detrimental to the
functioning of Camp Bondsteel in Kosovo. There was a large U.S. military
presence around Skopje as a mandated part of KFOR, and the conflict
between Macedonian and Albanian forces was within mortar range of
American base operations. Furthermore, this action had the full backing
and real-time knowledge of the host Macedonian government where the
American deployment was in place. Yet the White House wanted ultimate
control and veto over how the troops would be used in order to prevent
the possibility of confrontation and casualties—and indeed as commander-
in-chief, it was ultimately the U.S. president's responsibility to decide how
U.S. forces should be employed.

This case is emblematic of the difficulties that liberal democracies have
in doing peacekeeping well. The American public, as represented by its
leaders, has every right not to send its forces into harm's way for a reason
that it does not understand to be in the national interest. Yet to exercise
that right of democratic control over the military may very well impede the

effectiveness of an operation that ultimately protects American security. A U.S. Central Intelligence Agency report on the greatest foreign threats to the United States at the end of 2001 put Macedonian instability near the top of the list.[77] While it is always risky to engage in counter-factual analysis, thinking about what might have been, in this case the fact that the U.S. military took action without close political oversight was probably a good thing.

The Fickleness of Political Will

What the comparison between the colonialism of a hundred years ago and more recent complex peacekeeping operations highlights is the fact that great power liberal democracies are by nature inconsistent in their foreign military policies. They have a tendency to start off in high-minded directions that lack sufficient priority to ensure good follow-through. This is especially the case in circumstances like colonial occupation and peacekeeping, where perceived core national security interests are not at stake but the potential cost in lives and treasure is high. Politics demands responsiveness to what the public seems to want, and cohesion is often sacrificed as particular political administrations come and go.

This shouldn't come as a surprise to anyone. It does, however, suggest that the attempts made by liberal democratic states to direct foreign societies in particular directions are quixotic. The more tasks that either occupation authorities or peacekeepers have taken on, the more room for slippage there is. In the next chapter we will see how much harder this becomes in multilateral operations, where even military allies who would seem to share a vision of security can trip each other up because of their domestic political limits. What this means is that rather than trying to do too much too eagerly, the international community should concentrate on doing fewer things and doing them better, with more foresight and more communication with their domestic publics about why these few things matter.

FIVE

MILITARY TASKS AND MULTILATERALISM

Iraq, Summer 2003

"I know this is a frustrating time for you and that the high crime rate makes everything worse," said L. Paul Bremer III, Administrator of the Coalition Provisional Authority in Iraq, in his weekly radio address on Aug. 3, 2003. "We understand the desire of you, the Iraqi people, to end your fear of both political oppression and the depredations of common criminals. We are going to remove that fear from your lives."[1] But it remained unclear how these brave words would be translated into practice.

Some 139,000 U.S. troops remained on the ground, three months after President George W. Bush declared an end to major hostilities in Iraq. They were joined by around 21,000 personnel deployed by other countries, for a total force of 160,000.[2] More than half of the non-U.S. troops (11,000) were British, mostly concentrated in the troubled city of Basra; the remaining forces were contributed in smaller numbers by 17 additional countries including Italy, the Netherlands, and Denmark. By the end of September, these forces were scheduled to be augmented by 9,000 troops from a variety of mostly East European and South American countries led, by Poland and significantly financed by the U.S. These new soldiers would be sent in with a clear peacekeeping mission.[3] But both France and India—countries who were large troop donors to many of the complex peacekeeping missions of the 1990s—had made very public declarations that they would not send their forces to Iraq in the absence of an explicit United Nations

(continued)

Iraq, Summer 2003 (*continued*)

Security Council resolution to authorize their presence.[4] U.S. Secretary of State Colin Powell had reportedly been mulling over UN Secretary General Kofi Annan's suggestion that the U.S. propose such a resolution to the UNSC,[5] but senior Bush officials were reluctant to go forward with this, fearing that it would sap Bremer's authority and require Washington to share the reconstruction contracts that had previously been distributed to American firms.[6] By mid-August, the Bush administration was reported to have "abandoned" the notion of a UNSC resolution.[7]

What this meant is that American taxpayers continued to bear the vast majority of the expenses for the Iraqi occupation, and American troops continued to shoulder by far the largest responsibility for keeping order—a task that most of the troops considered onerous and thought they were ill-prepared to accomplish.[8] Even the civil affairs soldiers who were trained for humanitarian relief operations believed they were not suited to the kind of long-term occupation roles they were forced to play.[9] By the end of the summer there were approximately 1,000 civilians working in the Coalition Provisional Authority, but in practice it was coalition military forces—primarily the Americans—who continued to deal with most policing duties as well as a great deal of the reconstruction work. Given the demands on the forces' time and resources, this meant that a lot of the reconstruction was not getting done very quickly.

Iraq continued to make the international headlines because of the instability that plagued the country. British troops in Basra faced days of violent rioting over fuel shortages, in a city whose university had earlier been looted of all its books, equipment and furniture while no one from the outside did anything to stop it.[10] Reconstruction efforts in many major cities were stymied, because the specialized materials, parts and tools used for rebuilding such things as electrical grids were constantly being stolen out of half-finished projects that no one was guarding.[11] Highway bandits and carjackers targeted everyone in sight, including NGO humanitarian relief workers.[12] The general sense of the population seemed to be that all those military troops standing around were not good for much; they couldn't make life more secure, and the ham-handed raids they carried out in their search for cronies of Saddam Hussein ended up humiliating, injuring, and sometimes killing innocent civilians.[13]

American troops in the Baghdad neighborhood known as Sadr City were attacked by residents after a low-flying helicopter hovering over a transmission tower appeared to be trying to rip a Shiite flag from its post atop the building.[14] Since a major irritant in Somalia ten years before had been low-flying U.S. helicopters hovering over residential areas in the capital

Iraq, Summer 2003 (*continued*)

city of Mogadishu (where residents believed they were being spied upon in the bath, and where women complained of having their robes torn open by the backwash of air from the copter blades[15]), one might have thought that U.S. soldiers sent on what amounted to a peacekeeping mission would have been forewarned about these perceptions. Given the U.S. military organization's reluctance to think about peacekeeping, however, it is not surprising that such a lesson was not learned.

How could order be restored in Iraq, as the U.S. had promised it would be? To do so meant relying on the military leadership of a country that did not want the job. Unilateralism—or the modified version of it that the U.S. practiced with its closest allies—made the prospect of achieving beneficial social and political change in the country difficult to imagine. The United States did not appear to have the political will needed to establish the "empire" that its critics accused it of seeking.

Yet for a long time the United States also resisted the idea of reaching out to other states for assistance, if that meant giving up control over military activity. In the previous chapters we have seen that the political goals of complex peacekeeping operations—gaining control over political developments in foreign societies, for the sake of self-interest intertwined with humanitarian impulses—have in some ways resembled the political goals of imperialism as practiced by liberal states a century ago. The example outlined above shows how hard it is to do these things well *unilaterally*, or at best with the support of a few well-chosen allies. What this chapter will concentrate on, however, is the flip side of the coin. The task of achieving control is made much more complex when it is attempted in *multilateral* operations, like those in the Balkans, where more than one state is attempting to exert its political vision over a piece of foreign territory. This difficulty was not faced by the old colonial empires, who kept guard over their national possessions and kept each other out of their territories. It is a problem that has plagued the multilateral peacekeeping operations of the 1990s, and made the problem of trying to establish control abroad much harder—perhaps contributing to the Bush administration's initial unwillingness to have outsiders involved.

The idea that putting multiple actors in charge of an operation makes cohesive action difficult is already well explored, to some extent, in the existing literature on peacekeeping. It is regularly argued that the number of players involved on a mission should be limited, to try to make sure that they share common training and a common vision of what is needed. This is one reason why so-called coalitions of the willing seem to do a better job of restoring peace to war-torn societies than traditional UN-commanded operations. Traditional operations are too subject to the varying political whims of the large number of countries that donate troops to them, and also too dependent on forces that often have inconsistent expectations and differing qualities of skills and training. There is also now widespread recognition that private NGOs have different perspectives and interests from the states that send military forces to peacekeeping operations. A great deal of effort has been spent in the policy community in recent years to try to bridge the barriers between NGO and military leaders so that more unified operations can be put into place in the future.[16]

What has not been explored are the problems of achieving coordination even among close military allies, such as those in NATO, and between those military forces and their civilian counterparts who are linked by a supposedly common set of liberal western values. This chapter draws out these difficulties by looking at examples of coordination difficulties from the peacekeeping experiences in Bosnia and Kosovo, paying special attention to the interaction between military and civilian players in the international community and the roles played by NATO military personnel in these operations. While the international community in the Balkans has made a well intentioned and heavily funded effort to establish political control over societies torn by ethnic conflict, the means employed have not been sufficiently well coordinated to achieve these goals. Indeed the fact of multilateralism has often made cohesive actions impossible.

Since multilateralism is what legitimates these operations, it is politically unacceptable to suggest that a single, powerful entity (with the authority equivalent to an imperial state) ought to be in charge. Indeed in Iraq before it turned to the UN Security Council in October 2003, the U.S.-dominated coalition constantly faced accusations of imperialism. Without question that made the job of restoring order more difficult, because it emboldened the detractors of the occupation. Yet putting a single state in charge would seem to help ensure that the political aims sought have a chance of being coordinated with the use of military resources necessary to achieve them. (The more that is revealed in the press about the lack of coordination between the U.S. State Department and the Pentagon in planning for the Iraqi occupation,[17] however, the more any cohesive policy whatsoever seems doubtful, reinforcing the findings of the previous chapter.) In the Balkans there have been too many actors with competing values and interests who have tried to do what they believe is right in the peace operations, but have in the end created a muddled set of expectations for the local population. The international community as a whole has been unable to communicate a clear message, and therefore unable to exercise the kind of control that would in theory be necessary to move a society from one political system to another.

But it is not necessary to give up in despair; there is a political choice available that combines the best aspects of unilateral control with multilateral support for peacekeeping operations. This chapter contrasts the Balkans cases with the experience of the Interfet operation led by Australia in East Timor beginning in Fall 1999. While it is true that long-term stability and economic development in East Timor remain uncertain, the Australian Defense Force's ability to manage the conduct of the initial UN-authorized multinational military operation there from September 1999 through February 2000 (and even on into the UNTAET area in the crucial western sector) ensured clarity and consistency in the establishment of security in the country. Rather than approaching East Timor as an alliance of equals, the Australians took charge unambiguously, seeking multilateral participation and feedback but keeping responsibility for decisions at a national level. Such a model would have worked better for the U.S. in Iraq than the initial attempt at what amounted to unilateralism—and indeed, it was this model that the Bush administration seemed to embrace by Fall 2003, when UN support was finally sought and achieved. The only question was whether Washington had waited too long and acted too presumptuously toward other states to obtain genuinely enthusiastic participation in the operations.

The following section details some of the military tasks carried out in the Balkans, and shows how similar they are to the actions carried out (sometimes successfully, sometimes with too much brutality) by military organizations during the imperial era. The chapter goes on, though, to show how these tasks have been complicated in the Balkans by the necessity of multilateral coordination across NATO members and other representatives of the western community. Multilateralism makes complex military activity more difficult. Finally the Australian leadership of the Interfet mission in East Timor is explored, to show that there is a compromise solution possible to the dilemma of multilateral effectiveness.

The Use of NATO Military Force in the Balkans

There is a striking resemblance between the tasks that military personnel have been asked to do during today's complex peace operations and the tasks many military personnel were asked to do in colonial empires. Military troops serving on the NATO peacekeeping missions in Bosnia and Kosovo are routinely given duties that would be assigned to civilian police in calm and established societies. Military officers serving on these missions are also asked to coordinate humanitarian aid delivery in their areas of operation, working with NGOs and international aid agencies to select and prioritize funding for projects ranging from road reconstruction to small-business development. In other words, military personnel are being asked to take on responsibilities extending far beyond the standard tasks they are trained to do, and are being asked to do this in unstable foreign countries where the political consequences of their actions are uncertain.

There are four military tasks in particular in the Balkans that bear strong resemblance to colonial governorship activities, even though once again their goals and methods differ from what was practiced in the colonial era. First is riot control. The British army stationed in colonial India (where most officers were British, but most soldiers were Indian) was routinely asked to back up local police when riots occurred that challenged British rule.[18] One British general wrote an entire book on the subject in 1934, emphasizing the importance of limiting the use of force to the minimum amount necessary, since "the hostile forces are fellow citizens of the Empire, and . . . the military object is to re-establish the control of the civil power and secure its acceptance without an aftermath of bitterness."[19]

Similarly, in the SFOR operation in Bosnia in recent years, NATO military troops have often been asked to provide a "security ring" in areas where rioting is likely to occur. As in the colonial era, local police are usually given the responsibility for immediate control of the rioting itself. Military personnel, however, will guard the surrounding area to prevent outsiders from joining the melee, and to provide a sense of "presence" to try to deter violence. This was done, for example, by the Nordic/Polish brigade working with American troops to provide a safe and secure environment for a Croat religious pilgrimage to the Serbian-controlled town of Komusina in Aug. 2001;[20] by Spanish troops when rioting accompanied the attempt to reconstruct a destroyed Bosniac mosque in the Croatian-dominated town of Stolac in Dec. 2001;[21] and by British and Italian-led contingents working with Slovene, Czech, Portuguese, Dutch, and Canadian forces in Banja Luka throughout the early summer of 2001, when violent protests and counter-protests by both Serbian and Bosniac extremists repeatedly delayed the groundbreaking ceremonies for the reconstruction of the Ferhadija mosque destroyed in 1993 (at one point, visiting foreign dignitaries had to be evacuated by NATO troops from the site).[22]

British officers sometimes make the direct connection between their colonial experience and their approach to such peacekeeping activities today, citing as lessons learned from that era the preference for minimal use of force and the need to win the hearts and minds of the population.[23] Obviously what constitutes minimal use of force has changed over time. Sometimes in the colonial era, as in Egypt in 1919, it simply meant showing the British flag in the harbors and deploying troops in the cities, to remind the local population of the potential for violence if order were not kept.[24] But often for the British, it meant something harsher: giving clear warning before opening fire, and then targeting only the violent leaders of mob action;[25] or sometimes merely firing weapons over the rioters' heads.[26] In NATO peacekeeping operations today, it means relying mostly on presence as a deterrent, and using only nonlethal weapons and good protective equipment so that any loss of life is avoided as much as possible—something, as noted in the previous chapter, which is not always done well. But the parallels are clear: NATO troops today engage in riot control in order to allow outside forces (i.e., the international community) to impose their own sovereign vision on political society in the Balkans.

The second unusual military activity that bears some resemblance to the colonial governorship era is the meting out of rewards to villages in the local population who cooperate with the mission, and sanctions against those who would harm it. In other words, military forces reward or punish collectivities for the actions of individuals. This time the methods used are vastly different between the two time periods. In the colonial era village sanctions were sometimes taken to violent extremes by American, British and French forces. If gentler means failed to win the support of the population, colonial forces would destroy their crops and livestock as punishment.[27] (It should be noted that such activities were allowed under international law up through the early twentieth century.[28]) U.S. forces in the Philippines a hundred years ago would reward those who collaborated with the occupation, encouraging American trade with cooperative local governments in the Muslim Moro region, and allowing them to manage their own affairs (including turning a blind eye to local slavery) and to practice their own religion; but they would destroy the political hubs of groups who did not cooperate, occasionally massacring large numbers of civilians in the process.[29] French forces in Indochina called their policy "progressive occupation," where military posts gave preferential prices to traders as a reward for cooperation.[30] Yet French officers in Algeria in the 1840s were known to retaliate against Arab raiders by using their own traditional local means of warfare against them, the *razzia*; analyst Douglas Porch writes, "Blackened fields, destroyed fruit orchards, and devastated villages soon marked the passage of French columns," in what he calls "an orgy of brutality and excess."[31] While British forces were supposed to be trained to use restraint, by the 1920s future Prime Minister Winston Churchill, who then had responsibility for overseeing Britain's colonies, was championing the policy of "air control" (or aerial carpet bombing) against recalcitrant villages of the Iraqi Marsh Arabs in particular, who had declared a jihad against British occupation.[32] Clearly, that kind of violence is not practiced by NATO forces in the Balkans today (nor is it by American troops in post-Saddam Iraq).

Indeed much of the rewards and sanctions policy carried out by the international community in the Balkans in recent years has not been done through the use of force, but instead through the use of economic aid policy. The "Open Cities" program in Bosnia has already been discussed—a policy which targeted international reconstruction assistance to villages whose mayors expressed a willingness to allow and encourage refugee returns, and denied financial aid to those whose mayors opposed this goal, especially in areas where NATO peacekeepers were attacked by locals.[33] Military officers played a key role in this process, by talking to the local mayors as part of their regular patrols, and reporting their findings to the EU and UN coordinators.[34]

In some cases, military commanders have played an even more direct role in rewards and sanctions policy in the Balkans. This is because the military contingents, both through their own national means and through NATO civil-military coordination (CIMIC) programs, have aid funding at their disposal that they can disperse as they see fit. For example, a Canadian CIMIC team decided to cut off all SFOR-coordinated aid to the Bosnian town of Kotor Varos, because the town political leaders were unwilling to expend resources to help ensure the safety of returning refugees.[35]

There was at least one case in Kosovo where a sanctioning decision made by a NATO troop commander did have some unintended violent consequences, and where the victims were probably not the perpetrators of the original unrest. On July 1, 2000, the U.S. commander of KFOR Multinational Brigade East [MNB(E)], Brigadier General Randal Tieszen, suspended humanitarian assistance (except for emergency food and medical supplies) to the Serb population of the village of Strpce, after the UN civilian mission (UNMIK) building there was attacked by a mob who destroyed its facilities, stoned the police station, and stockpiled more rocks to throw at NATO troop patrols.[36] The mob was angry because a number of villagers had disappeared or been murdered while working in their fields, and they felt UNMIK and KFOR were not doing an adequate job of protecting them from Albanian retribution.

American forces placed simultaneous sanctions on the Albanian population in the town of Kamenica. In that town, villagers had insisted (despite

KFOR having denied them permission to do so) on adorning a new war memorial with an illegal symbol of the banned Kosovo Liberation Front paramilitary forces, who had been responsible for attacks carried out against Serb authorities. When Russian KFOR troops (deployed in the American-controlled sector) tried to intervene to remove the symbol, they were violently attacked by the Albanian crowd; the American sanctions were designed to punish that attack. This was perhaps an unusual incidence of U.S.-Russian cooperation in Kosovo; more often than not, American troops were suspicious of unauthorized Russian military activity in the American occupation sector.[37]

As part of the sanctions against Strpce, MNB(E) stopped providing the regular armed protection convoys it had previously given the ethnic Serb villagers, which had allowed them to cross Kosovar Albanian areas of Kosovo safely by bus and go into Serbia proper to shop, visit doctors, see family, or take school exams. Tieszen told a press conference, "You can't attack us and then put your hand out for support and aid."[38] On the day that the sanctions were imposed, a bus convoy of 300 villagers from Strpce was already in Serbia, and because of the new policy it was denied NATO protection for its return trip. These villagers decided to try to make it home anyway. Along the way they were blocked by ethnic Albanians, and the buses were stoned; three Serb villagers were injured. Within a week, the convoy service was restored, because the local government demonstrated good faith and support for UNMIK and KFOR.[39] In this case, the means used and the goals sought were significantly different from those of the colonial era; but a military commander used (in this case, by withdrawing) a tool of military force against a collective group in order to encourage cooperation with the political goals of an outside power.

The third unusual military activity which both colonialism and NATO peacekeeping in the Balkans share is the use of military force to support particular political figures over their detractors. In colonial times, military commanders would often forcibly replace particular local leaders with others more amenable to their control. For example, in Morocco, French General Louis-Hubert Lyautey had a powerful sultan replaced with his brother, a bookish man who happily withdrew to his study and allowed the French to run the country without much interference.[40] In the Philippines, American forces used divide-and-conquer tactics to reward elites who informed on each other, often by granting political offices to those who cooperated with them.[41]

An example from Bosnia shows that not that much has changed. In 1997, many in the international community believed that the success of the Dayton Accords hinged on the fate of one individual: the president of

Republica Srpska (the Serbian sector of Bosnia), Biljana Plavsic. Plavsic had originally been a hard-line Serbian nationalist, and she was later convicted of war crimes by the International Criminal Tribunal for the Former Yugoslavia and sentenced to 11 years in prison. However in the late 1990s she had not yet been prosecuted. She in fact had been invited to a number of international conferences on foreign aid policy. Because she had been exposed through these conferences to the aid conditionality practices used by the international donor community as it made decisions about who was deserving of funds, she had become convinced by June 1997 that cooperation with the Office of the High Representative (OHR) for Bosnia and with NATO's SFOR was necessary for the economic well-being of BiH's Serbian population. As a result, on June 28 she fired her own interior minister, a strong supporter of the Serbian hard-line faction, on charges of corruption.

Immediately, her government rose up against her, calling her actions unconstitutional under republican law and charging that she was working with the international community to undermine Bosnian Serb independence.[42] In early July, Plavsic traveled to Great Britain and on her return was temporarily placed under house arrest by Republica Srpska authorities. When she was released, she ordered the dissolution of the republic's parliament and called for new elections in September, actions that her government did not recognize and that led it to call for her to step down. While this did not quite constitute a civil war, it was certainly a civil standoff, between the rest of the republic's government on one side and Plavsic on the other. She was immediately placed under the armed protection of British SFOR troops.[43] Over the next several weeks, SFOR troops took control over hard-line Serb-controlled television stations that were broadcasting propaganda and threats against Plavsic and SFOR, and raided a number of local police stations, finding significant arms caches that convinced the international community that a coup was being planned against Plavsic.

Plavsic's new position as what amounted to an ally of the West was complicated by another underlying issue: NATO's recent attempt to capture a different indicted Serbian war criminal on Bosnian territory, Simo Drljaca. This attempt had ended in a shoot-out with British troops, and Drljaca was killed instead of being captured for trial. Following this incident, Serbian hardliners depicted NATO British forces on television as the reincarnation of the pro-Nazi Croatian Ustase from the World War II era, and labeled Plavsic as their stooge.[44] In other words, NATO troops were clearly coming down on one side of a very heated and nasty political battle inside Bosnia.

NATO troops continued to protect Plavsic. Perhaps the most stunning use of military force on her behalf came in September. Hardliners in the town of Banja Luka, where Plavsic was based, planned a demonstration rally against her on September 8. SFOR got word that the rest of what had been the Bosnian Serb government, based in the town of Pale and no longer recognized by the OHR as legitimate, intended to send dozens of busloads of armed and drunk supporters into Banja Luka to join the rally. The rump government thought it could create a melee and bring Plavsic down. NATO had already set up a number of checkpoints on the roads connecting the two areas, and it now used them to delay the progress of the buses—verbally, by having checkpoint guards engage in intentionally confusing conversations with the drunk drivers of the convoy, and physically, by sending out slow-moving vehicles to block the progress of the buses on the roads (and according to one report, by throwing spikes on the road in front of the first bus in line to cause its tires to puncture).[45] The armed and drunk hardliners never made it to the rally, which fizzled into an embarrassment. The broadcast of these events by moderate local media sources boosted Plavsic's support in the election, and she won.

The goals of the international community in this case were consistent with their liberal vision for Bosnia's future. Blocking violent protesters who were attempting what amounted to a coup was certainly something that served electoral democracy, too. Yet by taking one side in a constitutional struggle, NATO and the OHR demonstrated their willingness to enforce an outside political agenda on BiH society. It was the use of outside force that tipped the election in Plavsic's favor—not the political resources that were internal to Bosnian society. What made this case particularly ironic was that Plavsic was later indicted for committing war crimes during the hostilities in Bosnia. She turned herself in to the International War Crimes Tribunal for Yugoslavia, and is now in prison. In other words, NATO exerted its military might in order to support what amounted to one war criminal over another, for the sake of furthering the political interests of the West in undermining Serbian hardliners.

The fourth at least passing similarity between colonialism and NATO operations in the Balkans is the use of force to encourage demographic change—in the case of the peacekeeping operations, to undo the effects of ethnic cleansing. Obviously once again the goals and means differ. In the colonial era, populations were sometimes relocated by force in order to separate armed insurgents from civilians who might otherwise support them, for example by providing them with food and shelter. The British did this in Malaya as late as the early 1950s,[46] following the example the French used against the Tokolor population in Sudan in the late nineteenth century[47] and that the U.S. tried as a repeated temporary measure in the Philippines in the early twentieth century.[48] In the colonial era no one ever seemed to question the ethics of moving a population out of their current homes for a larger political end. If establishing stability required depriving rebel forces of their support base by forcible relocation, so be it.

In the Balkans, NATO military forces have certainly not forcibly relocated villages. In Bosnia, there is a process of ethnic eviction that usually must take place for displaced persons to return to the homes that they fled when ethnic cleansing was at its peak, since those houses are now occupied by families from ethnic groups whose paramilitaries drove out the original occupants during the war. But NATO has been very careful not to participate directly in that process. Instead, when SFOR troops hear about property claims during their routine patrols, they bring those claims to the attention of civilian authorities. SFOR also uses its mapping software to help in the process of verifying property claims, and it provides a presence that helps ensure security for returnees once they arrive.[49] Yet when an occupying family has to be evicted in order for an owner to return home, under the Displaced Persons Property Law Implementation Plan passed by the OHR in 1999, it is local police and local authorities who must manage the process, and SFOR will not intervene to make it happen.[50]

Yet in Kosovo American forces have been directly used to try to convince occupying Albanians to leave Serbian-owned homes, even though the U.S. troops say that they do not do evictions per se.[51] And certainly NATO troops have used force to try to convince hostile ethnic populations to *allow* minorities to return to their homes, after those minorities have been encouraged to return by UN authorities. Sometimes these NATO actions have aggravated violent clashes that NATO troops then have to control.

One of the best examples of this is the complex story of the divided city of Mitrovica in Kosovo. The last chapter talked about one incident from that case, but it is worth looking at as a whole in greater detail. Following the war and the major influx of refugee returns in Summer 1999, the northern half of the city remained almost completely ethnically Serbian, and the southern half became almost completely ethnically Albanian. A major bridge, heavily guarded by KFOR troops protected with barbed wire and other barricades, keeps a de facto demilitarized zone between the two sides—who each blame the other for wartime suffering.

In February 2000, a grenade was detonated inside a Serbian café in the north, and this provoked weeks of rioting by Serbs who blamed Albanians for the attack. Nine Mitrovica residents died in the riots. The immediate result was further ethnic separation, as 1,500 Albanians who had remained in the north fled south to safety.[52] In an effort to control the rioting, KFOR decided to move more forces into the city. The French troops who normally patrolled the northern sector were bolstered by an American battalion, as described in the last chapter, but to no effect. The rioting got worse, and several NATO troops were injured.[53] The next day, Albanians on the southern side of the city who said they wanted to return to the north clashed with British troops who refused to allow them over the bridge. Although UN officials had shouted out to the Albanian crowd from the top floor of a nearby building that returns would soon be possible, Serbian hardliners who were self-appointed "bridge guardians" had earlier warned that any mass attempt by Albanians to cross the bridge would be met with deadly force. The Serb hardliners backed up this threat with a huge counter-demonstration on their side of the bridge.[54]

As the violence of the Serbian demonstrations escalated, U.S. troops once again entered the Serbian sector, this time swooping down by helicopter at dawn. They arrested eight Serbs who were ringleaders of the violence, and seized Serb weapons while the French (this time) provided a security cordon. KFOR announced that Albanians forced from the north would soon begin returning to their homes under NATO protection.[55] KFOR then built a special new bridge across the dividing line, very near the existing bridge but with one end leading directly to the former Albanian area in the north (known as Little Bosnia). It was hoped that this would give the returnees an extra sense of security.[56]

The returns process began, with Albanians crossing the bridge into Little Bosnia, but the violence didn't stop. In early March a street fight broke out in the north between ethnic Albanians and Serbs, when an Albanian used a crowbar to attack a Serb who was taunting and threatening him. Fellow Serbs surged out to defend their compatriot, and a second Albanian shot one of these Serbs dead.[57] The Serb mob grew larger and angrier in response, and apparently some Albanians lobbed grenades into the mob. Seventeen French soldiers who were trying to control the rioting (but whom the Albanians viewed as pro-Serb, because of their failure to stop the earlier anti-Albanian violence in the north) were injured by the grenades, apparently accidentally.[58]

The unrest and violence continued throughout 2001. Numerous press reports document rioting and ethnic attacks by each side against the other, with NATO troops often caught in the middle—first as they attempted to protect convoys of Albanian returnees to the north, and then as they tried to contain retribution violence led by the Albanian returnees against the Serb population. The situation in Mitrovica remained far from settled at the time this book went to press. It is a good example of how the international community is continuing to use NATO troops to try to enforce an integrationist view for Kosovo—one that may not ultimately be sustainable in the absence of political will among its citizenry.

One set of events demonstrates what happens when all four of these unusual military activities—riot control, community rewards and sanctions, the support of particular political factions, and efforts at demographic control—come together. That case involves the actions taken by NATO troops in response to activism by the Croatian independence movement inside BiH in spring and summer 2001. Croat nationalists were not happy with the Dayton division of the country, and began agitating for the right to have their territory annexed to the state of Croatia instead.

In March 2001, Ante Jelavic, head of the Croat Democratic Union (HDZ) party (and the Croatian member of the joint BiH presidency who had earlier been removed by the OHR, as discussed in chapter 2), publicly demanded ethnic Croatian autonomy inside Bosnia. He asked all ethnically Croatian soldiers and police officers to stop recognizing the Muslim/Croat Federation authorities, who until that point had been their commanders. Since moderates had been elected to all of the open state and federation offices that past November, Jelavic's move was widely seen as a far-fetched ploy to keep the HDZ in power without democratic support.[59] Yet most of the approximately 8,000 ethnically Croat military troops in the Federation army deserted their posts in a show of support for the HDZ,[60] and more than 20 high-ranking officers publicly refused to follow the orders of the Federation command[61] in what NATO termed an "organized mutiny."[62] Some of the military installations were then occupied by the deserters, or by veterans' groups who supported the nationalist cause. SFOR commander Lieutenant General Michael Dodson, using the language of the Dayton Accords that gave SFOR responsibility for oversight of Bosnian weapons storage facilities, ordered all munitions at Croat facilities to be seized and the barracks themselves to be put under SFOR control.[63]

Simultaneously, Bosnian High Representative Petritsch—the man who had earlier fired Jelavic from the presidency—took control over the national bank that was responsible for financing the Croatian separatists in Bosnia, the Bank Hercegovacka (including its 10 local branches). Working with NATO, he used SFOR troops to protect OHR officials and UN police who seized the bank's records; he then suspended the existing bank managers and replaced the staff with his own provisional appointees.[64] SFOR troops faced ethnic Croatian rioters at the main bank branch in Mostar and at several local branches when they first tried to take over the bank on April 6. The rioters, including members of the Croatian police and army,[65] shouted "occupiers, occupiers" at those raiding the bank.[66] The international community representatives had to return to Mostar in the middle of the night two weeks later with 80 armored vehicles and 20 helicopters; British-led SFOR troops then blasted open the bank doors and vaults with explosives to achieve Petritsch's goals.[67] While this second operation was termed a successful use of SFOR force, it was widely criticized for being ham-handed and for aggravating ethnic tensions.

The Difficulty of Multilateralism

These cases demonstrate that while the goals of the international community were certainly not the same as those of earlier colonial governors, and while the means used to achieve those goals had been significantly moderated from that earlier point in history, there was still some degree of similarity in how military force was used in the two eras. But a closer examination of several of these examples indicates that the international community faces a problem in the Balkans that complicates the successful use of force for these purposes. While the international community would like, at least to some extent, to force the Balkans into a liberal democratic and ethnically integrated template of development, it is often impossible for various countries and nongovernmental actors, each operating under their own, independent set of liberal democratic norms, to force any consistent political vision on anyone else. In the above examples there were often too many liberal democratic players, each with their own set of deeply embedded philosophical norms (and organizational self-interests, which are often hard to disentangle from those norms) about how to do things to have a coherent outcome.

The players range from the individual NATO member states and their military organizations, who have different limiting rules about how their forces may be used abroad, to various UN agencies and NGOs who are naturally suspicious about the efforts of any military organizations to limit their activities. The result is that there is no way of establishing clear lines of control over what happens when. This multiplicity of operating procedures is not something that can be changed by clearer communication or better discussion; it is simply a fact of life in the liberal democratic international community.

Colonial occupations were also sometimes characterized by muddled lines of control. The French colonial army was notable for its tendency to ignore directives coming from Paris and to work around the titular local French civilian leaders on the ground. Officers in Africa acted without the permission of civilian authorities and often without their knowledge, sometimes starting new wars that French leaders would have preferred to avoid. This was especially common in areas of the empire that were deemed less important by Paris, and that as a result received less ministerial oversight.[68] Over time, this meant that the arrival or departure of a particular military commander could have an unsettling impact on the colony, as individual philosophies about how to treat indigenous culture and indigenous political leaders clashed.[69] In the Philippines, too, the differing personalities of American military governors and commanders often sent conflicting messages to the population about American goals and intentions, with some officials practicing a live and let live policy while others, like Leonard Wood, engaged in almost constant warfare and were famed for their brutality.[70]

Yet despite the personal vicissitudes of colonial rulers, and despite battles over civilian versus military control of colonial activity, there were nonetheless clear national goals of territory and profit (and sometimes conversion to Christianity) motivating the actions taken by the representatives of each empire. There was also a consistent background threat communicated to the populations of the British, French, and American empires alike that failure to comply with colonial rules would be met with force. There was no need for multilateral or international cooperation, and little political space was given at home to debate over what military organizations should or should not be doing while abroad.

In contrast, several of the examples described above of NATO military activities in Bosnia and Kosovo were constrained or weakened either by national limitations on how force might be used or by the fact that no one body was ever in real control of the actions taken on the ground. Let us reexamine some of these cases.

Multilateralism and the Use of Troops for Policing

As was mentioned in chapter 2, IFOR (the original NATO-led peace-keeping force in Bosnia) was criticized by the liberal international community for its failure to take action to ensure the safe integration of ethnic groups immediately following the Dayton Accords of 1995. The most glaring example of this was when military troops stood by as ethnic Serbs burned and looted apartments in the area surrounding the capital city of Sarajevo in early 1996.[71] The Dayton Accords stipulated that seven suburban municipalities, the scene of heavy fighting and ethnic cleansing during the civil war that were now occupied largely by ethnic Serbs, were to be transferred to the political control of the Muslim-Croat Federation. The suburbs sat at a height above Sarajevo, and the primary reason for the transfer was reportedly to ensure the safety of Sarajevo proper from sniper attacks. The transfer was also designed to ensure that Muslims and Croats driven from their homes during the war could safely return. But fueled at least in part by intimidation from Serbian paramilitary groups, most of the Serbian population living in these suburbs—both those who had lived there continuously since before the war, back when the suburbs were ethnically integrated, and those who as displaced persons from elsewhere had occupied homes left vacant by the ethnic cleansing of non-Serbs—deserted the area and migrated into Republica Srpska. As they left, the residents stripped the homes of everything of value, including wiring and plumbing, and Serbian arsonists burned some neighborhoods to the ground.

There was an International Police Task Force (IPTF) on the ground at that time as part of the Dayton Accords, under the control of the United Nations. But the IPTF was unarmed and was only mandated to provide supervision and oversight to local police forces, not to take any police actions itself—probably because the international community did not wish to take actions that might be seen as neocolonial. The local police forces, however, were dominated by ethnic nationalists who did not wish to see integration happen. The IPTF had no enforcement power, even though its Commissioner's Guidance Notes stated that the local police "must realign their missions from the protection of the state to the protection of citizen's rights."[72] Meanwhile NATO member states were unwilling to let IFOR military troops use force for anything except the military purposes outlined in the Dayton Accords. As a result, the international community was unable to accomplish the forcible integration it intended.

With the change of mandate that was associated with the transition between IFOR and SFOR, and also with the appointment of General Wesley K. Clark as the new commander of NATO (SACEUR),[73] this situation began to change. Yet both in SFOR and later in KFOR, military forces have been reluctant to intervene in untraditional ways, even when not doing so threatens the success of the NATO mission. Furthermore, military and civilian actions have not always been well coordinated. This lack of cohesion has been clear, for example, in response to ethnic rioting. In the case of the cornerstone laying at the Ferhadija mosque in Banja Luka in early May 2001, discussed above, a mob of several thousand protestors broke through the local police cordon and threatened members of the international community who were there to witness the celebration. The mob effectively imprisoned the American head of the Bosnian UN mission and the Austrian and British ambassadors to Bosnia (among others) in the nearby Islamic community building. High Representative Petritsch said that the violence was the fault of the Republica Srpska authorities, and wrote, "I am shocked that the Republika Srpska still appears to be a place with no rule of law, no civilized behavior, and no religious freedom."[74]

It would be surprising if he were truly shocked, however, and the international community should have been better prepared for violence. SFOR spokesperson (and Canadian Captain) Andrew Coxhead defended the British and Italian troops who helped evacuate the dignitaries but did not intervene in the rioting, saying, "It would be inappropriate for us to not allow the police to fulfill their duties. . . . SFOR intervention only would have occurred if the police had completely failed to resolve the situation."[75] Yet inaction here undermined the deterrent effect that the presence of those troops was supposed to have. Granting ownership of the peace process to the same Serb hardliners who had destroyed the mosque exactly eight years before was not an effective tactic to take.

When the ceremony was tried again weeks later, it succeeded. This time, the OHR used its appointments leverage to compel local authorities to deploy a more convincing police presence; under the threat of removing people from office, the OHR ensured that the police were instructed to defend whoever might be harmed. Perhaps more important, SFOR district commander General Rick Hillier (a Canadian) gave "Person Designated with a Special Status" standing to the Bosniac officials attending the ceremony, which legally allowed "SFOR to intervene, where and when it needs to, to protect people without waiting for any request of local authorities or the International Community."[76] In other words, the NATO deterrent was given teeth. When the international community really wanted to accomplish a political goal in Bosnia it could do so, but not always the first time around—and not without emphasizing that it would impose a political vision on the region with or without local consensus.

A similarly uncoordinated situation had actually been faced by the international community in the Croatian bank takeover crisis a month earlier. (Learning has not been a strength of the Bosnian peace mission.) According to one knowledgeable NATO official, the rules of engagement that were specified for the initial bank takeover effort were insufficient to allow SFOR to react as strongly as it might have once the rioting broke out. Each SFOR member state has the ability to "flash their red card," or to declare that a particular military order coming from the top is politically unacceptable for them to carry out. This NATO official said that when the rioting broke out, the Spanish contingent guarding the bank takeover flashed its red card, because Spanish military troops are not allowed to engage in riot-control activities. As a result the SFOR contingent assigned to the event was forced to withdraw.[77] A second NATO official confirmed that there was insufficient coordination among the various actors to craft an appropriate contingency plan in anticipation of the rioting, and also confirmed that Spain would not allow its troops to be used for riot control.[78] A Spanish military officer explained that Spain divides security activities into "blue box" and "green box" activities, and that while military troops may be used to provide perimeter security (the green box), they may not be used for immediate police actions (the blue box). He argues that SFOR lacked a good understanding of the real situation in Mostar, and that Spanish forces should never have been assigned to guard the bank takeover given the political situation there, since the SFOR command knew about the Spanish red card.[79]

Spanish troops were also reported to have loosely interpreted their orders at that time to intervene in the simultaneous Croatian barracks mutiny. They sent an unarmed contingent to one arms depot and simply watched as the rebel Croat forces operated there. French commanders, too, were reportedly reluctant to follow the orders of the American NATO commander. Major General Robert Meille said at a press conference, "They are rebels. But this is the problem of the government. It is not my problem."[80] The same French reluctance to follow the general NATO plan of operations has been noted in Mitrovica, Kosovo, where the French are known not to favor the ethnic reintegration plan that NATO and the UN are following.[81]

A different form of uncoordinated military activity might have hampered the actions taken on behalf of Plavsic in 1997. In that case, it was U.S. policy, particularly the "force protection" policy described in chapter 4—protecting the safety of U.S. troops in the field—that challenged the cohesion of the international community. As was noted in the previous chapter, U.S. policymakers widely believe that the American public will not tolerate casualties on peacekeeping missions. To respond to this democratic imperative, the notion goes, U.S. forces on such missions must be kept safe. In this case, U.S. troops who had been raiding the police stations that were suspected of stockpiling weapons for an anti-Plavsic coup withdrew after they were stoned and firebombed by a mob. The directive apparently came down from Washington that U.S. forces were not to risk casualties over an internal Bosnian political dispute.[82]

Later in that same set of incidents, U.S. troops confronted Serbian hardliners over control of a television station in the town of Bijeljina that was broadcasting attacks against NATO. But the deputy UN official in charge of the Bosnian mission, American diplomat Jacques Klein, negotiated a separate deal with the Serbian hardliners in an effort to stave off violence, apparently without the approval of the then-High Representative Carl Westendorp. On orders from Washington, the American troops turned over the station to the hardliners it had been confronting, despite the anger that this provoked in the OHR.[83] These actions did not seem, in the end, to undercut the effectiveness of the international community's pro-Plavsic efforts. They do, though, highlight the limits of liberal coalition cooperation when military activities become messy.

Multilateralism and Humanitarian Aid Decisions

It is not only police actions that reveal the limits of multilateralism. Efforts to direct humanitarian aid delivery, in order to reward or sanction local community behavior, also come up against limits on cohesive interpretation of how to express liberal values. The announcement of aid conditionality may have some effect on the behavior of those supposedly affected by it. Yet there are real limits to how well the diverse international community is able to coordinate who gets what aid. For example, the "Open Cities" conditional aid program in Bosnia is widely perceived by NATO officials to have been a failure. This is because once particular Bosnian mayors had convinced EU and UN donors that they embraced the Dayton Accords, little coordinated monitoring of their later actions proved feasible. There is much suspicion that the aid community was suckered into continuing to fund hard-line nationalists.[84]

In the case of military sanctioning, even if the CIMIC (Civil-Military Cooperation) aid that is under the control of SFOR or KFOR military troops is withheld, humanitarian NGOs are free to give independent help to whomever they like. Military contingents usually lack the authority to restrict their movements, because to limit participation in humanitarian aid delivery goes against UN principles. In the Bosnian example of Kotor Varos cited above, where the Canadian SFOR contingent attempted to sanction the town for its noncompliance with the Dayton Accords, "The team's efforts were undermined several days later when an NGO announced a major donation to the town. . . . With this NGO's money the mayor was able to ignore pressure to accept minority returns."[85]

In the American KFOR contingent's sanctioning of the Kosovo town of Strpce in July 2000, a number of NGOs were asked to withhold their aid and were denied U.S. CIMIC support for projects in that locale for the several days that the sanctions lasted. The NGOs were reportedly quite angry and made their views known in Washington.[86] Even the United Nations authorities who had been physically attacked in Strpce publicly distanced themselves from U.S. sanctions; the local UN administrator, a French citizen, "called the punishment 'politically stupid' and resigned."[87] In what may have been a delayed show of unity with the rest of the international community, a year later the new American commander of MNB(E), Brigadier General Bill David, presented the town of Strpce with gifts of a fire truck and a garbage truck in "a sign that the town was cooperating well with KFOR and UNMIK" and "to aid with cooperation in the future."[88]

The press reports of disagreements over targeted aid policy tend to portray them as philosophical debates over what the mandate of the international community should be. The question at the heart of these divides seems to be whether the international community should punish ordinary citizens for the ethnic intolerance of their representative officials, or whether aid should be given to everyone equally regardless of local political behavior. But private conversations with a variety of NATO civilian and military officials hint at a darker picture, revealing that some national military contingents have developed bad reputations for using aid to serve national commercial interests rather than shared humanitarian goals. No one wants to say which states are the culprits. In the words of British Colonel John Rollins, Deputy Director of CIMIC at SHAPE, however, "Bilateralism—even unilateralism—by national military contingents in theater is rife. This has been particularly true in Kosovo. . . . This undermines trust between the military and the humanitarian community on the ground."[89]

When all of these examples are put together, the picture that emerges is quite a bit different from the one presented at first, where the western international community was seen to be imposing a particular political future on the Balkans by force. What we see instead is a variety of national and nongovernmental actors trying their best—but often failing—to present a coherent message to the involved populations about what is expected of them. Peace operations in the Balkans may be an attempt to move those societies in a liberal democratic direction, but by their very nature such multilateral efforts cannot control social or political sovereignty very effectively. The inconsistencies of the international community provide loopholes for the opponents of the peace process to jump through, and leave local populations confused about what the international community is really trying to do. The mixed messages that the international military forces send about democracy versus fiat and about encouragement versus blackmail may indeed harm the long-term reputation of both the United Nations and NATO in the region.

Australia in Interfet

There is a counter-example of a multilateral peace enforcement mission, authorized by the UN Security Council and designed to impose a particular political outcome on a society, that worked well, at least in its initial stages. That is the Australian-led military mission in East Timor, which was deployed for six months in response to the violence that accompanied the country's independence referendum in Sept. 1999.

In one sense the Interfet operation impinged less on local sovereignty than did the peace enforcement missions in Bosnia and Kosovo, because a 78 percent vote in favor of independent statehood made the preferences of the East Timorese population clear. Most Timorese welcomed Interfet's presence.[90] Interfet was designed primarily to remove an occupying force that otherwise might not leave quickly, namely the Indonesians; it supported a political outcome that most Timorese preferred on their own. Yet much of the violence resulting from the ballot, and especially the continuing threats of retribution faced by the East Timorese, came not only (and perhaps not even primarily) from the outside Indonesian forces. Instead the violence was caused by local soldiers who were serving in the Indonesian military (the so-called "territorials" recruited from within East Timor itself), and from paramilitary militias whose political and economic interests were harmed by the Indonesian withdrawal.[91] Later, territorials and militia members who attempted to return home to East Timor also risked retaliatory lynching by the pro-independence parties, and had to be protected by outside military forces. In the absence of Interfet, locally motivated mob violence may very well have left East Timor permanently unstable and depopulated. In this sense, then, Interfet was also designed to impose a particular political outcome—independence and peaceful cohabitation, if not liberal democracy—on a society that would not have reached it on its own.

Two things set the well coordinated Interfet operation apart from the NATO operations in Bosnia and Kosovo. First, as Australian army analyst Alan Ryan demonstrates, Australia managed to keep centralized control over operational planning. Interfet did not suffer from the lack of cohesion found in the Balkans peace operations. Yet Interfet was a truly multinational operation. A great deal of negotiation by Australian authorities (both civilian diplomats and military attachés) was required in order to get other countries to contribute troops to Interfet, especially the members of ASEAN (the Association of South East Asian Nations) who were reluctant to take actions that might be seen as intervening in the internal affairs of Indonesia.[92] What this meant was that the roles taken by each of the force contributors on the ground had to be painstakingly designed to mesh, and then negotiated with the relevant foreign authorities, by the Interfet force commander, Australian Major General Peter Cosgrove.[93]

Australia was recognized unquestionably as the preponderant military power in the region, and therefore as the appropriate lead nation for the mission. When this fact was combined with the longstanding cooperative security arrangement that Australia had with New Zealand and Great Britain, which led to common doctrinal practices and understandings among those three countries (easing the process of joint, mission-specific contingency planning),[94] it meant that Australian military planners had the ability to make key decisions on their own, and then oversee their implementation through well coordinated negotiations with other forces.[95] One particular benefit of this system was that Australia was able to place well prepared and equipped combat forces in the most dangerous areas of East Timor, while ensuring that countries who were less willing to risk violence had their soldiers assigned to the humanitarian aid activities at which they excelled.[96] Australia thus sidestepped one of the most common difficulties of multilateral peacekeeping missions that are commanded by the UN, where troops are sometimes deployed into situations they are not equipped to handle.

Australia's leadership of the entire peacekeeping operation was also, ironically, made easier by the level of destruction that permeated the East Timorese countryside. Because East Timor was perceived to be a dangerous place, plagued not only by violence but also by poor roads, poor sanitation, and rampant disease that could harm the unprotected, the support of core combat forces was necessary in order for humanitarian aid to be delivered to outlying areas. Especially given the destruction of East Timor's infrastructure in the days following the ballot, humanitarian NGOs needed military backing to do their work. This meant that there was little opportunity for inconsistencies to arise in the approaches taken to the mission, since the military could effectively control where aid workers went. (In this sense, Interfet resembled the UNTAES mission described in chapter 2, where Special Representative Jacques Klein could veto the participation of certain NGOs in the work in Eastern Slavonia.)

The second factor which set Interfet apart from the Balkans was that the core combat forces who were involved in Interfet—the Australians, New Zealanders and British—were all prepared and trained to engage in a wide variety of atypical military activities on the ground, especially activities that blur the line between military and police action and humanitarianism. Each of these military forces pride themselves on their flexibility. The British (as noted above) see this as part of their colonial heritage. Many

Australian officers trace their own institutional preparedness in this regard to the fact that their military doctrine was originally borrowed from the British model. They especially credit Australian participation in the British counterinsurgency campaign in Malaya in the 1950s.[97] Brigadier Mark Evans, commander of the Australian army brigade (3RAR) that led Interfet into East Timor in Sept. 1999, had himself served earlier as an officer for the British army in Northern Ireland.[98] Particularly important in this tradition is the notion that if the troops are able to win the hearts and minds of the local population, they then receive information from the locals that enhances their ability to fulfill their missions successfully.

The Australian forces were particularly well prepared for the kinds of activities that peacekeeping entails. In the 1980s and 1990s, as the threats associated with the cold war declined, Australian tactical flexibility was reinforced by the fact that commanders were planning for the possibility of low-level counterinsurgency operations. In particular, they thought it was likely that at some point the Australian Defence Forces (ADF) would be called on to defend Australia from harassment or sabotage arising from instability in the South Pacific.[99] One senior Australian officer said that as a result, the ADF trains extensively in activities like disarmament and detention of hostile individuals and small groups.[100] Another pointed out that the ADF emphasizes training in what is called "services-protected personnel evacuation," or cases where Australian diplomats and other civilians need emergency evacuation from a hostile political environment abroad. This officer argued that complex humanitarian missions are in many ways similar to evacuation missions: in both cases forces need to establish an entry point and then extend their control to additional preselected areas; in evacuation missions this system brings people out, and in complex humanitarian missions it brings relief supplies and troops in.[101]

Furthermore, the ADF had previous experience on peace operations to use in its Interfet preparations. The Chief of the Australian General Staff in the mid-1990s, Lieutenant General John Sanderson, had commanded the military component of the UN peacekeeping mission in Cambodia (UNTAC), whose mission changed midstream to include guarding refugees, arresting and detaining human rights violators, and securing the safety of the electoral process and of unarmed UN personnel.[102] Sanderson stressed in Cambodia the importance of keeping negotiation channels open with forces who might be hostile to mission success, and his advice was actively sought and applied as the ADF was putting together the Interfet mission. Beyond UNTAC, several senior ADF officers who trained and led some of the contingents going into East Timor had earlier served on the United States–commanded UNITAF mission in Somalia. The Australian component on that UNITAF mission was proud of its success in winning the hearts and minds of both the local Somali population and the NGO community in its area of operations,[103] and this helped cement the lessons of the British model. Australia learned a different set of lessons from Somalia than the Americans had.

This combination of resources held by the ADF—centralized control over mission planning and execution, and the willingness of the core combat forces to engage in flexible military action—meant that Interfet was able to send a clear and coherent message to the local population, one that integrated its various components. It went in to East Timor prepared for battle if necessary, with an all-encompassing UN mandate backed by a tough deterrent force, but it preferred to avoid bloodshed if possible and its personnel were sympathetic to the concerns of the local population. The ADF would take whatever actions were necessary to restore a sense of security among the East Timorese, including police actions if required, and the brunt of any hostility would be faced by forces prepared to take casualties.

Of course, the Interfet mission was temporary. It ended in February 2000, when the more complex and multifaceted UN mission to East Timor, UNTAET, was deployed. There was a high degree of continuity in the military personnel used in the two missions—over 70 percent of the soldiers on the final rotation of Interfet stayed for the first rotation of UNTAET,[104] and Australia and New Zealand remained the dominant forces in the volatile Western sector of East Timor. But the transfer to UN authority significantly expanded the purposes of the mission to include democratization, civil society, and economic development tasks, and at that point the variety of international organizations descending on East Timor exploded. UN personnel on the mission were harshly criticized for their obvious displays of wealth on the ground, their lack of organization, their wastage of resources, and the slow pace of the inclusion of local East Timorese in civil management activities.[105] Once the goals of the international community became more complex, the ability to maintain cohesion over operations was lost. As previous chapters have noted, it is not clear at this point that the attempt to create a functioning, independent, liberal democratic state in East Timor will work over the long term.

The Dilemmas of Liberal Democratic Intervention

Today's acceptance of multilateralism as a badge of legitimacy could be seen as presenting a conundrum. On the one hand, peacekeeping missions cannot afford to be exclusionary. The goal of imposing a particular form of political sovereignty on a troubled society is a controversial one, and this means that the international community, if it seeks that goal, cannot afford to have prominent countries be told that their troops aren't wanted on the mission. Nor can it tell those countries that their national command authority will be usurped. NGOs will certainly not allow themselves to be subjected to control by military forces whose motives they suspect. (Not surprisingly, they complained about the control that Australian forces exerted over their activities during Interfet, even as they expressed appreciation for the ADF's assistance in getting them where they needed to go.) It is already hard enough to garner sufficient political will to put well designed complex peace missions together. If important actors are not given a voice in such missions, then those missions will be hampered by inadequate resources—as the United States discovered in its postwar occupation of Iraq.

Even if an actor with an abundance of national resources had sufficient interest to lead a mission alone, accusations of old-fashioned colonial intentions would taint the operation and ultimately play into the hands of the local opposition. Again, Washington discovered this in the early months of the Iraqi occupation. Liberal democratic actors tend not to trust the motives of unilateralists. Indeed, one of the reasons that Australia was so keen to create an ASEAN-supported multinational coalition from the start of Interfet was to preempt the accusations of ethnic European colonialism that later arose in both Indonesia and Malaysia.

When all the voices that want a say in mission design and execution are heard, however, the result is a cacophony of competing norms and interests that often undermines operational coherence. The result can be a security quagmire, where too many opportunities are created for revisionists to subvert the international community's goals while seeking their own ends. NATO is widely perceived to be a more effective military actor than the UN is in general, but even NATO does not function as a consistent force on peace missions. A liberal democratic style of complex intervention results in messy outcomes.

The Australian lead role in Interfet provides a hybrid model of how this can be done better. The goal was simple: to restore order. The technique, which necessitated a great deal of cooperation between Australian military commanders and diplomats, was clever: keep control of the mission, while encouraging others to participate in ways appropriate to their resources. The outcome was a multilaterally supported operation that retained its coherence remarkably well, and is cited as one of the few unquestioned successes of UN peacekeeping. It is time that the United States, when it intervenes in places like Afghanistan and Iraq, learns from the Australian experience on Interfet. Multilateralism is manageable, if it is done right.

SIX

SECURITY AS A STEP TO PEACE

Why Peacekeeping Still Matters

In recent years a new trend has emerged in world affairs. The United States, usually with the support of a few selected allies, has gone to war far from its borders for the explicit purpose of replacing existing political regimes with ones more congenial to U.S. interests and values. Whether the stated goals were humanitarian, as in Kosovo, or designed to protect Americans from the threat of terrorism, as in Afghanistan and (according to President George W. Bush) Iraq, these military interventions have gone forward without United Nations Security Council authorization.

Yet despite deep-seated official U.S. skepticism about UN capabilities and political motives, sooner or later Washington has been forced to turn back to some form of multilateralism to get the support it needs to ensure security and reconstruction in these countries after the wars are over. While it is now common to refer to the United States as a new imperial power, the truth is that the U.S. acting alone lacks the political will to establish a real empire. Americans do not want to devote the time and resources (in terms of both troop numbers and financing) that are necessary for a long-term occupation regime to succeed. Unlike the colonial era of a century ago, the public sees too little gain to justify the expenditure of lives and tax dollars that a long-term unilateral occupation entails. There is neither much profit nor much competitive strategic value to be had from controlling territory far from home.

It is not surprising, then, that U.S.-led NATO intervention in Kosovo without UN approval was followed by a UN-authorized complex peace-keeping operation, as Clinton administration officials turned over duties of reconstruction and reestablishing order to the international community even as Washington preserved a key role for itself in the mission. U.S.-led intervention in Afghanistan was again followed by a UN-authorized complex peacekeeping operation in the capital of Kabul, even though Washington insisted on maintaining military control over outlying, less stable areas of the country for almost two years afterward. In October 2003, finally UN authorization was sought and achieved for a country-wide complex peacekeeping operation under NATO command. And while the U.S. resisted turning to the UN in Iraq, eventually the UN Security Council authorized a U.S.-commanded complex security keeping operation there, too. In July 2003, both India and France had disappointed U.S. officials by refusing to send troops to the country in the absence of such a resolution. As violence—including against UN humanitarian facilities in the country—skyrocketed, it became evident that American troops lacked both the resources and political support back home to do the job of keeping security by themselves, and eventually a compromise resolution was passed by the UN in October 2003. Meanwhile a new peacekeeping mission was getting underway in Liberia as well, and in early 2004 events in Haiti once again led the U.S. to turn to the UN to authorize a new operation there. Around the globe there are simmering conflicts that could burst onto the headlines at any moment, calling out for peacekeeping forces to be deployed.

This means that as time goes on, the lessons of the complex peacekeeping operations of the 1990s remain relevant, despite the American predilection for unilateral action.

The dilemmas outlined in this book are not going away any time soon. Tensions will continue between the desire to control political developments on the ground and the lack of political will to do so. There will also be ongoing strains between the requirements that operations be on the one hand cohesive, and on the other legitimized through multilateralism and local ownership of the peace process. Given the political realities of the world we live in, what do the perspectives presented here tell us about how these dilemmas can be resolved?

Lack of State Will

The colonial operations carried out by liberal states at the turn of the twentieth century and the complex peacekeeping operations of more recent years had one key component in common, despite all their differences.

They were characterized by the desire of outsiders to control political events happening on the ground abroad. Whether for self-interested security motives or genuine humanitarianism, western liberal democratic states wanted these foreign regions to adopt more of the values and institutions of the western liberal democratic world. In more recent times this goal was shared by significant portions of the peace-kept populations, but a substantial fraction of the target population has in each case opposed the international presence, which is why the use of robust military force has been necessary. While the balance of reasons for undertaking these operations shifted between the two eras, favoring state self-interest in the former period and humanitarianism in the latter, the desire for foreign control over political and social institutions was a constant.

Perhaps the most important lesson to come out of the preceding chapters is that even when liberal democratic states appear to have strong interests in gaining control over foreign societies, they will almost always lack the political will to follow through on their plans with cohesive, well designed operations. Competing political goals get in the way. It has become a truism to make this argument about peacekeeping. UN corridors frequently echo with laments about the absence of political will among member states. But this characteristic of liberal democracies isn't new; an absence of political will was a defining characteristic of the colonial period as well. Colonial hegemony as practiced by the U.S., France, and Great Britain often lacked cohesion and consistency, because the capitals did not have the will or the resources to adequately oversee the man-on-the-spot. This was the case even when empire was seen as being central to how states defined their competitive standing in the international system, and when foreign territory was such an important possession that the capitals decided to send out personnel to occupy it. Ultimately, this lack of consistency is one of the things that led to colonialism's failure, because insufficient oversight was associated with on-the-ground brutality, as well as with mixed messages about which political values the empires held most dear.

What this means is that the lack of political will to do things right and well in foreign countries is not just an artifact of modern peacekeeping operations, and it is not something that is likely to be solved just by authorizing lead states or so-called coalitions of the willing to act. The problem goes beyond the willingness of interested states to lead operations; it extends to the willingness to maintain sufficient political interest to coordinate those operations well once they are in place. There is unlikely ever to be sufficient political will in the current international system by any liberal democratic state or coalition to put together a coherent, long-term operation whose purpose is to direct political developments abroad. This fact should matter to the international community, because it implies that the lack of forceful will when dealing with peace operations and governorship of foreign countries is a permanent feature of the foreign policy of powerful states.

There is a tendency among peacekeeping analysts and advocates to try to persuade countries like the United States to act with more will on peacekeeping operations. The Brahimi Report issued by the UN Secretary General in 2000, for example, is filled with suggestions about how member states (and the United States in particular is often implied in its criticisms) must create mandates for operations that match the resources available to them, and must follow through on their good intentions with adequate financing and personnel.[1] What is missing from that report is the question of exactly where the political will to do this is going to come from. Similarly many authors seem to approach the future in the belief that if the great powers are simply criticized enough for their failure to act or to act cohesively and rationally in peacekeeping, then eventually they can be made to act. Dozens of books have been written that urge the United Nations and/or the United States to do more and to do peacekeeping better.[2]

But one thing the comparison to colonialism brings out is how little things have changed in the past hundred years. Despite an enormous revolution in norms, for example, that makes blatantly colonial behavior now unacceptable, international society has not adopted a norm that manages to create political will where there is none, no matter how good the cause might seem. What this means for policy planners is that we should *expect* a lack of will and consistency, rather than being surprised by its absence. In the colonial era the key characteristic associated with this inconsistency was man-on-the-spotism, as the capitals' intentions were undermined by colonial officials in the field. In the current era, it may be the privileging of casualty avoidance over peacekeeping mission accomplishment, or the notion that military forces can't do policing even when there's no one else to do it.

In both eras, this inconsistency has been unavoidable, given the vicissitudes of public attention in liberal democratic states and the relatively low priority that both military occupation and peacekeeping have held on the agenda in comparison to preparing for major war. Rather than simply lamenting this lack of political will, the international community should figure out how peacekeeping operations can be better deployed *given* that they will often occur with poor coordination, with mixed and even incompatible goals, and with insufficient funding and resources. For those who truly want to transform the politics and culture of foreign societies in the name of liberal democracy, there should be no expectation that complex peacekeeping operations—or anything else demanding coordinated liberal democratic state action—are the best way to accomplish it.

Why Germany and Japan Don't Work as Models

In theory, might it not be possible for liberal democracies to impose political control abroad, through a carefully directed military occupation policy? After all, critics might point out, military occupation worked just fine to turn Germany and Japan into functioning liberal democracies after World War II. But what sets those two cases apart from both the colonial regimes that preceded them and the complex peacekeeping operations that arose later was the balance of political opportunity and will, between the occupiers and the occupied.

World War II was a total war, fought by the United States and its European allies at great cost, in the belief that their survival as independent states (and as an overarching liberal democratic society) depended on victory. This meant that in the occupation era, the political will of the occupiers to ensure the success of reforms was immense, because everyone was frightened about what a resurgence of Japanese or German militarism would mean. Simultaneously, the level of civilian destruction in both Japan and Germany was horrific, following lengthy fire-bombing campaigns in both countries and the use of atomic weapons in Japan. On both sides, World War II was seen as a total war, and on both sides, enemy civilians were considered fair targets. The allies fought on until they were able to wrest unconditional surrender from their enemies. For the populations of occupied Japan and Germany, this meant that there was no credible political alternative to bowing to the conquerors. The victors had demonstrated their political will to win at any cost. Since resistance would only cause a prolongation of warfare and further suffering, violent opposition to the occupiers was rare.

Bush administration officials who wished to make the occupation of Iraq seem typical in historical terms claimed in August 2003 that there were frequent attacks against U.S. occupation troops in Germany by renegade Nazis immediately after the war.[3] However, the definitive U.S. Army history of the postwar German occupation negates this. While threats of violence against U.S. troops were issued, and rumors of anti-American violence abounded, actual attacks were rare—and many appeared to be personal vendettas against soldiers whose relative wealth and prestige made them attractive to German women in a time of hardship.[4] Most crime in postwar Germany actually involved black marketeering, rather than anti-Americanism, and tended to be associated with displaced ethnic German foreigners who did not want to go back to their countries of origin. In the words of a major review published by the RAND Corporation think tank in mid-2003, "no resistance of consequence emerged [following the surrender of German armed forces] or at any time thereafter."[5] Incidentally, the low level of anti-American violence in both countries was probably also partly explained by the fact that neither German nor Japanese officials from the old regimes would have been welcome to use surrounding countries to plot further actions against the allies, since nearby territories had been the primary victims of what were particularly cruel empires.

There are many who explain the success of democratization in Germany and Japan as being based on those societies' ethnic homogeneity, or pre-existing acceptance of Western values (Japan actually went through a very pro-American cultural period at the turn of the twentieth century). Yet those factors do not explain their acceptance of outside domination at the hands of the Americans and others. Good evidence has emerged in recent years that the American occupations of Germany and Japan were rather ugly, and not uniformly welcomed by their inhabitants, at least not to the degree that popular lore in the United States has suggested. The Japanese were burdened by grinding postwar poverty, near-starvation diets, disease and overcrowding, a corrupt government, and looting and economic sabotage that lasted for several years after Tokyo's 1945 capitulation. Furthermore, many locals recognized the irony of having democracy imposed from on high. Yet any Japanese attempts to criticize or even lampoon the occupation forces for their contributions to these problems were censored by the American military.[6] Meanwhile, the Germans immediately after the war suffered under an American directive that limited relief supplies, including food, to what was necessary to prevent the outbreak of rioting and disease. The nation that was the aggressor in the war was not to be given any favoritism in its immediate aftermath. Agricultural products were requisitioned from farmers by the occupation force, and hunger was common, even as U.S. troops patronized the thriving black market.[7] It was not until several years later that the Marshall Plan lent a helping hand to German recovery.

Yet rebellion was rare, at least in part because there were no credible alternatives to submission to the occupation authorities, especially among people who were exhausted and in despair. This meant that the American public was not confronted with regular reports of casualties among the occupying troops, as they are today for the cases of Afghanistan and Iraq. No one in Germany or Japan thought they could make the occupiers go home. (And yet the pressure to bring the boys home was high in the United

States anyway; that was one of the major reasons why the initial occupying force in Germany was quickly replaced by a specially recruited constabulary military force.[8]) In comparative terms, this means that despite their complexity, their physical hardship, and the hard moral decisions that had to be made, the occupations of Japan and Germany were relatively easy duty for the troops who manned them in comparison to today's efforts. There was no room for domestic political spoilers.

Most peacekeeping operations today, as well as other occupations designed to bring order to unstable areas of the world, will not share these political characteristics with Japan and Germany. The liberal democratic states of today for the most part do not feel that their survival is threatened by postwar Bosnia, Kosovo, Afghanistan, or Iraq, and therefore do not have the will to ensure that major occupations last indefinitely. Despite the shock of September 11 and the spate of related terrorist attacks that have followed, the threat emanating from particular foreign states does not seem large enough to warrant a permanent foreign governing presence. While President Bush's September 2002 National Security Strategy highlighted the dangers posed by "weak states" and "chaos" in the fight against terror,[9] the focus of domestic debates by Summer 2003 was on the need to bring U.S. troops home from Afghanistan and Iraq, not on the question of whether anarchy in those territories posed ongoing threats for core U.S. national security interests. Bush's statement also listed the need to combat "disease, war, and desperate poverty" in Africa as a strategic priority linked to combating terrorism, yet both the Pentagon and significant members of the U.S. Congress were reluctant to endorse sending U.S. troops as peacekeepers to the failed African state of Liberia in 2003.

Because of the power of information technology in the modern world, people on the ground in Afghanistan and Iraq were well aware of American ambivalence, and even of the history of similar ambivalence in Somalia. So attacks against U.S. troops and their allies in both Afghanistan and Iraq continued, as their perpetrators hoped to convince the American public that it was high time to withdraw. And since most of today's conflicts reflect regional tensions that extend far beyond state borders, opponents to peacekeeping and occupation regimes can often find nearby supporters to turn to for outside help. When these things are combined, it means that spoilers today have plenty of reason to believe that credible alternatives to internationally mandated solutions exist, if they just hold on long enough to put themselves in a better political position. A repeat of Japan and Germany is unlikely. The need for robust, combat-prepared forces in peacekeeping operations who are willing to stay the course over the long term to achieve security is not going to disappear anytime soon.

Tasks for the Military

In both the colonial era and in complex peacekeeping operations, the effects of low political will in the capitals have been magnified by military organizations who accorded a relatively low priority to occupation duties. In the colonial era this was associated with massacres and atrocities that went against rational thinking about how to gain control over a foreign society. In the current era it is associated with inadequate attention to the less glamorous aspects of security. Preparing for policing is sacrificed to preparing for war-fighting, even though adequate international police forces are not available to quell the riots and the humanitarian aid convoy raids that undercut effective peace operations—and even though societal anarchy is now associated with opportunities for terrorism. As we saw in the cases of Haiti in 1994, and Bosnia and Kosovo in the years that followed, many western military organizations today are uncomfortable with the notion of policing. They either try to avoid doing it even when circumstances thrust it upon them, or they do it without adequate attention to the need to get and keep local opinion on their side. Their mindsets are often not geared toward hearts and minds campaigns.

But as we saw in the case of Australia in East Timor, there are liberal democratic military organizations who can do policing well in difficult circumstances. The Australian Defence Force guarded the borders, protected humanitarian aid convoys, secured first towns and then the outlying areas against rebels and bandits, and (when necessary) confronted militia members directly and detained them in rebuilt prisons. And perhaps surprisingly, one positive lesson that the colonial era provides is that when military troops are well trained and supervised, they can take on these tasks and still retain their reputation for military toughness. It is hard to accomplish this; it requires constant oversight and a consistent policy at higher levels of rewarding soldiers for their positive actions and punishing them when they break good conduct norms. But military effectiveness and peacekeeping effectiveness are not at odds with each other. This means that there is room for change in the area of what military troops are prepared to do on peacekeeping operations. The lack of flexibility in some military organizations' approach to peacekeeping is something that can be improved.

State leaders in liberal democracies can instruct the military commanders under their control to raise the priority they give to peacekeeping. Of course, to make this change also takes political will. It requires change in defense budget priorities, so that more attention is paid to having large numbers of high-quality personnel prepared to serve abroad for extended periods. In the case of the U.S. Army in particular, this would mean relying less on reserve forces, who are difficult to deploy for long periods of time on hazardous operations because of their emotional and financial attachments to jobs and families at home. Instead, the United States would have to increase the size of active duty troops—and pay the costs of the salaries, benefits, and hazard pay that goes along with the decision to hire a larger volunteer force. Political debate on this point had begun by fall 2003, and it was clear that the cost would be in the billions.[10]

It also requires undertaking what might become a pitched bureaucratic fight, as top military leaders are instructed that their job is not just to plan, deter, and win wars, but to make sure their troops are ready to keep the peace well, too. Military organizations for the most part do not like going to war, because they are the ones who suffer the consequences of battle. But when they are sent into dangerous situations they would rather fight and win through force than restrain their fire power to win the peace. It is a well-established chestnut of civil-military relations theory that military organizations prefer to go on the offense and take the initiative, and to follow what has become known as the "Powell Doctrine" in the United States (after the thinking of then-Chairman of the Joint Chiefs of Staff General Colin Powell): use decisive force, and have an exit strategy after the battle is won.[11] Long-term peacekeeping and occupation don't fit this template.

Hence doctrinal innovation would need to be ingrained into military organizations to make the change last. In many ways this would require a revolution in how the U.S. military in particular thinks of itself, since U.S. leadership (or at least support) appears necessary for most peacekeeping operations to go forward these days. It would demand that political leaders appoint as their top military advisers and commanders people who share a belief that foreign anarchy is a source of domestic danger. As time goes on, it has become clear that there are senior officers in the U.S. armed forces who believe that some variation on that kind of transformative policy would serve U.S. security interests.[12] Yet they are far from the majority. Major doctrinal innovation in military organizations is most easily undertaken by powerful insiders, not by civilian outsiders who can be sidelined or undercut by those who have something to lose from change.[13] Any change will therefore likely be slow and bumpy.

The amount of training time allocated to policing actions and other flexible uses of force and restraint would have to be increased. The change would require making room for a focus on people skills and cultural awareness, not just technology skills, in military training. This obviously can be done, because it is something that U.S. Special Operations Forces, for example, already do. But it would involve shaking up standard operating procedures, and that will likely threaten those who have succeeded in the current environment. In particular, soldiers and officers who excel at peace-keeping duties would have to be given as great a chance at promotion to the top ranks as people who excel at war-fighting; as in colonial times, promotion incentive structures will otherwise reward those who go for the glory. But given the level of postwar casualties that American troops have experienced in Iraq in particular, the time may now be ripe for such a revolution to occur. It is clear that the current system is not working well enough, and this may mean that a critical mass inside the military bureaucracy can be convinced that change is inevitable.

There are other alternatives. If the U.S. military and citizenry decide that America should not do peacekeeping, only war-fighting, then one alternative choice is to go home after the hot-war phase is over. If diplomatic channels are used with sufficient effectiveness, perhaps the European states and Canada can be convinced to do all the multilateral peacekeeping jobs that will rise up in the future. Obviously, this was not done during the Iraq crisis; the decision to act unilaterally undercuts the ability to gain postwar support. Such a division of labor would also require the gathering of political will in allied countries to enact massive increases in defense budgets and military recruitment, as well as to cooperate with the United States, at a time when antimilitarism is strong and suspicion of American imperial intentions runs high. Given that this scenario is unlikely, another alternative would be American isolationism—a refusal to become involved abroad militarily. Yet the cost of this latter decision would be standing by as witnesses not only to future Bosnias and Rwandas, but to the growth of anarchy that al Qaeda finds so conducive to its activities.

Change in the way that the U.S. military defines its role is hence in some sense the easiest, and is certainly the most rational, solution to the new problems faced in international security today. Such a change will only be possible in a liberal democratic state like the U.S. if the public is explicitly told every time there is deployment of troops to a peacekeeping or occupation operation that casualties are to be expected, and that those casualties are an acceptable cost of an action that is in accordance with core U.S. security interests. This will again mean that political will must be exercised by state leaders. There is a great deal of evidence that the American public does not object to casualties on peacekeeping operations per se. It only objects to the idea of sacrificing American lives for an unclear purpose.[14] Making this argument will be a challenge for policymakers, one that requires spending political capital to convince a reluctant public that peace and order in a far-off foreign country matters for domestic tranquility. Given the experience of September 11, however, as well as continuing evidence of the existence of transnational terrorist networks that operate from unstable regions, a convincing case can be made for the idea that preventing anarchy abroad is in not just the national interest, but the interests of the western world and its values in general.[15]

Limiting the Goals

Resolving both of these problems—recognizing that foreign political intervention will not be coherent, and convincing both the military and the public to get on board for greater levels of peacekeeping activity—will be easier if one fundamental shift is made in the approach to peacekeeping operations: intervention should not try to accomplish so many abstract goals. It is hard to make the case that it is in U.S. interests to create a functioning democracy in Iraq, in the face of mounting evidence that many Iraqis do not share American views of what their own political future should be. It is also hard to continue to argue that Kosovo will be at peace only when it is ethnically integrated, given that the calmest areas there are the ones where ethnic homogeneity is the highest, and the ethnically split city of Mitrovica remains the least stable. It would be easier to make the case that preventing anarchy in Iraq, by providing a minimal level of public security until a stable state can get up and running, is a way to stem the threat of terrorism that may reach beyond Iraqi borders. It was, after all, anarchy that allowed al Qaeda to train and flourish in Afghanistan before September 11. It would also be easier to make the case that the purpose of having troops in Kosovo is to ensure that people don't kill each other in large numbers while they are sorting out on their own what kind of future for that territory makes the most long-term sense.

The history presented here suggests that given the difficulty liberal democracies have in imposing coherent political influence over foreign societies, the limited goal of establishing security over the medium term is more likely to be achievable. In the colonial era, attempts to instill supposedly western values throughout the empire ultimately backfired, as the population recognized the inconsistencies in the policies of the imperial states. In many cases it appears that it was the brutality of the imperialists, rather than their humanitarianism, that most influenced the later development of politics in postcolonial territories. While complex peacekeeping operations have not been so brutal, the inconsistencies within the liberal democratic values they have proclaimed, as well as the inevitable lack of cohesive follow-through on planning, have demonstrated that the notion of imposing liberal democracy abroad is a pipedream. Hence in Bosnia we have a supposed democracy overseen by a foreigner with veto power over election results; in Kosovo we have public arguments between U.S. military officials, UN officials, and NGOs about who is politically deserving of assistance, while the international overseers are so suspicious of their charges that constitutional self-determination is not allowed; and in East Timor the international community has created a brand new country that relies on foreign assistance to function even as foreign influence is resented.

What makes more sense in peacekeeping and occupation operations is to provide security for countries in the aftermath of war and civil unrest, while the politics are sorting themselves out. This would in some sense mean taking back a more traditional model of peacekeeping, where the goals are limited to stopping the violence and preventing its resurgence. But it would mean doing it better than has been done in the past, by recognizing that what is needed are robust military forces that are applied flexibly to meet the real needs of the societies where they are sent. They must expect to do riot control when new governments choose policies that threaten old interests. They must expect to protect humanitarian aid deliveries when bandits threaten the highways. They must expect to pull guard duty, when new governments lack the security forces to defend key installations. They must also go in with the expectation that they will need to stay on the ground for several years, until a new domestic government can pull itself into place—and that they will have to put a lot of resources and effort into training new security forces on the ground to take their place when they leave.

It is not enough to go into an unstable country, forcibly unseat an old regime, hold new elections, and then leave. The international community learned this in Cambodia and repeated the mistake in Haiti in 1994. It is also not sufficient to provide a cordon against outside interference while allowing internal rioting and other forms of political violence to continue. The international community learned this in the IFOR deployment in Bosnia, and then had the lesson repeated many times during the SFOR period in Bosnia and the KFOR deployment in Kosovo when coordination between the NATO command and individual military units broke down. (Many of these latter instances—for example the Bank Hercegovacka takeover attempt by the OHR in Bosnia, or the UN's efforts to forcibly integrate Kosovars back into the Serbian-dominated area of Mitrovica— simultaneously showcase the difficulties of maintaining political and military consistency when the goal is to bend domestic political situations to the international community's desires.) Providing security in foreign society requires changing expectations, especially Washington's expectations, about what it is that military forces do.

What I propose here is a narrower definition of "security" than what many from the NGO community, for example, would prefer. What I mean by security is what the seventeenth-century British philosopher Thomas Hobbes meant when he talked about the role of the state, the so-called leviathan, in holding anarchy at bay. Security, from this perspective, means that commerce can be practiced, and the arts can flourish, because most people don't fear for their lives on a daily basis.[16] It does not imply that society is perfect, or even particularly just; it merely means that society is capable of functioning. Borders are controlled, terrorism is curtailed, and the government does not face constant threats of violent overthrow.

To many voices from the liberal international community, this definition is inadequate. It is only the achievement of basic human rights for everyone that constitutes true security. While ultimately this broader definition may be correct, my point here is that these broader goals cannot be accomplished by force, unless that force is applied consistently over a period of many years, perhaps until a generational change takes place. The international community does not seem capable of accomplishing this; it cannot even decide, in peace-kept countries like Bosnia, to allow human rights courts to function without interference when its own security interests are threatened. If human rights are to be protected, perhaps it is better done through the "spotlight" effect, where NGOs publicize human rights shortcomings and convince liberal democratic western states to withhold aid and put other political pressure on such countries. It is already asking a lot of military organizations to do basic security tasks well, and it would be more realistic to tailor our expectations to their capabilities.

Solving the Dilemma of Multilateralism

The search for multilateral support for peacekeeping intervention makes all of these issues even harder to solve. The greater number of states that are involved in a mission, the less likely it is that the aims will be coherent, and that all of the troops involved will be capable of carrying out flexible duties well. Multilateralism leads to a greater chance for slippage. Yet international involvement is necessary for operations to be considered legitimate. This matters not just for the intervening forces, but also for the new governments that emerge out of the chaos of conflict. For them to be able to establish any sense of popular support and longevity, they must not be seen as the puppets of a single outside, outlier state. In other words, they must not be seen as the beneficiaries of imperialism. Instead, they need to be seen as representatives of the will of the international community as a whole.

While multinational control over a mission often leads to incongruity and disarray, as we have seen in both Bosnia and Kosovo, it is possible to work through the UN to get UNSC support for an operation and multilateral participation in it, while keeping operational command in a single, interested country. We saw this in the example of Australia's leadership of the Interfet mission to East Timor. Something similar has already begun to emerge in Afghanistan, where NATO has taken over the peacekeeping mission that works alongside American military operations in the country. It may emerge in Iraq if the United States can convince other states to send troops to the UN-authorized mission now under its command. What this book would predict, however, is that the NATO mission in Afghanistan will soon encounter political conflicts that undermine its efficacy, as interference from the various involved European capitals erupts over how force should be employed. The result, if Bosnia and Kosovo are any clue, is that mixed and confusing messages will be sent to the local population about what the international community intends. It would have been better for the United States to take on leadership of a Chapter Seven mission in Afghanistan from the start, with NATO country support rather than NATO command. This may emerge now in Iraq, although the hard face of American unilateralism throughout most of 2003 may undercut Washington's ability to gain diplomatic support for the kind of operation it now prefers to see waged.

A New Model of Security Building

There is no model for any kind of political behavior, including international intervention, that is perfect. There is also no model that will fit each new case to a tee. Any new model can be credibly critiqued by naysayers, as well as advocates of the current system who fear that change will leave things worse off. Certainly, each new peacekeeping case will demand flexibility in thinking, to respond to the details of the situation on the ground. But this book suggests that rather than lament the failures of peacekeeping as we now know it, it may be time to think of the problem in a new way.

A new model that I call security-keeping would give up the notion that political change can be forced on a foreign country, except perhaps in the rare circumstance of the aftermath of a total war like World War II. In this new model, the goal of military peacekeeping or occupation would no longer be to direct foreign countries along a path of liberalization or democratization. This model therefore stands in direct opposition to the thinking of the idealists in the current administration of George W. Bush, those like Paul Wolfowitz (who some have called the "democratic imperialists") who believe that the United States can convince others to adopt its political system by using force to get rid of dictators.[17] The goal of this new model would furthermore not be to enforce the provisions of a treaty imposed on a society by outsiders, as in the Dayton Accords in Bosnia. It would not be to force ethnic integration on a recalcitrant society, as in Kosovo, or to right the wrongs of a past conflict. It is instead based on a fundamental belief that outsiders, no matter how well intentioned, cannot credibly force that kind of change on others. After the initial creation of a new government for a country, it would not attempt to control the direction of election and appointment results, as in the Balkans, or to favor a particular notion of government structure, as happened in East Timor.

Instead, the militarily supported peacekeeping mission would have one and only one overarching purpose: to provide security—along a country's borders, in support of humanitarian aid delivery, and for the purpose of establishing broad-scale public order—until a new indigenous government can take over those functions itself. The mission would be led by a state who has a strong interest in a stable outcome in the territory. That state would have military troops trained for flexible policing duties, and would reward soldiers and officers with promotion for good performance of such actions. The intervening lead state should furthermore be determined to stay the course until stability is achieved. State leaders must convey to their own public why providing stability to the foreign country in question is in the clear national interest. They must also communicate the expectation that casualties will occur in a difficult environment, and that the loss of soldiers, while regretted, will be accepted as inevitable.

As in the case of the Interfet mission in East Timor, the lead state would be responsible for choosing its partners in the operation, and of assigning the forces of all willing donors to tasks where they would be appropriately used. Some contributors would provide strong security for humanitarian aid delivery, border control, and government functioning; others would train new domestic security forces, or help rebuild roads, humane but secure prisons for violent opposition leaders, and electricity grids. The lead state would put its own continuing resources into helping select and train a domestic constabulary force for the target country—in other words, a force designed over a space of several years to replace the security functions served by the peacekeepers. The understanding going in would be that the peacekeeping force would remain in place until this new, domestic security force was capable of taking its place—and that this might mean making a commitment of many years. As we have learned in many recent peacekeeping operations, the domestic security force would have to be supported by some form of functioning judicial system, as well, so that those arrested for committing violent acts were not simply released and put back on the street. This model works only when there is a clear security interest at stake in acting, since it requires high levels of political will. In other cases, where purely humanitarian goals are at stake, there may be no alternative to the disorderly current model of multilateral effort that we now use.

For all of its flaws, the example of Afghanistan may provide a good, if incomplete, picture of how this new model of security-keeping can be initially set up in conflict-ridden societies. The international community as a whole, as represented by the UN and a special representative of the UN Secretary General, can work with and encourage domestic factions to meet with each other and select a new government that the majority of those factions find (at a minimum) acceptable. Leadership in this state-creation endeavor may still have to come from interested states, as it did in the case of Afghanistan from the ongoing influence and pressure of the United States representative on the ground, Zalmay Khalilzad. The outcome, as in the case of the selection of President Karzai, will never be perfect. The selection process will always be controversial, and there will always be accusations that the process is rigged. Nonetheless the initial leadership of the new country will at least be seen to be supported from many directions, and will not be easily lampooned as a simple flunky of a single neoimperialist state. This was not done in Iraq; the United States did not seek multilateral support for the choices it made in appointing Iraq's interim governing council. This choice undoubtedly weakened the legitimacy of the new proto-government in the eyes of the Iraqi people.

Afghanistan also provides at least a rudimentary example of how the turnover of security functions to a new state can proceed. Training of an indigenous Afghan security force is moving forward, but its success has been limited because powerful factions in the country have not been willing to work with the new government. Here is where more determination and a wider deployment area by the initial peacekeeping force could have made a difference. If the international community's real goal was to provide stability in the country—something that is now becoming clearer, as the expansion of the peace force continues—then peacekeepers in Afghanistan, led by an American command and well armed and well protected, should have been deployed immediately throughout the country with the explicit statement that they were there to provide order on behalf of the new government. This should have happened even as other American soldiers continued their anti-al Qaeda mop-up activities.[18] Such an internationally mandated presence would have provided a visible reminder to the population as a whole that the international community did not support recalcitrant warlords. Indeed, as time went on this system was adopted. For example, U.S. civil affairs troops made it clear that they would only provide humanitarian assistance—for example by helping build new water wells—to regional governors in Afghanistan who publicized the good works that Karzai was doing for their regions.[19] Early success in restoring order may also have attracted more Afghanis to work in the new domestic security forces, by making the central government appear stronger and more worthy of support.

As this book was going to press, the international community was given the opportunity to do this in Haiti the second time around. We can hope that a clear message will be communicated to the Haitian people: that international forces are in the country in order to provide support to the constitutionally formed government that replaces the departing Aristide regime. We can hope that this time around some interested state stays the course, to ensure that security is provided until the new government can create a functioning civil police system for itself. This time around, we can hope that the job is not left to an ad hoc collection of international police forces whose training and qualifications vary. While Pentagon forces were severely overextended because of continuing instability in Iraq and Afghanistan, a glimmer of hope was provided by the French presence in the initial UN-authorized intervention force in Haiti in March 2004. Perhaps this time around, the French gendarmerie can step in as the interim security force that the new Haitian government so badly needs.

The primary goal of peacekeeping in this model would then be to do what it takes to help this new government gain control over the country. That means paying special attention to the problems of border control, so that the circulation of weapons, rebels, and the contraband goods that fund them can be limited. It also means providing a presence throughout the territory of the new regime, so that everyone understands that the international community is watching what happens. Troops should expect to face rioters, and should have adequate equipment and training to allow them to protect themselves from such things as stones and bottle rockets without shooting into crowds in response. They should not have to withdraw in the face of such opposition, as the Americans initially did in Mitrovica. And until a new domestic security force is formed, this new model sees no realistic alternative to having foreign military forces provide a rudimentary justice system. It is impossible for an international military force to prevent or even investigate every post-conflict crime of looting or retribution, as was made clear in Haiti in 1994. It is also impossible for that force to end organized criminal activity on the territory, as we have learned in Kosovo. But enough troops should be placed in major areas of tension to deter disruption by convincing the locals that violent criminal activity will not be tolerated. If the laws governing society are being set by local authorities in the capital, rather than by outsiders (who can be said not to understand the situation on the ground), it should be easier to gain popular support for the occupation authorities—even when, as on the 1990s peacekeeping missions in Haiti, Kosovo and East Timor—neither the methods of detective work nor the jails holding violators are ideal.

How would this model work in a country divided by ethnic hatred, as in Bosnia or Kosovo? The answer is that in this model, the international community would abandon the long-standing idea that it has the right to confer legitimate sovereign statehood on some territories but not others. In a society where a single state is impossible to hold together without the use of outside force, as Bosnia still appears to be and as Kosovo is likely to become, multiple regional authorities would be tolerated. A number of proposals have surfaced in recent years about alternatives to statehood for territories too small, too divided, or too economically weak to function as real states in the international system. Jeffrey Herbst has proposed this as a solution for state failure in sub-Saharan Africa,[20] and Chaim Kaufmann has explored the relatively taboo topic of partition in the Balkans.[21] The idea of partition has even been raised, along with a great deal of controversy, by Leslie Gelb as a potential future for Iraq.[22] More thought should be put toward the question of how territorial self-determination might exist in areas that are too small to have the full trappings of statehood, such as independent economic sovereignty. Especially in an era when supra-state structures like the European Union are coming into their own, it is time for the international community to think outside of the current box that says that states *per se* have unique juridical rights that they can in turn extend to others. In the Balkans, in this model, the goal of security-keeping would be to stop people from killing each other, not to force them to live together in ethnic harmony. The international community needs to recognize that liberal democratic paternalism is not a long-term solution to the continuing existence of illiberal beliefs.

This doesn't mean that the United Nations wouldn't still be involved in questions of humanitarian assistance, economic development, elections monitoring, or political and judicial reform. There would certainly still need to be cooperation between civilian and military agencies in coordinating the disbursal of assistance, and in making the transition from international security provision to the creation of functioning domestic security forces. The initial setting up of a government, whether by election as in Cambodia or Haiti, or by council as in Afghanistan, would still be encouraged and overseen by the international community acting as a whole. The training of new domestic security forces would also need to be supported by an international civilian police presence, and not just by military officers. But beyond that initial effort, political reforms would be suggested, rather than mandated, by outsiders. The goal of security-keeping would be to prevent and prosecute violence to forestall the possibility of anarchy, not to achieve liberal political outcomes.

If we lived in a world where the political will of liberal democratic states to intervene abroad with coherence were abundant, it would not be necessary to put these kinds of limits on the goals of peacekeeping operations. It is not that there is anything wrong with the desire by liberal democracies to share their philosophical political visions with others. That ideal world, however, does not exist. By focusing on doing one thing—security keeping—that is central to the self-interests of the international community, and doing it well, peacekeepers would have a much better chance of actually establishing longstanding peace and stability in the troubled areas of the world where they are deployed.

How would this ideal model differ from the examples of complex military peacekeeping discussed in this book? Unlike the case of intervention in Haiti in 1994, there would be more effort made to actively restore public order and establish faith in the new government, not just to ensure that elections occur and then turn order over to local chance. There would have to be more of a commitment to stay for a longer term. But unlike the peacekeeping operations in Bosnia and Kosovo, there would be no attempt by outsiders to impose a particular political outcome on the country, beyond cementing the authority of leaders (and in these cases, this might mean several regional leaders) who were minimally acceptable to both the international community and a variety of domestic factions. If the territory in question had a tendency anchored in a long history of animosity to divide itself along ethnic lines, division would be allowed by the international community. The presence of well armed and well protected troops would be used to encourage such a partition to happen as peacefully and with as little bloodshed as possible, and those troops would stay until there was a reasonable guarantee that the remaining minority groups could expect to be physically protected by whatever new government emerged in their area. In other words, unlike the example of IFOR in Sarajevo, well armed troops would not stand by as city districts were set ablaze by separatist forces. Muslim enclaves in the Serbian region of Bosnia would still be protected, as would Serbian enclaves in Kosovo. But unlike the examples of SFOR and KFOR, the international community would not actively encourage or induce the return of displaced minorities to geographic areas where they had no reasonable chance of being welcomed in the next generation, and would not force a particular constitution on any territory.

In Haiti in 1994, as well as in Bosnia and Kosovo, there was a misplaced hope that international civilian police forces would be able to provide public order. They did not arrive in sufficient time or with sufficient training or desire to do so. Unlike those cases, in this new model there would no longer be an expectation that UN police could fill the security gap. Instead, flexibly trained and deployed military troops would be willing to deal with whatever situation came their way, and would go in with the understanding that they would stay as long as was necessary. Perhaps, if a sufficient number of troops were available, this could be done by American military police or the French gendarmerie. We will see if this is indeed what happens in Haiti the second time around, as the 2004 intervention gives way to a follow-on police force. But if sufficient specialized troops are not available, regular combat forces will have to learn to be peacekeepers, too. East Timor provides perhaps the best existing example of a case where this latter kind of policy has worked. Yet the abrupt departure of most of the international community may have put the long-term success of that case in jeopardy. As this book was going to press, the UN was intending to leave the country entirely by May 2004, even as the new Malaysian commander of the UN peacekeeping force there expressed continuing concern about both cross-border raids from former militia members and internal clashes between clans in East Timor itself in a situation of economic despair.[23] In this new model, an end-state of stable security replaces an artificial end-date set in advance, as the measure of operational success.

Future Interventions

This new model of security-keeping cannot provide a solution to the dire problem of the lack of political will to respond to humanitarian crises. It will not prevent future Rwandas from happening, and it cannot speed the reaction of even self-interested countries to the kinds of tragedies that engulfed Haiti, Bosnia, and East Timor in the 1990s. Perhaps, though, if the idea becomes ingrained that the purpose of the international community is only to supply security until new regimes can do it for themselves, and not to engender lasting liberal-democratic political change, it will be easier to gain both popular and military support for such missions. Especially if a stronger link can be made in the public mind between anarchy and the opportunity for terrorism to flourish, intervention to overcome anarchic violence will become more acceptable and politically popular.

This new model is by definition flawed and incomplete. It does not answer the question of how the international community should deal with war crimes, for example. It does not provide a template of how to stop retribution killings in post-conflict situations, nor does it explain how a reliable new security force can be formed from the ruins of a police state. But despite these gaps, it may help generate a new way of looking at the problem of peacekeeping.

The comparison of recent peacekeeping operations to the era of colonialism as practiced by liberal democratic states has highlighted the fact that imposing control over a foreign society is not possible using liberal democratic means. No matter how noble our intentions, we face limitations in our capabilities and in the effects that our actions can have. In places like Bosnia and Kosovo, the international community has spent enormous resources in trying to create liberal societies; yet the fact remains that occupation is the only thing that guarantees their functioning. In places like Haiti, a large expenditure of resources in the end created no change, and a decade later the international community was called back in again. The people were replaced, but the system was not. Instead of trying to change societies, we should change our expectations. A return to the goal of keeping the peace, rather than imposing change, will lead to more realistic policies that have a better chance of reaching their goals.

NOTES

1. Peace, or Change?

1. "Report of the Panel on United Nations Peace Operations," A/55/305-S/2000/809; available at www.un.org/peace/reports/peace-operations/.

2. Robert C. Owen, "Aerospace power and land power in peace operations," *Airpower Journal* 13, no.3 (Fall 1999): 4–22.

3. Michael W. Doyle, *Empires* (Ithaca: Cornell University Press, 1986), p. 19.

4. John Laughland, "UN Tyranny in Bosnia," *The Spectator*, May 5, 2001.

5. John Laughland, "UN Tyranny in Bosnia," *The Spectator*, May 5, 2001; Max Boot, "America Must Keep the Peace," *Wall Street Journal*, Apr. 22, 2002; Michael Ignatieff, "Nation-Building Lite," *New York Times Magazine*, July 28, 2002; and Ignatieff, "When a Bridge Is Not a Bridge," *New York Times Magazine*, Oct. 27, 2002.

6. Boot, *The Savage Wars of Peace: Small Wars and the Rise of American Power* (New York: Basic Books, 2002).

7. Ignatieff, "Nation-Building Lite."

8. Ignatieff, "When a Bridge Is Not a Bridge."

9. John Gerard Ruggie, "Multilateralism: The Anatomy of an Institution," in *Multilateralism Matters: The Theory and Praxis of an Institutional Form*, ed. Ruggie (New York: Columbia University Press, 1993), p. 11.

10. Lisa L. Martin, "The Rational State Choice of Multilateralism," in ibid., p. 92.

11. Roland Paris, "Peacebuilding and the Limits of Liberal Internationalism," *International Security* 22, no. 2 (Fall 1997): 54–89; Jack Snyder and Karen Ballentine, "Nationalism and the Marketplace of Ideas," *International Security* 21, no. 2 (Fall 1996): 5–40; Snyder, *From Voting to Violence: Democratization and Nationalist Conflict* (New York: W.W. Norton, 2000).

12. Michael J. Kelly, *Restoring and Maintaining Order in Complex Peace Oper-*

ations: The Search for a Legal Framework (Boston: Kluwer Law International, 1999).

13. Julie Mertus, "Reconsidering the Legality of Humanitarian Intervention: Lessons from Kosovo," *William and Mary Law Review* 41, no. 5 (May 2000): 1743–87.

14. Nicholas Lemann, "After Iraq," *The New Yorker*, Feb. 17–24, 2003; James Atlas, "A Classicist's Legacy: New Empire Builders," *New York Times*, May 4, 2003; and Ivo H. Daalder and James M. Lindsay, *America Unbound: The Bush Revolution in Foreign Policy* (Washington, DC: Brookings, 2003).

15. Col. (Ret.) John R. Ballard, *Upholding Democracy: The United States Military Campaign in Haiti, 1994–1997* (Westport, Conn.: Praeger, 1998), p. 25; U.S. Deputy Secretary of Defense Paul Wolfowitz, testimony before the Senate Armed Services Committee, "Situation in Afghanistan," Federal News Service, June 26, 2002, as reported in the Lexis/Nexis Congressional Universe Online Database.

16. A similar point is made by Roland Paris, "International Peacebuilding and the 'Mission Civilisatrice,' " *Review of International Studies* 28, no. 4 (Oct. 2002): 637–56.

2. Peacekeeping and Control

1. Fareed Zakaria, "The Rise of Illiberal Democracy," *Foreign Affairs* 76, no. 6 (Nov./Dec. 1997): 22–43.

2. While some would call the truce observation missions that the UN began to deploy in 1947 "peacekeeping," the term was not explicitly used until the 1956 Suez crisis, and it was the UNEF I mission deployed in response to that crisis that set the standard definition of what "classic" peacekeeping involved. For a clear discussion of the definition and history of traditional peacekeeping, see William J. Durch, *The Evolution of UN Peacekeeping: Case Studies and Comparative Analysis* (New York: St. Martin's Press, 1993).

3. See Larry L. Fabian, *Soldiers Without Enemies: Preparing the United Nations for Peacekeeping* (Washington, D.C.: Brookings, 1971); Carsten Holbraad, *Middle Powers in International Politics* (London: Macmillan, 1984); and Andrew F. Cooper, ed., *Niche Diplomacy: Middle Powers after the Cold War* (New York: St. Martin's Press, 1997). The intellectual inspiration for the literature on middle powers is Robert O. Keohane, "Lilliputians' Dilemmas: Small States in International Politics," *International Organization* 23, no. 2 (Spring 1969): 291–310.

4. "UN Peacekeeping: Some Questions and Answers," prepared by the UN Department of Public Information, Sept. 1998, and available on the web at www.un.org/News/facts/peacefct.htm.

5. Lewis Mackenzie, *Peacekeeper: The Road to Sarajevo* (Toronto: Douglas and McIntyre, 1993), pp. 21–22.

6. Ibid., p. 38.

7. Author's off-the-record conversation with a retired colonel, Lester Pearson Peacekeeping Center, Nova Scotia, Mar. 1999.

8. The United Nations' goal in ONUC was to restore law and order in Congo following the pull-out of Belgian colonial forces. UN peacekeepers ended up taking sides with the government against a rebel faction in the province of Katanga,

but the attributes of the mission were so controversial and so out of synch with the expectations of the UN system that ONUC remained a unique case until the end of the cold war. Indar Jit Rikhye, Michael Harbottle, and Bjorn Egge, *The Thin Blue Line: International Peacekeeping and Its Future* (New Haven: Yale University Press, 1974), pp. 71–92.

9. Erwin A. Schmidl, "Police Functions in Peace Operations: A Historical Overview," in *Policing the New World Disorder: Peace Operations and Public Security,* ed. Robert B. Oakley, Michael J. Dziedzic, and Eliot M. Goldberg (Washington, DC: National Defense University Press, 1998), available at www.ndu.edu/inss/books/policing/chapter1.html.

10. A review of this literature would be a chapter in itself. Two influential and comprehensive edited volumes are William J. Durch, ed., *UN Peacekeeping, American Politics, and the Uncivil Wars of the 1990s* (New York: St. Martin's Press, 1996), and Olara A. Otunnu and Michael W. Doyle, eds., *Peacemaking and Peacekeeping for the Next Century* (Lanham, Md.: Rowman & Littlefield, 1998). For a history of UN thinking about peacekeeping from 1989 through the Rwandan case in 1994, see Michael Barnett, *Eyewitness to a Genocide: The United Nations and Rwanda* (Ithaca: Cornell University Press, 2002), pp. 22–48.

11. Lakhdar Brahimi, chair, "Report of the Panel on United Nations Peace Operations," A/55/305-S/2000/809, Aug. 17, 2000, available at www.un.org.

12. J.M. Sanderson, "UNTAC: Successes and Failures," in *International Peacekeeping: Building on the Cambodian Experience,* ed. Hugh Smith (Canberra: Australian Defence Studies Centre, 1994), pp. 15–31, and Cheryl M. Lee Kim and Mark Metrikas, "Holding a Fragile Peace: The Military and Civilian Components of UNTAC," in *Keeping the Peace: Multidimensional UN Operations in Cambodia and El Salvador,* ed. Michael W. Doyle, Ian Johnstone and Robert C. Orr (New York: Cambridge University Press, 1997), pp. 107–33.

13. James A. Schear and Karl Farris, "Policing Cambodia: The Public Security Dimensions of U.N. Peace Operations," in *Policing the New World Disorder: Peace Operations and Public Security,* ed. Robert B. Oakley, Michael J. Dziedzic, and Eliot M. Goldberg (Washington, D.C.: National Defense University Press, 1998), pp. 69–102.

14. This process is described well by Roland Paris, *At War's End: Building Peace after Civil Conflict* (New York: Cambridge University Press, 2004 [in press]), chapter 5.

15. Kenneth Allard, lecture on "Cooperation, Command and Control: Lessons Learned or Lessons Identified?" in Capt. Leif Ahlquist, ed. *Cooperation, Command and Control in UN Peacekeeping Operations* (Stockholm: Swedish War College Department of Operations, 1996), p. 98.

16. The movie was based on the book by Mark Bowden, *Black Hawk Down: A Story of Modern War* (New York: Atlantic Monthly Press, 1999).

17. John L. Hirsch and Robert B. Oakley, *Somalia and Operation Restore Hope: Reflections on Peacemaking and Peacekeeping* (Washington, D.C.: U.S. Institute of Peace Press, 1995); Lynn Thomas and Steve Spataro, "Peacekeeping and Policing in Somalia," in *Policing the New World Disorder* ed. Oakley, et al., pp. 175–214.

18. The Republic of Somaliland, a chunk of territory which is governed by one

of the warring rebel groups but is not recognized by any state as sovereign, has maintained a measure of economic and social stability since its founding in 1991. It does not include Somalia's capital of Mogadishu.

19. Philip Gourevitch, *We Wish to Inform You that Tomorrow We Will Be Killed with Our Families: Stories from Rwanda* (New York: Farrar, Straus and Giroux, 1998); Michael Barnett, *Eyewitness to a Genocide: The United Nations and Rwanda* (Ithaca: Cornell University Press, 2002).

20. Dallaire's estimate was largely supported by a major conference of both military and civilian policy leaders sponsored by the Carnegie Commission on Preventing Deadly Conflict; see Scott R. Feil, *Preventing Genocide: How the Early Use of Force Might Have Succeeded in Rwanda* (New York: Carnegie Corporation, April 1998). For a well regarded dissenting view, but one that nonetheless is critical of the international community for its failure to act more quickly as the Rwandan situation progressed, see Alan J. Kuperman, *The Limits of Humanitarian Intervention: Genocide in Rwanda* (Washington, DC: Brookings, 2001). A definitive report of events in this case is "Report of the Independent Inquiry into the Actions of the United Nations During the 1994 Genocide in Rwanda," Dec. 15, 1999, commissioned by UN Secretary General Kofi Annan and available at www.un.org.

21. See James R. Davis, *The Sharp End: A Canadian Soldier's Story* (Vancouver, BC: Douglas and McIntyre, 1997).

22. UN Secretary General Kofi Annan commissioned a major internal investigation of the Srebenica events and presented the resulting report to the General Assembly: "The Fall of Srebenica: Report of the Secretary General Pursuant to General Assembly Resolution 53/35," A/54/549, Nov. 15, 1999, available at *http://www.un.org/peace/srebrenica.pdf*. Also see Richard Holbrooke, *To End a War* (New York: Random House, 1998), pp. 68–70.

23. Boutros Boutros-Ghali, "An Agenda for Peace: Preventive Diplomacy, Peacemaking, and Peacekeeping," A/47/277—S/24111, June 17, 1992, available at *www.un.org/Docs/SG/agpeace.html*.

24. These reconstruction efforts did not always involve a military component; soldiers were not involved in UN peacekeeping efforts in El Salvador or Nicaragua, for example. It is only those operations that did include a military component that I will be considering here.

25. Stephen John Stedman, "Spoiler Problems in Peace Processes," *International Security* 22, no. 2 (Fall 1997): 5–53.

26. "Charter of the United Nations," available at *www.un.org/aboutun/charter/index.html*. Sometimes these operations are referred to as "peace enforcement" missions, but since the term "peace enforcement" has also been used to refer to bombing campaigns against aggressive states, such terminology can become confusing. "Peacekeeping" will remain the term used throughout this book.

27. Kofi Annan, "Two Concepts of Sovereignty," *The Economist*, Sept. 18, 1999; Annan, "Report of the Secretary General on the Work of the Organization," General Assembly Official Records A/54/1, Aug. 31, 1999, available at *www.un.org*; Annan, "We the Peoples: The Role of the United Nations in the 21st Century (The Millennium Report)," UN Department of Public Information DPI/2103, Mar. 2000.

28. David Jablonsky and James S. McCallum, "Peace Implementation and the Concept of Induced Consent in Peace Operations," *Parameters* 29, no. 1 (Spring 1999): 54–70, available at http://carlisle-www.army.mil/usawc/Parameters/99spring/jablonsk.htm.

29. Jarat Chopra, *Peace-Maintenance: The Evolution of International Political Authority* (New York: Routledge, 1999).

30. Chopra, "The Space of Peace-Maintenance," *Political Geography* 15, no. 3–4 (1996): 340.

31. Michael W. Doyle, "The New Interventionism," *Metaphilosophy* 32, no. 1/2 (Jan. 2001): 220–21.

32. Neta C. Crawford, *Argument and Change in World Politics: Ethics, Decolonization, and Humanitarian Intervention* (New York: Cambridge University Press, 2002), p. 429.

33. Richard Caplan, *A New Trusteeship? The International Administration of War-torn Territories*, Adelphi Paper 341 (London: International Institute for Strategic Studies, 2002), p. 10.

34. Jacques Paul Klein, "Sharing Political Space in Peacemaking: The Case of Bosnia and Herzegovina," International Peace Academy Seminar, Vienna, Austria, July 7, 2000; available at *http://www.unmibh.org/news/srsgspe/2000/07juloo.asp*.

35. Caplan, *A New Trusteeship*, p. 15.

36. Klein, "Sharing Political Space in Peacemaking."

37. Caplan, *A New Trusteeship*, p. 27.

38. Michael W. Doyle, "Warmaking and Peacemaking: The United Nations' Post-Cold-War Record," in *Turbulent Peace: The Challenges of Managing International Conflict*, ed. Chester Crocker, Fen Hampson, and Pamela Aall (Washington, D.C.: U.S. Institute of Peace Press, 2001), p. 546.

39. Michael Bailey, Robert Maguire, and J. O'Neil G. Pouliot, "Haiti: Military-Police Partnership for Public Security," in *Policing the New World Disorder: Peace Operations and Public Security*, ed. Oakley, et al., p. 215.

40. John R. Ballard, *Upholding Democracy: The United States Military Campaign in Haiti, 1994–1997* (Westport: Praeger, 1998), pp. 25–28.

41. Joseph W. Kinzer, "Vision for the End State for the United Nations Military Force," memo, Dec. 28, 1994, as reprinted in U.S. Army Peacekeeping Institute, "Success in Peacekeeping: United Nations Mission in Haiti: The Military Perspective," U.S. Army Chief of Staff Haiti After Action Review (Carlisle Barracks, Penn.: U.S. Army War College, no date), p. 23.

42. Ballard, *Upholding Democracy*, p. 213.

43. Margaret Daly Hays and Gary F. Weatley, *Interagency and Political-Military Dimensions of Peace Operations: Haiti—A Case Study* (Washington, DC: National Defense University Press, 1996), available at *www.ndu.edu/inss/books/haiti/haithome.html*.

44. Bailey, Maguire and Pouliot, "Haiti," pp. 222–24.

45. Ibid., pp. 224–25.

46. The most damning accounts of U.S. military inaction, which many U.S. military officers believe are exaggerations, are provided by Bob Shacochis, *The Immaculate Invasion* (New York: Penguin, 1999).

47. Ballard, *Upholding Democracy*, p. 120.

48. Ibid., pp. 114–15.

49. Bailey, Maguire and Pouliot, "Haiti," pp. 235–40.

50. Ballard, *Upholding Democracy*, p. 211.

51. See Larry Rohter, "U.N. Troops to Leave Haiti as Feeble as They Found It," *New York Times*, Dec. 4, 1997; and Steven Lee Myers, "Full-Time U.S. Force in Haiti to Leave an Unstable Nation," *New York Times*, Aug. 26, 1999. This analysis was confirmed in an off-the-record e-mail interview by the author with a high-ranking U.S. Army officer who had been stationed in Haiti, January 2003.

52. Hays and Weatley, *Interagency and Political-Military Dimensions of Peace Operations: Haiti.*

53. "Where Racketeers Rule," *The Economist*, Feb. 2, 2002.

54. Off-the-record email interview by the author, Jan. 2003.

55. For encyclopedic descriptions, see the NATO website (*www.nato.int*), as well as Laura Silber and Allan Little, *Yugoslavia: Death of a Nation* (New York: Penguin, 1996); Richard Holbrooke, *To End a War* (New York: Random House, 1998); Ivo H. Daalder and Michael E. O'Hanlon, *Winning Ugly: NATO's War to Save Kosovo* (Washington: Brookings, 2000), and Wesley K. Clark, *Waging Modern War: Bosnia, Kosovo, and the Future of Conflict* (New York: Public Affairs, 2001).

56. Andy Bair and Michael J. Dziedzic, "The International Police Task Force," in *Lessons from Bosnia: The IFOR Experience*, ed. Larry Wentz (Washington, DC: Command and Control Research Program, Office of the Assistant Secretary of Defense, April 1998), available on the web at *www.dodccrp.org/bostoc.htm*.

57. For a description of the complex process by which the operations of the OHR are overseen, see its website: *www.ohr.int*.

58. Ibid.

59. See "Political Situation in Bosnia and Herzegovina (November 2001)," *SFOR Informer* no. 126, Nov. 14, 2001, available on the web at www.nato.int.

60. Ibid.

61. Sgt. Kerensa Hardy, "OHR Involvement Reaches Far and Wide in BiH Progression," *SFOR Informer* no. 113, May 16, 2001, available on the web at www.nato.int.

62. NATO/SFOR Joint Press Conference (including statements by representatives from the OHR and the UN Commission on Human Rights), Jan. 22, 2002; available on the web at www.nato.int.

63. For examples, see Gerald Knaus and Felix Martin, "Travails of the European Raj," *Journal of Democracy* 14, no. 3 (July 2003): 60–74; Keith Brown, "Unraveling Europe's Raj," *Foreign Policy* no. 139 (Nov./Dec. 2003): 84; and the exchange between Knaus, Martin, and Brown, "Do Bosnians Want Democracy?" *Foreign Policy* no. 141 (Mar./Apr. 2004): 13.

64. See the General Framework Agreement, available on the NATO website at *www.nato.int/ifor/gfa/gfa-home.htm*.

65. Kevin Ong, rapporteur, "The UN, Europe and Crisis Management," conference report (Paris: International Peace Academy et al., October 2000), pp. 5–8, and Elizabeth M. Cousens, "Building Peace in Bosnia," in *Peacebuilding as Politics: Cultivating Peace in Fragile Societies*, ed. Cousens and Chetan Kumar (Boulder, Colo.: Lynne Rienner, 2001), pp. 113–52.

66. A good brief summary is provided on the NATO website at http://www.nato.int/sfor/docu/d981116a.htm.

67. David Chandler, *Bosnia: Faking Democracy after Dayton* (Sterling, Va.: Pluto Press, 1999), p. 3.

68. Chandler, *Bosnia*, pp. 11–28.

69. The agreement is available on the NATO website at http://www.nato.int/kosovo/docu/a990609a.htm.

70. UNMIK webpage, http://www.unmikonline.org/intro.htm.

71. Ibid.

72. Simon Chesterman, "Kosovo in Limbo: State-Building and 'Substantial Autonomy,' " Project on Transitional Administrations Report (New York: International Peace Academy, Aug. 2001), p. 4.

73. Daniel Simpson, "A Restive Kosovo, Officially Still Serbian, Squirms under the Status Quo," *New York Times*, Dec. 29, 2002.

74. Bob Breen, *Mission Accomplished East Timor: The Australian Defence Force Participation in the International Forces East Timor (INTERFET)* (Crows Nest, New South Wales: Allen and Unwin Australia, 2000), pp. 1–2; Lincoln Wright, "Secret Defence Papers Show 'Conspiracy' at Highest Level," *Canberra Times*, Nov. 24, 1999, as reported in the Lexis/Nexis Academic Universe online database.

75. Jarat Chopra, "The UN's Kingdom of East Timor," *Survival* 42, no. 3 (Autumn 2000), p. 37fn 2.

76. Breen, *Mission Accomplished East Timor*, pp. 6–13.

77. Chopra, "The UN's Kingdom of East Timor," pp. 27–39; Jonathan Steele, "Nation Building in East Timor," *World Policy Journal* 19, no. 2 (Summer 2002): 76–87; Caplan, *A New Trusteeship*, p. 48.

78. Steele, "Nation Building in East Timor."

79. Chopra, "The UN's Kingdom of East Timor," p. 31.

80. Simon Chesterman, "Justice under International Administration: Kosovo, East Timor and Afghanistan," Transitional Administrations Project Report (New York: International Peace Academy, Sept. 2002), p. 7.

81. UN Security Council Resolution 1410, May 17, 2002, available at www.un.org.

82. Steele, "Nation Building in East Timor."

83. "A New Year in East Timor," *Sydney Morning Herald*, Jan. 6, 2003, as reported in the Lexis/Nexis Academic Universe online database.

84. Steele, "Nation Building in East Timor."

85. A. E. Afigbo, "Men of Two Continents: An African Interpretation," in *African Proconsuls: European Governors in Africa*, ed. L. H. Gann and Peter Duignan (New York: Free Press, 1978), p. 529.

86. Niall Ferguson, *Empire: The Rise and Demise of the British World Order and Its Lessons for Global Power* (New York: Basic Books, 2003).

3. State Interests, Humanitarianism, and Control

1. See Tony Smith, *America's Mission: The United States and the Worldwide Struggle for Democracy in the Twentieth Century* (Princeton: Princeton University

Press, 1994), pp. 37–59; Brian McAllister Linn, *Guardians of Empire: The U.S. Army and the Pacific, 1902–1940* (Chapel Hill: University of North Carolina Press, 1997), pp. 5–50; and Linn, "Cerberus' Dilemma: The U.S. Army and Internal Security in the Pacific, 1902–1940," in *Guardians of Empire: The Armed Forces of the Colonial Powers, c. 1700–1964*, ed. David Kilingray and David E. Omissi (New York, Manchester University Press, 1999), pp. 114–36.

2. Max Boot, *The Savage Wars of Peace: Small Wars and the Rise of American Power* (New York: Basic Books, 2002).

3. Frank Hindman Golay, *Face of Empire: United States-Philippine Relations, 1898–1946* (Madison: University of Wisconsin Center for Southeast Asian Studies, 1998), p. 112; Linn, *Guardians of Empire*, pp. 38–39.

4. Smith, *America's Mission.*

5. Ibid.

6. Ibid.

7. Jeffrey Herbst, *States and Power in Africa: Comparative Lessons in Authority and Control* (Princeton: Princeton University Press, 2000), pp. 81–82; Philip D. Curtin, *The World and the West: The European Challenge and the Overseas Response in the Age of Empire* (New York: Cambridge University Press, 2000), pp. 16–17. French colonial policy was particularly variable across time and place as the assimilationist policies of the 1870s failed to produce the results Paris wanted; see William B. Cohen, *Rulers of Empire: The French Colonial Service in Africa* (Stanford: Hoover Institution Press, 1971); D. K. Fieldhouse, *Colonialism 1870–1945: An Introduction* (London: Weidenfeld and Nicolson, 1981), pp. 36–45; Alice L. Conklin, *A Mission to Civilize: The Republican Idea of Empire in France and West Africa, 1895–1930* (Stanford: Stanford University Press, 1997).

8. Ethan A. Nadelmann, "Global Prohibition Regimes: The Evolution of Norms in International Society," *International Organization* 44, no. 4 (Autumn 1990): 479–526; Martha Finnemore and Kathryn Sikkink, "International Norm Dynamics and Political Change," *International Organization* 52, no. 4 (Autumn 1998): 887–917; and Neta C. Crawford, *Argument and Change in World Politics: Ethics, Decolonization, and Humanitarian Intervention* (New York: Cambridge University Press, 2002). While Finnemore and Sikkink do say that "norm conformance can often be self-interested," they argue that the "logic of appropriateness" can be separated from instrumental reasons to explain norm conformance (p. 912).

9. Curtin, *The World and the West*, p. 39.

10. This is the major theme of Fieldhouse, *Colonialism.*

11. Lance E. Davis and Robert A. Huttenback, *Mammon and the Pursuit of Empire: The Political Economy of British Imperialism, 1860–1912* (New York: Cambridge University Press, 1986), pp. 306–7.

12. Ibid., p. 109, 311.

13. Ibid., p. 110.

14. Michael W. Doyle, *Empires* (Ithaca: Cornell University Press, 1986). Also see James J. Cooke, *New French Imperialism 1880–1910: The Third Republic and Colonial Expansion* (Hamden, Conn.: Archon Books, 1973).

15. Herbst, *States and Power in Africa*, p. 64.

16. Davis and Huttenback, *Mammon and the Pursuit of Empire*, p. 311.

17. Doyle, *Empires*, p. 246; Crawford Young, *The African Colonial State in Comparative Perspective* (New Haven: Yale University Press, 1994), pp. 84–86.

18. For an in-depth review of the British experience with private colonialism, see T. A. Heathcote, *The Military in British India: The Development of British Land Forces in South Asia, 1600–1947* (New York: Manchester University Press, 1995).

19. Herbst, *States and Power in Africa*, p. 75.

20. Robert H. Jackson, *Quasi-states: Sovereignty, International Relations, and the Third World* (New York: Cambridge University Press, 1990), p. 60; Conklin, *A Mission to Civilize*, p. 12; Herbst, *States and Power in Africa*, pp. 64–65.

21. Curtin, *The World and the West*, p. 208.

22. Young, *The African Colonial State in Comparative Perspective*; Heathcote, *Military in British India*; Conklin, *Mission to Civilize*.

23. The need for self-financing colonies is a major theme of Fieldhouse, *Colonialism*. Also see Young, *African Colonial State in Comparative Perspective*, pp. 123–24.

24. Conklin, *Mission to Civilize*.

25. See Stig Förster, Wolfgang J. Mommsen, and Ronald Robinson, eds., *Bismarck, Europe, and Africa: The Berlin Africa Conference 1884–1885 and the Onset of Partition* (London: Oxford University Press, 1988).

26. Daniel Philpott, "Liberalism, Power, and Authority in International Relations: On the Origins of Colonial Independence and Internationally Sanctioned Intervention," *Security Studies* 11, no. 2 (Winter 2001/2): 117–63.

27. In addition to the example of Leonard Wood in the Philippines cited above, a prominent case was the Amritsar massacre ordered by British officers in colonial India in 1919. See Major General Charles W. Glynn, *Imperial Policing* (London: Macmillan, 1934), pp. 52–63, and Lawrence James, *Imperial Rearguard: Wars of Empire, 1919–85* (New York: Brassey's, 1988), pp. 60–63.

28. Gerrit W. Gong, *The Standard of 'Civilization' in International Society* (Oxford: Clarendon Press, 1984), p. 39.

29. Conklin, *Mission to Civilize*.

30. For a detailed discussion of indirect rule and "native administration," see John E. Flint, "Frederick Lugard: The Making of an Autocrat (1858–1943)," in *African Proconsuls: European Governors in Africa*, ed. L.H. Gann and Peter Duignan (New York: Free Press, 1978), pp. 290–312. Also see Fieldhouse, *Colonialism*, pp. 33–34, and Jackson, *Quasi-states*, pp. 14–15.

31. Doyle, *Empires*, pp. 181–82; Conklin, *Mission to Civilize*, p. 96.

32. Ronald Robinson, "The Excentric [sic] Idea of Imperialism, With or Without Empires," in *Imperialism and After: Continuities and Discontinuities*, ed. Wolfgang J. Mommsen and Jürgen Osterhammel (Boston: Allen & Unwin, 1986), pp. 267–89.

33. Doyle, *Empires*, pp. 41–2.

34. Herbst, *States and Power in Africa*, p. 91.

35. Curtin, *The World and the West*, p. 276.

36. Anthony Clayton, *The British Empire as a Superpower, 1919–39* (London: Macmillan, 1986), p. 162.

37. Moshe Gershovich, *French Military Rule in Morocco: Colonialism and its Consequences* (London: Cass, 2000), p. 71.

38. A. S. Kanya-Forstner, *Conquest of the Western Sudan: A Study in French Military Imperialism* (London: Cambridge University Press, 1969), p. 272.

39. A. E. Afigbo, "Men of Two Continents: An African Interpretation," in *African Proconsuls*, ed. Gann and Duignan, pp. 523–34.

40. Quoted in Cohen, *Rulers of Empire*, p. 11.

41. See especially Timothy Mitchell, *Colonising Egypt* (Berkeley: University of California Press, 1991), pp. 69–81, and Conklin, *Mission to Civilize*, pp. 75–84.

42. Gong, *The Standard of 'Civilization' in International Society*.

43. Conklin, *Mission to Civilize*; Mitchell, *Colonising Egypt*.

44. Mitchell, *Colonising Egypt*.

45. Horst Gründer, "Christian Mission Activities in Africa in the Age of Imperialism and the Berlin Conference of 1884–1885," in *Bismarck, Europe, and Africa*, Förster, et al., eds., pp. 85–103. Also see L. H. Gann, "The Berlin Conference and the Humanitarian Conscience," in ibid., pp. 323–24, and Davis and Huttenback, *Mammon and the Pursuit of Empire*, p. 6.

46. Conklin, *Mission to Civilize*, pp. 52–4.

47. Virgil L. Matthew, Jr., "Joseph Simon Gallieni (1849–1916)," in *African Proconsuls*, ed. Gann and Duignan, pp. 80–108.

48. G. Wesley Johnson, "William Ponty and Republican Paternalism in French West Africa (1866–1915)," in *African Proconsuls*, ed. Gann and Duignan, pp. 127–56; Young, *African Colonial State in Comparative Perspective*; Conklin, *Mission to Civilize*; Linn, *Guardians of Empire*.

49. PBS, "The 2nd Presidential Debate: A Newshour with Jim Lehrer Transcript," Oct. 11, 2000, available at http://www.pbs.org/newshour/bb/election/2000debates/2ndebate2.html.

50. One exception may have been the humanitarian intervention in Somalia in 1993, which was genuinely focused on the purpose of ending starvation in the country. This was not really the kind of complex mission described in this book, however, because there was not much concerted effort put in Somalia toward encouraging good governance and real political change.

51. See Margaret Daly Hays and Gary F. Weatley, *Interagency and Political-Military Dimensions of Peace Operations: Haiti—A Case Study* (Washington, DC: National Defense University Press, 1996), available at *www.ndu.edu/inss/book/haiti/haithome.html*; Michael Bailey, Robert Maguire, and J. O'Neil G. Pouliot, "Haiti: Military-Police Partnership for Public Security," in *Policing the New World Disorder: Peace Operations and Public Security*, ed. Robert B. Oakley, Michael J. Dziedzic, and Eliot M. Goldberg (Washington, DC: National Defense University Press, 1998); and Bob Shacochis, *The Immaculate Invasion* (New York: Penguin, 1999).

52. Hays and Weatley, *Interagency and Political-Military Dimensions of Peace Operations*.

53. John R. Ballard, *Upholding Democracy: The United States Military Campaign in Haiti, 1994–1997* (Westport, Conn.: Praeger, 1998), p. 77.

54. Christopher Marquis, "U.S. Declines To Use Force To Put Down Haitian Strife," *New York Times*, Feb. 18, 2004.

55. Christopher Marquis, "Aristide Flees after a Shove from the U.S.," *New York Times*, March 1, 2004. The fact that it was the attack by armed Aristide supporters on the Haitian Coast Guard that pushed the U.S. over the line in deciding to intervene was confirmed by the author in an off-the-record interview with a Pentagon official, Washington, DC, March 2004.

56. An advertisement was placed in the New York Times by the American Jewish Committee, the American Jewish Congress, and the Anti-Defamation League in August 1992 urging American intervention in Bosnia; a description of this and similar actions appears in Richard Cohen, "It's Not a Holocaust: Rhetoric and Reality in Bosnia," *Washington Post*, Feb. 28, 1993. In 1995, the U.S. Holocaust Memorial Museum sponsored an ecumenical ceremony urging unspecified international action in Bosnia; see Judith Weinraub, "Never Again: Religious Leaders Protest Carnage in Bosnia," *Washington Post*, Aug. 4, 1995; both as reported in the Lexis-Nexis Academic Universe online database.

57. For example, see Kenneth Roth, executive director of Human Rights Watch, letter to the editor, "U.S. Hesitates on Kosovo," *New York Times*, Sept. 21, 1998, as reported in the Lexis-Nexis Academic Universe online database.

58. Carlo Scognamiglio-Pasini, "Increasing Italy's Input," *NATO Review* 49, no. 2 (Summer 2001): 26–27.

59. Richard Holbrooke, *To End a War* (New York: Modern Library, 1998), pp. 360–61; David S. Yost, *NATO Transformed: The Alliance's New Roles in International Security* (Washington, DC: U.S. Institute of Peace, 1998), pp. 197–99. Also see David Chandler, *Bosnia: Faking Democracy after Dayton* (Sterling, Va.: Pluto Press, 1999), pp. 182–86.

60. James Cotton, "East Timor and Australia—Twenty-Five Years of the Policy Debate," in *East Timor and Australia: AIIA Contributions to the Policy Debate*, ed. James Cotton (Canberra: Australian Defense Studies Center, 1999), pp. 1–20.

61. Michael Evans, *Forward from the Past: The Development of Australian Army Doctrine, 1972–Present*, Study Paper 301 (Duntroon, ACT: Australian Land Warfare Studies Center, 1999), and Robert Wall, "Modernization, Stability Top RAAF's Agenda," *Aviation Week and Space Technology*, 154, no. 22 (May 28, 2001): 46.

62. Two civilian Australian defense analysts affirmed this in off-the-record conversations with the author.

63. Philpott, "Liberalism, Power, and Authority in International Relations," p. 148.

64. Most recently this has influenced the thinking of U.S. Defense Secretary Donald M. Rumsfeld. See Thom Shanker, "Rumsfeld Favors Forceful Actions to Foil an Attack," *New York Times*, Oct. 13, 2002.

65. Holbrooke, *To End a War*, pp. 360–72.

66. While the full text of the directive has not been declassified, the State Department press briefing which accompanied its publication stated that the first factor to be used in determining whether or not U.S. troops should participate on a peacekeeping mission was whether or not "participation advances U.S. interests." "President Clinton Signs New Peacekeeping Policy," White House Office of the Press Secretary, May 5, 1994, available at http://www.fas.org/irp/offdocs/pdd25.htm.

67. Philip Gourevitch, *We Wish to Inform You that Tomorrow We Will be*

Killed with Our Families: Stories from Rwanda (New York: Farrar Straus and Giroux, 1998); Linda Melvern, *A People Betrayed: The Role of the West in Rwanda's Genocide* (New York: Zed Books, 2000).

68. John R. Bolton, then-Senior Vice President of the American Enterprise Institute, "United States Policy on United Nations Peacekeeping," statement before the U.S. House of Representatives International Relations Committee, Oct. 11, 2000, as reported in the Lexis/Nexis Congressional Universe online database.

69. Carl Honore, "Britain Takes on New Role as World Peacekeeper," *Houston Chronicle*, Jan. 13, 2002.

70. Peter Caddick-Adams, "Civil Affairs Operations by IFOR and SFOR in Bosnia 1995–1997," *International Peacekeeping* 5, no. 3 (Autumn 1998): 147; Cpl. David Thomas, "Sipovo's New Information Centre," *SFOR Informer* no. 105 (Jan. 24, 2001), available at www.nato.int.

71. Hays and Weatley, *Interagency and Political-Military Dimensions of Peace Operations: Haiti.*

72. Ballard, *Upholding Democracy*, p. 119.

73. Shacochis, *The Immaculate Invasion*, p. 189.

74. U.S. Army Peacekeeping Institute, "Success in Peacekeeping: United Nations Mission in Haiti: The Military Perspective," U.S. Army Chief of Staff Haiti After Action Review Report (Carlisle Barracks, Penn.: U.S. Army War College, no date), p. 11.

75. This is one of the themes of Shacochis, *The Immaculate Invasion.*

76. Paddy Ashdown, "What I Learned in Bosnia," *New York Times*, Oct. 28, 2002.

77. One exception may be Saudi Arabia, which is known to give aid in Bosnia that is tied to fundamentalist proselytizing among secular Muslims. Some NATO representatives believe that this undermines the goal of multiethnic tolerance in the country. See Daniel Simpson, "Where Did All That Money in Bosnia Go?" *New York Times*, Feb. 16, 2003.

78. Maj. Marie Richter, "A New Turovi," *SFOR Informer* no. 119, Aug. 8, 2001, and 1st Lt. Luis Sanchez, "Helping People: German CIMIC Takes Action," *SFOR Informer* no. 120, Aug. 20, 2001, both available at *www.nato.int/sfor*. This was confirmed by two senior members of the NATO International Military Staff in an off-the-record interview with the author at NATO HQ in Brussels, Jan. 2002.

79. Off-the-record interview with a senior civilian NATO representative, NATO HQ, Brussels, Jan. 2002.

80. 1st Lt. Kristoffer Egeberg, "When Words Can't Describe," *SFOR Informer* no. 114, May 30, 2001; 2nd Lt. Alexandre Barbé, "Small Creek, Great Expectations," *SFOR Informer* no. 115, June 13, 2001; Thierry Domin, "Podvidaca Road Brings Entities Closer," *SFOR Informer* no. 123, Oct. 3, 2001; available at *www.nato.int.*

81. 1st Lt. Luis Sanchez, "Operation Domino," *SFOR Informer* no. 117, July 11, 2001; Sanchez, "Italian CIMIC Team Helps Gorazde Community," *SFOR Informer* no. 120, Aug. 22, 2001; Sanchez, "The Road to Peace," *SFOR Informer* no. 125, Oct. 31, 2001; available at www.nato.int.

82. Capt. Karine Chapleau, "Electricity for Three Villages," *SFOR Informer*

no. 107, Feb. 21, 2002, available at www.nato.int.

83. Cpt. Nicolas Girault, "Providing Comfort: Ambassadors in MND SW," *SFOR Informer* no. 117, July 11, 2001, available at www.nato.int.

84. Bradd C. Hayes and Jeffrey I. Sands, *Doing Windows: Non-Traditional Military Responses to Complex Emergencies* (Newport, R.I.: Naval War College Center for Naval Warfare Studies, 1997), p. 79.

85. 1st Lt. Kristoffer Egeberg, "For a Smoother Aid Process," *SFOR Informer* no. 110, Apr. 4, 2001, available at www.nato.int.

86. Laura Kay Rozen, "New Bosnia Tack: Reward 'Open' Towns," *Christian Science Monitor*, Aug. 1, 1997, and Martin Walker, "EU Rewards Bosnians Who Back Peace," *London Guardian*, Jan. 23, 1998, both as reported by the Lexis/Nexis online news service.

87. Capt. Karine Chapleau, "Employment Boost in Gornji Vakuf," *SFOR Informer* no. 108 (Mar. 7, 2002); Chapleau, "More Help to the Community," *SFOR Informer* no. 109 (Mar. 21, 2001); Chapleau, "Women Are Making a Difference," *SFOR Informer* no. 111 (Apr. 18, 2001); Sgt. Peter Fitzgerald, "New Funding Source for MND-SW CIMIC Projects," *SFOR Informer* no. 123 (Oct. 3, 2001); Capt. Vance White, "Small Business—Big Expectations," *SFOR Informer* no. 125 (Oct. 31, 2001), available at www.nato.int.

88. International Crisis Group (ICG), "The Continuing Challenge of Refugee Return in Bosnia and Herzegovina," Balkans Report no. 137 (Brussels: ICG, Dec. 2002), pp. 4–5.

89. For an example, see Cpl. Jean-Philippe Lavigne, "Kotorsko," *SFOR Informer* no. 124, Oct. 17, 2001, available at www.nato.int.

90. ICG, "The Continuing Challenge," pp. 10–11, 14–16.

91. Ibid., pp. 19–21.

92. Herbst, *States and Power in Africa*, pp. 71–72.

93. "The Berlin Conference: The General Act of Feb. 26, 1885," chap. 1, art. VI, as excerpted at *http://web.jjay.cuny.edu/~jobrien/reference/ob45.htm*.

94. Suzanne Miers, "Humanitarianism at Berlin: Myth or Reality?" in *Bismarck, Europe, and Africa*, ed. Förster, Mommsen and Robinson, pp. 343–44.

95. Jackson, *Quasi-states*, pp. 69–73.

96. Miers, "Humanitarianism at Berlin;" and Gann, "Berlin Conference and Humanitarian Conscience."

97. Gann, ibid., p. 321.

98. Geoffrey de Courcel, "The Berlin Act of 26 February 1885," in *Bismarck, Europe, and Africa*, ed. Förster, Mommsen and Robinson, p. 256.

99. Jackson, *Quasi-states*, pp. 60–61.

100. Mitchell, *Colonising Egypt*, p. 166.

101. Jörg Fisch, "Africa as *terra nullius*: The Berlin Conference and International Law," in *Bismarck, Europe, and Africa*, ed. Förster, Mommsen and Robinson, pp. 347–75.

102. Nadelman, "Global Prohibition Regimes," p. 484.

103. Jackson, *Quasi-states*, pp. 73–74. Also see William Bain, "The Political Theory of Trusteeship and the Twilight of International Equality," *International Relations* 16, no. 1 (2003): 59–67.

104. Townsend Hoopes and Douglas Brinkley, *FDR and the Creation of the U.N.* (New Haven: Yale University Press, 1997); Stanley Meisler, *United Nations: The First Fifty Years* (New York: Atlantic Monthly Press, 1995), pp. 1–20.

105. Evan Luard, *The United Nations: How It Works and What It Does*, 2nd ed., rev. Derek Heater (New York: St. Martin's Press, 1994), pp. 19–20; James S. Sutterlin, "The Past as Prologue," in *The Once and Future Security Council*, ed. Bruce Russett (New York: St. Martin's, 1997), p. 8.

106. Barry O'Neill, "Power and Satisfaction in the Security Council," in *The Once and Future Security Council*, ed. Russett, p. 63.

107. Nigel Thalakada, "China's Voting Pattern in the Security Council, 1990–1995," in *The Once and Future Security Council*, ed. Russett, pp. 83–118.

108. Kofi A. Annan, "Report of the Secretary General on the Work of the Organization," UN General Assembly Report A/54/1, Aug. 31, 1999, available at *www.un.org*; Annan, "Two Concepts of Sovereignty," *The Economist*, Sept. 18, 1999.

109. Kimberly Marten Zisk, "Making and Keeping the Peace," in *A Global Agenda: Issues Before the 55th General Assembly of the United Nations*, ed. John Tessitore and Susan Woolfson (New York: Rowman & Littlefield, 2000), pp. 1–3.

110. Kofi A. Annan, *"We the Peoples:" The Role of the United Nations in the 21st Century* (New York: United Nations, 2000), pp. 47–8.

111. Simon Chesterfeld, "Kosovo in Limbo: State-Building and 'Substantial Autonomy,' " Report of the Project on Transitional Administrations (New York: International Peace Academy, Aug. 2001).

112. Nicholas Lemann, "After Iraq: The Plan to Remake the Middle East," *The New Yorker*, Feb. 17–24, 2003; and James Atlas, "A Classicist's Legacy: New Empire Builders," *New York Times*, May 4, 2003.

4. Political Will and Security

1. Factual material in this vignette is taken from the following sources: Dexter Filkins, "The Anxiety of Postwar Afghans," *New York Times*, Mar. 31, 2002; Amy Waldman, "Courted by U.S. and Iran, an Afghan's Influence Rises," *Times*, Apr. 3, 2002; Pamela Constable, "Afghan Officials Say Forces Foiled Sabotage," *Washington Post*, Apr. 5, 2002; Susan B. Glasser and Peter Baker, "Surge of Violence Threatens Plans for Afghanistan," *Post*, Apr. 12, 2002; Baker, "In Kabul, an Unroyal Welcome," *Post*, Apr. 14, 2002; "UN Running out of Funds for Refugees," Associated Press, Apr. 17, 2002, as reported by www.nytimes.com; Kathy Gannon, "Afghan Warlord Fighting Kills 25," *Post*, Apr. 29, 2002; Baker and Glasser, "Traces of the Enemy Near Pakistan Border," *Post*, Apr. 30, 2002; Mary Beth Sheridan, "Militia Leader Given Ultimatum on Standoff," *Post*, May 24, 2002; Philip Smucker, "A Fight to Feed Hungry Afghanistan," *Christian Science Monitor*, June 3, 2002; and Anthony Davis, "Kabul's Security Dilemma," *Jane's Defence Weekly*, June 12, 2002, as reported in the Earlybird online news service.

2. See Kimberly Zisk Marten, "Defending Against Anarchy: From War to Peacekeeping in Afghanistan," *The Washington Quarterly* 26, no. 1 (Winter 2002–3): 35–52.

3. S/RES/1510, Oct. 13, 2003, available at www.un.org.

4. Eric Schmitt and David E. Sanger, "Looting Disrupts Detailed U.S. Plan to Restore Iraq," *New York Times*, May 19, 2003; Marc Santora, "Scholars Complain of Feeling Helpless as They See Their Campus Destroyed," *New York Times*, May 19, 2003.

5. Sabrina Tavernise, "Americans Try to Quell Arab-Kurd Flare-Up," *New York Times*, May 21, 2003.

6. Michael E. Gordon, "Allies to Begin Seizing Weapons from Most Iraqis," *New York Times*, May 21, 2003.

7. Lawrence James, *Imperial Rearguard: Wars of Empire, 1919–85* (New York: Brassey's, 1988), p. 31; Douglas Porch, "Bugeaud, Galliéni, Lyautey: The Development of French Colonial Warfare," in *Makers of Modern Strategy from Machiavelli to the Nuclear Age*, ed. Peter Paret et al. (Princeton: Princeton University Press, 1986), p. 403; Moshe Gershovich, *French Military Rule in Morocco: Colonialism and its Consequences* (London: Cass, 2000), pp. 7–8; Brian McAllister Linn, *Guardians of Empire: The U.S. Army and the Pacific, 1902–1940* (Chapel Hill: University of North Carolina Press, 1997), p. 47; Linn, "Cerberus' Dilemma: The U.S. Army and Internal Security in the Pacific, 1902–1940," in *Guardians of Empire: The Armed Forces of the Colonial Powers, c. 1700–1964*, ed. David Kilingray and David E. Omissi (New York: Manchester University Press, 1999), p. 123.

8. A. S. Kanya-Forstner, *The Conquest of the Western Sudan: A Study in French Military Imperialism* (Cambridge: Cambridge University Press, 1969); William B. Cohen, *Rulers of Empire: The French Colonial Service in Africa* (Stanford: Hoover Institution Press, 1971); John E. Flint, "Frederick Lugard: The Making of an Autocrat (1858–1943)," in *African Proconsuls: European Governors in Africa*, ed. L. H. Gann and Peter Duignan (New York: Free Press, 1978), pp. 290–312; Alice L. Conklin, *A Mission to Civilize: The Republican Idea of Empire in France and West Africa, 1895–1930* (Stanford: Stanford University Press, 1997); Gershovich, *French Military Rule in Morocco*; Jeffrey Herbst, *States and Power in Africa: Comparative Lessons in Authority and Control* (Princeton: Princeton University Press, 2000).

9. Philip D. Curtin, *The World and the West: The European Challenge and the Overseas Response in the Age of Empire* (New York: Cambridge University Press, 2000), pp. 48–9.

10. Cohen, *Rulers of Empire*.

11. James, *Imperial Rearguard*, passim; Maurice Willoughby, *Echo of a Distant Drum: The Last Generation of Empire* (Sussex, UK: The Book Guild, Ltd., 2001), pp. 263–64.

12. James, *Imperial Rearguard*, p. 33; Cohen, *Rulers of Empire*, pp. 14, 23; Porch, "Bugeaud, Galliéni, Lyautey," p. 403; Gershovich, *French Military Rule in Morocco*, p. 7.

13. Porch, "Bugeaud, Galliéni, Lyautey," p. 403.

14. Ibid., p. 376.

15. T. A. Heathcote, *The Military in British India: The Development of British Land Forces in South Asia, 1600–1947* (New York: Manchester University Press, 1995), pp. 126–27.

16. D. K. Fieldhouse, *Colonialism 1870–1945: An Introduction* (London: Weidenfeld and Nicolson, 1981), p. 23; Michael W. Doyle, *Empires* (Ithaca: Cornell University Press, 1986), p. 178; Willoughby, *Echo of a Distant Drum*, p. 263.

17. Willoughby, ibid., p. 263.

18. James, *Imperial Rearguard*; Kanya-Forstner, *Conquest of the Western Sudan*; Gershovich, *French Military Rule in Morocco*.

19. Kanya-Forstner, *Conquest of the Western Sudan*, pp. 58–60; Flint, "Frederick Lugard," p. 298.

20. While Great Britain acted independently by intervening in a military peacekeeping role in Sierra Leone, and France did so in Cote d'Ivoire, neither of these operations involved the intrusive political intervention that characterizes the cases analyzed in this book.

21. White House spokesperson Ari Fleischer, press briefings, Jan. 16 and 28 and Apr. 18, 2002, available at *www.whitehouse.gov*; Sec. of Defense Donald Rumsfeld, press briefings, Federal News Service, Feb. 26, Mar. 6, and Mar. 25, 2002; Rumsfeld, Pentagon briefing, reported on CNN Live Event/Special, Apr. 17, 2002; Rumsfeld, testimony before the U.S. Senate Armed Services Committee, *Operation Enduring Freedom*, Federal News Service, July 31, 2002; Dep. Defense Sec. Paul Wolfowitz, comments summarized by *ABC News Transcripts*, Sept. 6, 2002.

22. William P. Hamblet and Jerry G. Kline, "Interagency Cooperation: PDD 56 and Complex Contingency Operations," *Joint Forces Quarterly* no. 24 (Spring 2000): 92–7.

23. Briefing, 96th Civil Affairs Battalion (Airborne), Ft. Bragg, NC, Aug. 2002.

24. "Beyond Jointness: The Civil-Military Dimensions of Peace Operations and Humanitarian Assistance," National Defense University Symposium, June 2–3, 1999, available online at www.ndu.edu/inss/peaceops/ffjun0299.htm.

25. "The Clinton Administration's Policy on Managing Complex Contingency Operations: Presidential Decision Directive, May 1997," unclassified White Paper summarizing PDD-56; available online at www.fas.org/irp/offdocs/pdd56.htm.

26. Rowan Scarborough, "Study Hits White House on Peacekeeping Missions," *Washington Times*, Dec. 6, 1999. The consulting firm was A.B. Technologies, and the quotation comes from a briefing prepared for senior military personnel.

27. Eric Schmitt, "Forces Strained in Iraq Mission, Congress Is Told," *New York Times*, Sept. 10, 2003.

28. Steven Lee Myers, "Army to Shorten Tours of Reserves Serving Overseas," *New York Times*, Mar. 5, 2000.

29. Peter Viggo Jakobsen, "The Emerging Consensus on Grey Area Peace Operations Doctrine: Will It Last and Enhance Operational Effectiveness?" *International Peacekeeping* 7, no. 3 (Autumn 2000), p. 48.

30. John L. Hirsch and Robert B. Oakley, *Somalia and Operation Restore Hope: Reflections on Peacemaking and Peacekeeping* (Washington, D.C.: United States Institute of Peace Press, 1995).

31. Author's off-the-record interview with two mid-ranking military officers at SHAPE, Mons, Belgium, Jan. 2002; confirmed by the author's off-the-record interview with several officials at the U.S. Mission to NATO, Brussels, Jan. 2002.

32. Lynn Thomas and Steve Spataro, "Peacekeeping and Policing in Somalia,"

in *Policing the New World Disorder*, ed. Oakley, Dziedzic, and Goldberg, available at www.ndu.edu/inss/books/policing/chapter6.html.

33. William Langewiesche, "Peace Is Hell," *Atlantic Monthly* 288, no. 3 (Oct. 2001): 51–80.

34. Langewiesche, "Peace Is Hell." I was privileged to accompany one such patrol in Vitina, Kosovo in April 2002 as part of the annual NATO trip of the Council on Foreign Relations.

35. Bradd C. Hayes and Jeffrey I. Sands, *Doing Windows: Non-Traditional Military Responses to Complex Emergencies* (Newport, R.I.: Naval War College Center for Naval Warfare Studies, 1997), p. 68.

36. Christopher Bellamy, "Combining Combat Readiness and Compassion," *NATO Review* 49, no. 2 (Summer 2001): 9–11.

37. Author's off-the-record interview with officials at the U.S. mission to NATO, Jan. 2002.

38. See Spc. Marshall Thompson, "Cav Scouts Observe the FYROM Border," *Falcon Flier* (the newsletter of U.S. Task Force Falcon in Kosovo) June 15, 2001; Spc. Maria Jarmillo, "1–41st Field Artillery Controls the Roads," *Falcon Flier* Aug. 1, 2001; and Lt. Dieter Ortmeyer, Jr., "The Fate of Illegal Border Crossers," *KFOR Online News Report* Sept. 27, 2001, available at www.kforonline.com.

39. Anthony D. Sinnott, "A Good Reputation Is the Best Force Protection," *Marine Corps Gazette* 84, no. 6 (June 2000): 45–46.

40. Dana Priest, *The Mission: Waging War and Keeping Peace with America's Military* (New York: W. W. Norton, 2003), pp. 356–59.

41. Carlotta Gall, "Serbs in Kosovo Town Stone U.S. Troops, Who Retreat," *New York Times*, Feb. 21, 2000.

42. Priest, *The Mission*, p. 359.

43. Jeffrey Smith, "Serb Mob Confronts U.S. Soldiers," *Washington Post*, Feb. 21, 2000.

44. Priest, *The Mission*, pp. 324, 334–5.

45. Sgt. Gary Peterson, "Cordon and Search Keeps Kosovo Safe and Secure," *Falcon Flier*, Aug. 1, 2001.

46. Author's off-the-record interview with staff at the U.S. mission to NATO, Brussels, Jan. 2002.

47. For examples, see Chuck Call and Michael Barnett, "Looking for a Few Good Cops: Peacekeeping, Peacebuilding and CIVPOL," *International Peacekeeping* 6, no. 4 (Winter 1999): 43; David Last, "Organizing for Effective Peacebuilding," *International Peacekeeping* 7, no. 1 (Spring 2000): 82–84; Jakobsen, "The Emerging Consensus on Grey Area Peace Operations Doctrine," pp. 36–56; General Sir Rupert Smith, Deputy Supreme Allied Commander of Europe, interviewed in *NATO Review* 49, no. 2 (Summer 2001): 24–25, available at www.nato.int; Wesley K. Clark, *Waging Modern War: Bosnia, Kosovo, and the Future of Conflict* (New York: Public Affairs, 2001), pp. 53–55; and John McFarlane and William Maley, "Civilian Police in United Nations Peace Operations: Some Lessons from Recent Australian Experience," Australian Defence Studies Centre Working Paper 64, Canberra, Apr. 2001, pp. 7–8.

48. Major General Sir Charles W. Gwynn, *Imperial Policing* (London: Macmillan,

1934); Anthony Clayton, "'Deceptive Might': Imperial Defense and Security, 1900–1968," in *The Oxford History of British Empire, vol. VI: The Twentieth Century*, ed. Judith M. Brown and Wm. Roger Louis (New York: Oxford, 1999), p. 290.

49. Jason DeParle, "Riots in Los Angeles: General and Troops Have Domestic Mission," *New York Times*, May 3, 1992, as reported in the Lexis/Nexis Academic Universe online database.

50. Carol Goar, "Mohawk Crisis a Classic Case of Might not Making Right," *Toronto Star*, Sept. 1, 1990, as reported in the Lexis/Nexis Academic Universe online database.

51. Rod Thornton, "The Role of Peace Support Operations Doctrine in the British Army," *International Peacekeeping* 7, no. 2 (Summer 2000): 41-63.

52. Christopher Bellamy, "Combining Combat Readiness and Compassion," *NATO Review* 49, no. 2 (Summer 2001): 9–11.

53. John Hillen, "Debate: Can Soldiers Be Peacekeepers and Warriors?" *NATO Review* 49, no. 2 (Summer 2001): 16–20.

54. Congressional Budget Office, "Making Peace While Staying Ready for War: The Challenges of U.S. Military Participation in Peace Operations," 99-J-932–46, Washington, D.C., Dec. 1999, as reported by the Lexis/Nexis Academic News Service online database.

55. Brig. General (Ret.) David L. Grange, "Making Peacetime Engagement Work," *Naval Institute Proceedings* 127, no. 7 (July 2001): 30–34, and Bill Nash, "Debate: Can Soldiers Be Peacekeepers and Warriors?" *NATO Review* 49, no. 2 (Summer 2001): 16–20.

56. Samuel P. Huntington, *The Soldier and the State: The Theory and Politics of Civil-Military Relations* (Cambridge: Harvard University Press, 1957), p. 11.

57. Ibid., pp. 354–72.

58. Morris Janowitz, *The Professional Soldier: A Social and Political Portrait* (New York: Free Press, 1960).

59. Ibid., p. 419.

60. Michael J. Dziedzic, "Introduction," in *Policing the New World Disorder*, available at www.ndu.edu/inss/books/policing/intro.html.

61. David W. Foley, Commandant of the U.S. Army Military Police School, "Appendix B," in *Policing the New World Disorder*, available at www.ndu.edu/inss/books/policing/appendixb.html.

62. Schmidl, "Police Functions in Peace Operations;" "History of the U.S. Constabulary 10 Jan 46–31 Dec 46," Historical Division, Headquarters European Command, APO 757, U.S. Army Center of Military History Historical Manuscripts Collection 8–3.1 CA 37; available at www.army.mil/cmh-pg/reference/cstb-46.html.

63. Michael Dziedzic, "Introduction," in *Policing the New World Disorder*.

64. Alexandre Peyrille, "Inexperienced UN Police Hampering Law Enforcement in Kosovo," Agence France-Presse, Nov. 5, 2001, as reported in the ClariNet online news service. Also see Michael J. Kelly, "Legitimacy and the Public Security Function," in *Policing the New World Disorder*, available at www.ndu.edu/inss/books/policing/chapter11.html.

65. Priest, *The Mission*, pp. 371–72.

66. See Robert B. Oakley, Michael J. Dziedzic, and Eliot M. Goldberg, eds., *Policing the New World Disorder: Peace Operations and Public Security* (Washington, DC: National Defense University Press, 1998); Rachel Bronson, "When Soldiers Become Cops," *Foreign Affairs* 81, no. 6 (Nov./Dec. 2002):122–32.

67. Deborah D. Avant, *Political Institutions and Military Change: Lessons from Peripheral Wars* (Ithaca: Cornell University Press, 1994), p. 2.

68. Peter D. Feaver, "The Civil-Military Problematique: Huntington, Janowitz, and the Question of Civilian Control," *Armed Forces and Society* 23, no. 2 (Winter 1996): 149–78.

69. Eliot A. Cohen, "Why the Gap Matters," *The National Interest* 61 (Fall 2000): 38–48; and *Supreme Command: Soldiers, Statesmen, and Leadership in Wartime* (New York: Simon and Schuster, 2002).

70. Steven Kull and I. M. Destler, *Misreading the Public: The Myth of a New Isolationism* (Washington, DC: Brookings, 1999), pp. 81–112; James Burk, "Public Support for Peacekeeping in Lebanon and Somalia: Assessing the Casualties Hypothesis," *Political Science Quarterly* 114, no. 1 (Spring 1999): 57–78.

71. Justin Huggler, "Hatred, Fear and a Stench of Death in the Village that Symbolizes a Nation Slipping into Civil War," *The Independent* (London), June 28, 2001, as reported in the Lexis/Nexis Academic Universe online database.

72. Konstantin Testorides, "Government Claims Rebel Surrender in Aracinovo," Associated Press, June 24, 2001, as reported in the Lexis/Nexis Academic Universe online database.

73. Author's off-the-record interview with two mid-ranking officers at SHAPE, Mons, Belgium, Jan. 2002; confirmed in author's off-the-record interview with several officials at the U.S. mission to NATO, Brussels, Jan. 2002.

74. Author's off-the-record interview with officials at the U.S. mission to NATO, Jan. 2002.

75. Michael R. Gordon, "For G.I.'s, a Balkan Road of Neither War nor Peace," *New York Times*, July 17, 2001, as reported by the Lexis/Nexis Academic Universe online database.

76. Ibid.

77. Elizabeth Sullivan, "CIA Warns of 7 Hotspots, Likely Conflict," *Cleveland Plain Dealer*, Jan. 14, 2002, as reported in the Lexis/Nexis Academic Universe online database.

5. Military Tasks and Multilateralism

1. Coalition Provisional Authority website, *http://cpa-iraq.org/transcripts/weekly8aug03.pdf*.

2. The numbers were published in Steven R. Weisman with Felicity Barringer, "U.S. Abandons Idea of Bigger UN Role in Iraq Occupation," *New York Times*, Aug. 14, 2003.

3. Vernon Loeb, "U.S. to Fund Polish-Led Peacekeeping Force," *Washington Post*, July 29, 2003.

4. Kifner, "India Decides Not to Send Troops;" Elaine Sciolino, "France Declines U.S. Calls for Iraq Force," *New York Times*, July 16, 2003.

5. Colum Lynch, "More Cover for Peacekeeping Nations Debated," *Washington Post*, July 17, 2003.

6. Vernon Loeb and Colum Lynch, "U.S. Cool to New UN Vote," *Washington Post*, Aug. 2, 2003.

7. Weisman with Barringer, "U.S. Abandons Idea of Bigger UN Role."

8. Daniel Williams and Rajiv Chandrasekaran, "U.S. Troops Frustrated with Role in Iraq," *Washington Post*, June 20, 2003.

9. Rajiv Chandrasekaran, "Inexperienced Hands Guide Iraq Rebuilding," *Washington Post*, June 25, 2003.

10. Richard A. Oppel Jr. and Robert F. Worth, "Riots Continue over Fuel Crisis in Iraq's South," *New York Times*, Aug. 11, 2003; Marc Santora, "Scholars Complain of Feeling Helpless as They See Their Campus Destroyed," *New York Times*, May 19, 2003.

11. Edmund L. Andrews and Susan Sachs, "Iraq's Slide into Lawlessness Squanders Good Will for U.S.," *New York Times*, May 18, 2003; Jackie Spinner, "Thefts Plague U.S. Contractors' Efforts in Iraq," *Washington Post*, June 20, 2003.

12. David R. Baker, "Many Highways in Iraq Lead to Trouble," *San Francisco Chronicle*, Aug. 5, 2003.

13. Theola Labbe, "U.S. Raids in Iraq Net 'Dolphins' among 'Sharks,' " *Washington Post*, Aug. 8, 2003; Jon Lee Anderson, "Iraq's Bloody Summer," *The New Yorker*, Aug. 11, 2003.

14. Anthony Shadid, "Flag Is Flash Point in a Baghdad Slum," *Washington Post*, Aug. 14, 2003.

15. Mark Bowden, *Black Hawk Down: A Study of Modern War* (New York: Grove/Atlantic, 1999).

16. For prominent examples, see Michael C. Williams, *Civil-Military Relations and Peacekeeping*, Adelphi Paper 321 (New York: Oxford University Press, 1998); Bruce R. Pirnie, *Civilians and Soldiers: Achieving Better Coordination* (Santa Monica: RAND, 1998); and Pamela Aall, Daniel Miltenberger and Thomas G. Weiss, *Guide to IGOs, NGOs, and the Military in Peace and Relief Operations* (Washington, D.C.: United States Institute of Peace Press, 2000).

17. Peter Slevin and Dana Priest, "Wolfowitz Concedes Iraq Errors," *Washington Post*, July 24, 2003.

18. Lawrence James, *Imperial Rearguard: Wars of Empire, 1919–85* (New York: Brassey's, 1988), p. 29, 58.

19. Maj. General Sir Charles W. Gwynn, *Imperial Policing* (London: Macmillan, 1934), p. 14.

20. Cpt. Jean-Philippe Lavigne, "NPBG Monitors Pilgrimage of 6,000 to Komusina," *SFOR Informer* no. 120 (Aug. 22, 2001), available at www.nato.int.

21. 1st Lt. Pedro Fernández Vicente, "Arson in Stolac," *SFOR Informer* no. 128 (Dec. 12, 2001), available at www.nato.int.

22. Deutsche Presse-Agentur, May 7, 2001, as reported by the Lexis-Nexis online news service; Cpl. Nicolas Girault, "Second Cornerstone Ceremony," *SFOR Informer* no. 116 (June 27, 2001), available at www.nato.int.

23. Rod Thornton, "The Role of Peace Support Operations Doctrine in the British Army," *International Peacekeeping* 7, no. 2 (Summer 2000): 41–62.

24. Anthony Clayton, " 'Deceptive Might': Imperial Defense and Security, 1900–1968," in *The Oxford History of the British Empire, vol. IV: The Twentieth Century*, ed. Judith M. Brown and Wm. Roger Louis (New York: Oxford, 1999): p. 287.

25. Gwynn, *Imperial Policing*, p. 26.

26. James, *Imperial Rearguard*, p. 65.

27. Ibid., pp. 46–47.

28. Brian McAllister Linn, *Guardians of Empire: The U.S. Army and the Pacific, 1902–1940* (Chapel Hill: University of North Carolina Press, 1997), p. 17.

29. Ibid., pp. 38–45.

30. Douglas Porch, "Bugeaud, Galliéni, Lyautey: The Development of French Colonial Warfare," in *Makers of Modern Strategy from Machiavelli to the Nuclear Age*, ed. Peter Paret et al. (Princeton: Princeton University Press, 1986), p. 388.

31. Ibid., pp. 380–81.

32. James, *Imperial Rearguard*, pp. 70–77; Clayton, *Deceptive Might*, p. 290.

33. Laura Kay Rozen, "New Bosnia Tack: Reward 'Open' Towns," *Christian Science Monitor*, Aug. 1, 1997, and Martin Walker, "EU Rewards Bosnians Who Back Peace," *London Guardian*, Jan. 23, 1998, both as reported by the Lexis/Nexis online news service.

34. Rozen, "New Bosnia Tack," ibid.

35. Sgt. Sean Pollack, "Civil-Military Cooperation: A New Tool for Peacekeepers," *Canadian Military Journal* 1, no. 3 (Aug. 2000), available at *www.journal.dnd.ca*.

36. KFOR Press Update, July 4, 2000, available at www.nato.int; "Serb Convoy Blocked in Eastern Kosovo," Agence France Presse, July 5, 2000, and Richard Mertens, "Nudge Toward Order in Kosovo," *Christian Science Monitor*, July 11, 2000, both as reported in the Lexis/Nexis online news service.

37. Dana Priest, *The Mission: Waging War and Keeping Peace with America's Military* (New York: W. W. Norton, 2003), pp. 289–90.

38. Mertens, "Nudge Toward Order."

39. Dave Clark, "Serbian Enclave Simmers as Escorted Envoy Returns," Agence France Presse, July 7, 2000, as reported by the Lexis/Nexis online news service.

40. Moshe Gershovich, *French Military Rule in Morocco: Colonialism and its Consequences* (London: Frank Cass, 2000), p. 65.

41. Linn, *Guardians of Empire*, p. 45.

42. John L. Cirafici, "SFOR in Bosnia in 1997: A Watershed Year," *Parameters*, Spring 1999: 80–91; "Plavsic Calls for 'Constructive Approach' to Dayton Accords," Agence France Presse, June 3, 1997, "Bosnian Serb President Dismisses Pro-Karadzic Hardliner," Agence France Presse, June 28, 1997, and Bosnian Serb News Agency SRNA, June 28, 1997, as reported by the BBC Summary of World Broadcasts, June 30, 1997, all as reported by Lexis/Nexis online news service.

43. "Bosnian Serb Military to Remain Neutral in Government Crisis," Deutsche Presse-Agentur, July 2, 1997, "President Declares Bosnian Serbs' Parliament Dissolved," Deutsche Presse-Agentur, July 3, 1997, and Jovana Gec, "Parliament

Moves to Oust Bosnian Serb President," Associated Press, July 5, 1997, all as reported by Lexis/Nexis online news service.

44. These events are summarized by Cirafici, "SFOR in Bosnia."

45. Cirafici, "SFOR in Bosnia;" Brig. General (Ret.) David L. Grange, "Task Force Eagle and the Battle of the Buses," *Military Review* 80, no. 2 (Mar./Apr. 2000): 89–91; and Clark, *Waging Modern War*, pp. 92–96.

46. Clayton, "Deceptive Might," pp. 296–98.

47. A. S. Kanya-Forstner, *The Conquest of the Western Sudan: A Study in French Military Imperialism* (Cambridge: Cambridge University Press, 1969), p. 195.

48. Brian McAllister Linn, "Cerberus' Dilemma: The US Army and Internal Security in the Pacific, 1902–1940," in *Guardians of Empire: The Armed Forces of the Colonial Powers, c. 1700–1964* (New York: Manchester University Press, 1999), p. 121.

49. 1st Lt. Luis Sanchez, "Providing Hope: Ambassadors in MND-SE," *SFOR Informer* no. 117 (July 11, 2001) and 2nd Lt. Bruno Ménard, "You Said RRTF?" *SFOR Informer* no. 118 (July 25, 2001), both available at www.nato.int.

50. Sgt. Kerensa Hardy, "PLIP Works to Place Families in Pre-War Homes," *SFOR Informer* no. 116 (June 27, 2001), available at www.nato.int.

51. One example of this is described in detail by Priest, *The Mission*, pp. 372–84.

52. Steven Erlanger, "Torn Mitrovica Reflects West's Trials in Kosovo," *New York Times*, Feb. 27, 2000, as reported in the Lexis/Nexis online news service.

53. Jeffrey Smith, "Serb Mob Confronts U.S. Soldiers," *Washington Post*, Feb. 21, 2000, and Carlotta Gall, "Serbs in Kosovo Town Stone U.S. Troops," *New York Times*, Feb. 21, 2000, both as reported in the Lexis/Nexis online news service.

54. Jeffrey Smith, "NATO, Ethnic Albanians Clash," *Washington Post*, Feb. 22, 2000, as reported in the Lexis/Nexis online news service.

55. Elena Becatoros for AP, "U.S. Troops Seize Weapons on Serb Side of Kosovo City," *Fort Worth Star Telegram*, Feb. 24, 2000, as reported in the Lexis/Nexis online news service.

56. Erlanger, "Torn Mitrovica."

57. AP, "NATO Troops Hurt in Street Fight," *The Australian*, Mar. 9, 2000, as reported in the Lexis/Nexis online news service.

58. Carlotta Gall, "Dozens Wounded as Violence Erupts Anew in Divided Kosovo City," *New York Times*, Mar. 8, 2000, as reported in the Lexis/Nexis online news service.

59. Ivana Sekularac, "Rise of Croat Nationalism Call for Another War," Agence France Presse, Mar. 17, 2001, as reported in the Lexis/Nexis online news service.

60. Ivana Sekularac, "Peacekeepers Will Not Prevent Bosnian-Croatian Deserters from Returning," Agence France Presse, Apr. 12, 2002, as reported in the Lexis/Nexis online news service.

61. "SFOR Urges Bosnian Croats to Remain Loyal to Joint Army," Deutsche Presse-Agentur, Mar. 22, 2001, as reported in the Lexis/Nexis online news service.

62. 1st Lt. Javier Donesteve, "Return to Normality," *SFOR Informer*, May 30, 2001, available at www.nato.int.

63. Roy Gutman with Juliette Terzieff, "Bank Job in a Battle Zone," *Newsweek*, Apr. 30, 2001, as reported in the Lexis/Nexis online news service.

64. John Phillips, "NATO Soldiers Back Bosnian Bank Seizure," *The London Times*, Apr. 7, 2001, as reported in the Lexis/Nexis online press service.

65. "NATO Force Accuses Bosnian Croat Police, Soldiers of Organizing Riots," Agence France Presse, Apr. 11, 2001, as reported in the Lexis/Nexis online news service.

66. Phillips, "NATO Soldiers Back Bosnian Bank Seizure."

67. Gutman with Terzieff, "Bank Job in a Battle Zone."

68. Kanya-Forstner, *Conquest of Western Sudan*.

69. Porch, "Bugeaud, Galliéni, Lyautey."

70. Linn, *Guardians of Empire*, pp. 37–40.

71. Elizabeth M. Cousens, "Building Peace in Bosnia," in *Peacebuilding as Politics : Cultivating Peace in Fragile Societies*, ed. Cousens and Chetan Kumar, with Karin Wermester (Boulder, CO: Lynne Reiner, 2000), pp. 113-52; and Michael J. Dziedzic and Andrew Bair, "Bosnia and the International Police Task Force," in *Policing the New World Disorder: Peace Operations and Public Security*, ed. Robert B. Oakley et al. (Washington, D.C.: National Defense University Press, 2002), available at www.ndu.edu/inss.

72. Dziedzic and Bair, ibid.

73. Bruce R. Pirnie, *Civilians and Soldiers: Achieving Better Coordination* (Santa Monica: RAND, 1998), p. 74.

74. "Bosnian Serb Police Complete Evacuation in Banja Luka," Deutsche Presse-Agentur, May 7, 2001, as reported in the Lexis-Nexis online news service.

75. Quoted in Cpl. Sébastien Pisani, "Reconciliation Stumbles over a Stone," *SFOR Informer* no. 113 (May 16, 2001), available at www.nato.int.

76. Capt. Nicolas Girault, "Second Cornerstone Ceremony," *SFOR Informer*, June 27, 2001, available at www.nato.int.

77. Off-the-record interview, NATO HQ, Brussels, Belgium, conducted by the author in January 2002.

78. Off-the-record interview, NATO SHAPE (Supreme Headquarters of Allied Powers in Europe), Mons, Belgium, conducted by the author in January 2002.

79. Off-the-record interview, SHAPE, conducted by the author in January 2002.

80. Gutman with Terzieff, "Bank Job in a Battle Zone."

81. Priest, *The Mission*, p. 352.

82. Colin Soloway, "US Troops Hand Over TV Station to Karadzic," *London Daily Telegraph*, Sept. 3, 1997, and Colin Nickerson, "Hostility on All Fronts," *Boston Globe*, Sept. 8, 1997, both as reported in the Lexis/Nexis online news service.

83. Nickerson, "Hostility on All Fronts." For the official Pentagon view which does not mention any directive, see "DOD News Briefing," M2 Presswire, Sept. 3, 1997, as reported in the Lexis/Nexis online news service.

84. Off-the-record interview with two International Military Staff officers at NATO HQ, and with a knowledgeable civilian staff member at SHAPE, Belgium, conducted by the author in Jan. 2002.

85. Pollack, "Civil-Military Cooperation."

86. Off-the-record interview with a knowledgeable American military officer deployed in Kosovo at that time, New York, conducted by the author in Aug. 2001.

87. Mertens, "Nudge Toward Order in Kosovo."

88. Spc. Marshall Thompson, "Brig. General David Presents New Trucks to City of Strpce," *Falcon Flier* (newsletter of KFOR U.S. Task Force Falcon), Aug. 1, 2001, available at www.tffalcon.hqusareur.army.mil.

89. John Rollins, "Operational Models of Civil-Military Cooperation: Possibilities and Limitations," *Humanitarian Exchange* (magazine of the Humanitarian Practice Network) no. 19 (Sept. 2001): 54.

90. James Cotton, "Against the Grain: The East Timor Intervention," *Survival* 43, no. 1 (Spring 2001): 138.

91. Alan Castle, Australian Contingent Commander of the UNAMET police force, interviewed by Rob Long, "On the Ground in East Timor: The State of Law and Order," *St. Mark's Review* no. 180 (Summer 2000): 13; and Bob Breen, *Mission Accomplished East Timor: The Australian Defence Force Participation in INTERFET* (Crows Nest, NSW: Allen and Unwin Australia, 2000), p. 48. Good descriptions of the history of Indonesian recruitment and training of local East Timorese forces are provided by John Martinkus, *A Dirty Little War* (Victoria: Random House Australia, 2001), passim.

92. Alan Ryan, *Primary Responsibilities and Primary Risks: Australian Defence Force Participation in the International Force East Timor*, Study Paper 304 (Duntroon, ACT: Australian Land Warfare Studies Center, 2000), pp. 39–60. Also see *East Timor in Transition, 1998–2000: An Australian Policy Challenge* (Canberra: Department of Foreign Affairs and Trade, 2001), pp. 134–39, and Breen, *Mission Accomplished East Timor*, pp. 160–61.

93. P. J. Cosgrove, "Complex Questions: A Commander's Perspective," *Royal United Services Institute (RUSI) Journal* (London) 146, no. 1 (Feb. 2001): 31–35; Ryan, *Primary Responsibilities and Primary Risks*, pp. 63–66.

94. Ryan, Primary Responsibilities and Primary Risks, p. 85; John Crawford and Glyn Harper, *Operation East Timor: The New Zealand Defence Force in East Timor, 1999–2001* (Auckland: Reed, 2002), pp. 22–24, 43–44.

95. Ryan, *Primary Responsibilities and Primary Risks*, pp. 102–3.

96. Ibid., p. 95.

97. This was mentioned to the author in several off-the-record interviews with current and retired high-ranking officers having command roles in peace operations, Australia, Feb.–Mar. 2002. See Lt. Col. Neil C. Smith, *Mostly Unsung: Australia and the Commonwealth in the Malayan Emergency, 1948–1960* (Melbourne: Mostly Unsung Military History Research and Publications, 1989), esp. p. 29; and Michael Evans, *Forward from the Past: The Development of Australian Army Doctrine, 1972-Present*, Study Paper 301 (Duntroon, ACT: Australian Land Warfare Studies Center, 1999), pp. 5–7.

98. Breen, *Mission Accomplished East Timor*, p. 53.

99. Evans, *Forward from the Past*. I am grateful to Alan Ryan for elucidating this linkage for me.

100. Off-the-record interview, Canberra, Australia, conducted by the author in Mar. 2002.

101. Off-the-record interview, Canberra, conducted by the author in Mar. 2002.

102. Cheryl M. Lee Kim and Mark Metrikas, "Holding a Fragile Peace: The Military and Civilian Components of UNTAC," in *Keeping the Peace: Multidimensional UN Operations in Cambodia and El Salvador*, ed. Michael W. Doyle, Ian Johnstone and Robert C. Orr (New York: Cambridge University Press, 1997), pp. 119–20; John Sanderson, "UNTAC: Successes and Failures," in *International Peacekeeping: Building on the Cambodian Experience*, ed. Hugh Smith (Canberra: Australian Defence Studies Center, 1994), pp. 19–25.

103. Off-the-record interviews with three officers who served in UNITAF, conducted by the author in Canberra, Mar. 2002.

104. Lt. Cmdr. Steve Dunning and Barbara Reis, "East Timor Transition Begins," Australian Defence Public Affairs Organization statement, available at http://pandora.nla.gov.au/parchive.

105. Ryan, *Primary Responsibilities and Primary Risks*, p. 112; Jarat Chopra, "The UN's Kingdom of East Timor," *Survival* 42, no. 3 (Aut. 2000): 27–39.

6. Security as a Step to Peace

1. Available at http://www.un.org/peace/reports/peace_operations/

2. For prominent examples covering a variety of issues, see Michael Barnett, *Eyewitness to a Genocide: The United Nations and Rwanda* (Ithaca: Cornell University Press, 2002); Max Boot, *The Savage Wars of Peace: Small Wars and the Rise of American Power* (New York: Basic Books, 2002); Report of the International Commission on Intervention and State Sovereignty, *The Responsibility to Protect* (Ottawa: International Development Research Centre, 2001); Ramesh Thakur and Albrecht Schnabel, *United Nations Peacekeeping Operations: Ad Hoc Missions, Permanent Engagement* (New York: United Nations Press, 2001); and Bob Shacochis, *The Immaculate Invasion* (New York: Penguin, 1999)

3. Eric Schmitt, "2 U.S. Officials Liken Guerrillas to Renegade Postwar Nazi Units," *New York Times*, Aug. 26, 2003.

4. Earl F. Ziemke, *The U.S. Army in the Occupation of Germany, 1944–46* (Washington, D.C.: US Army Center of Military History, 1990), pp. 354–55, 437–38.

5. James Dobbins, et al., *America's Role in Nation-Building from Germany to Iraq* (Santa Monica: RAND, 2003), p. 21.

6. John W. Dower, *Embracing Defeat: Japan in the Wake of World War II* (New York: W. W. Norton, 1999).

7. Ziemke, *The U.S. Army in the Occupation of Germany*.

8. Dobbins, et al., *America's Role in Nation-Building*, pp. 9–10.

9. George W. Bush, "The National Security Strategy of the United States of America," Sept. 2002, available at http://www.whitehouse.gov/nsc/nss.pdf.

10. Mark Thompson and Michael Duffy, "Is the Army Stretched Too Thin?" *Time*, Sept 1, 2003.

11. For an excellent discussion of how this applies to questions of coercive diplomacy and nontraditional military operations, see Barry M. Blechman and Tamara Cofman Wittes, "Defining Moment: The Threat and Use of Force in Amer-

ican Foreign Policy since 1989," in *International Conflict Resolution after the Cold War*, ed. Paul C. Stern and Daniel Druckman (Washington, D.C.: National Academy Press, 2000), pp. 90–122.

12. See Dana Priest, *The Mission: Waging War and Keeping Peace with America's Military* (New York: W.W. Norton, 2003).

13. Kimberly Marten Zisk, *Engaging the Enemy: Organization Theory and Soviet Military Innovation* (Princeton: Princeton University Press, 1993).

14. Steven Kull and I. M. Destler, *Misreading the Public: The Myth of a New Isolationism* (Washington, DC: Brookings, 1999), pp. 81–112; James Burk, "Public Support for Peacekeeping in Lebanon and Somalia: Assessing the Casualties Hypothesis," *Political Science Quarterly* 114, no. 1 (Spring 1999): 53–78.

15. Kimberly Zisk Marten, "Defending against Anarchy: From War to Peacekeeping in Afghanistan," *The Washington Quarterly* 26, no. 1 (Winter 2002/3): 35–52.

16. Thomas Hobbes, *Leviathan*, ed. C.B. Macpherson (New York: Penguin, 1977).

17. See Ivo H. Daalder and James M. Lindsay, *America Unbound: The Bush Revolution in Foreign Policy* (Washington, D.C.: Brookings, 2003).

18. Marten, "Defending against Anarchy."

19. Jeffrey Herbst, "Responding to State Failure in Africa," *International Security* 21, no. 3 (Winter 1996/7): 120–44.

20. Chaim Kaufmann, "Possible and Impossible Solutions to Ethnic Civil Wars," *International Security* 20, no. 4 (Spring 1996): 136–75.

21. "Challenge for UN Force in Timor Leste," *New Straits Times*, Aug. 16, 2003, as reported in the Lexis/Nexis Academic Universe online news service.

22. Leslie H. Gelb, "The Three-State Solution," *New York Times*, Nov. 25, 2003.

INDEX

Afghanistan: British imperial troops in, 57; complex peacekeeping operations in, goals of, 5; multilateral peacekeeping force in, 3, 158; NATO forces in, 95, 158; security-keeping, as model for, 160–161; security situation, summer 2002, 93–95; UN intervention in, 146; U.S. unilateral peacekeeping in, 12
Afigbo A. E., 57
Africa, 73, 86–87, 151
African-American lobbying groups, 76
aid. *See* humanitarianism
Aideed, Mohammed, 29
air control (aerial carpet bombing), 126
air strikes, NATO, in Bosnia and Herzegovina, 46
airport security, 1
al Qaeda terrorist network, 48
Albanians, ethnic, in Kosovo, 22, 50, 78
Algeria, 125
Allard, Kenneth, 29
American Jewish Committee, 177n56
American Jewish Congress, 177n56
Amritsar massacre, 175n17
anarchy, effects of, 155
Annan, Kofi A., 27, 36, 37, 90, 120
Annex 1A (of Dayton Accords), 49
Annex 10 (of Dayton Accords), 47
Anti-Defamation League, 177n56
Apocalypse Now (Coppola), 108–109

Aracinovo, Macedonia, 114–118
Aristide, Jean-Bertrand, 41, 75–76
armed soldiers, citizens, psychological effects on, 2
Army Reserve troops (U.S.), 104
Army (U.S.), 153
ASEAN (Association of South East Asian Nations), 140
Ashdown, Paddy, 83
Association of South East Asian Nations (ASEAN), 140
Australia: Australian Defence Forces, 123, 142–143, 152; Australian Federal Police, 112; defense policy, 79; East Timor and, 19, 53, 79–80; INTERFET, role in, 123, 140–143
Avant, Deborah, 113

Baghdad, Iraq, 96
balance of power politics, 61
Balkans: international oversight of, 14; multilateralism in, problems of, 122–123; politicians, military support for, 127–129; rewards and sanctions in, 126–127; riot control, 124–125; U.S. military activities in, 106–107. *See also* Bosnia and Herzegovina; Kosovo; Macedonia; NATO
Ballard, John, 44
Ballentine, Karen, 9

Index compiled by Fred Leise

Banja Luka, Bosnia and Herzegovina, 124, 129, 135–136
Bank Hercegovacka, 132–133, 136–137, 156
Basra, Iraq, 119, 120
Bellamy, Christopher, 110
benign colonialism, 37–38
Berlin Conference General Act, 86–87
BiH. *See* Bosnia and Herzegovina
Bijeljina, Bosnia and Herzegovina, 137–138
Bismarck, Otto von, 86
Black Hawk Down (Bowden), 30
blue box activities, 137
Boot, Max, 7, 16
border control, 161
boredom, in early peacekeeping operations, 26
Bosnia and Herzegovina (BiH), 46–50; Banja Luka, 124, 129, 135–136; Bijeljina, 137–138; Croatian independence movement, 132–133; ethnic evictions, 130; future of, 57, 58; government, 47, 48; humanitarian efforts in, 83–85; Ignatieff on intervention in, 7; international oversight of, 14; Komusina, 124; Kotor Varos, 126, 138; lessons learned in, 156; liberal international community's beliefs about, 47; Little Bosnia (Mitrovica), 131; minority returns, 85; NATO intervention in, 78; oversight of, philosophical contradiction in, 49; peacekeeping operations in, 5, 45–50; peacekeeping operations in, context of, 40–41; politicians, NATO military support for, 127–129; Sarajevo, 48, 134–135; sovereignty issues, 45, 91; Srebrenica, ethnic massacre in, 32–33; Stolac, 124; U.S. activities in, 104, 106–107
Bosniacs (Bosnian Muslims), 46–47, 124
Boutros-Ghali, Boutros, 33–34
Bowden, Mark, 30
Brahimi, Lakhdar, 27
Brahimi Report ("Report of the Panel on United Nations Peace Operations," United Nations), 4–5, 27, 148
Bremer, L. Paul, III, 119
Britain. *See* Great Britain
Bush, George W., 75, 151
Bush Administration, 3, 14–15, 15, 149, 158–159

Cambodia, 28, 76, 156
Camp Able Sentry (Macedonia), 115, 117
Camp Bondsteel (Kosovo), 115, 117
Canada, 25, 26, 84–85, 110

Canadian International Development Agency (CIDA), 84–85
carbinieri (Italy), 111
carpet bombing, aerial, 126
casualties, acceptance of, 154
Cédras, Raoul, 76
Central Intelligence Agency, 118
Chandler, David, 49–50
change, local ownership of, 10
Chapter 7 (UN Charter), missions authorized under, 48, 51, 53, 55
Chechnya, 36
Chesterman, Simon, 52
China, 88, 89
Chopra, Jarat, 37, 54–55
Christian missionaries, 74
Churchill, Winston, 126
CIDA (Canadian International Development Agency), 84–85
civic liberalism, 70–71, 81
civil affairs officers, 103
civil conflicts: Cambodia, 28–29; Rwanda, 30–32; Somalia, 29–30; UN involvement in, 26–27. *See also* Bosnia and Herzegovina (BiH)
civil-military coordination (CIMIC), 84, 126, 138
civilian police, 112
civilizations, clash of, 73
civilizing missions, 74
Clark, Wesley K., 135
clash of civilizations, 73
class, as means of social control in colonialism, 63
Clinton, Bill, 82, 103
Coalition Provisional Authority (Iraq), 120
coalitions of the willing, 102, 122
Cohen, Eliot, 114
cold war, 81
colonial control. *See under* foreign control
colonial military actions, 62
colonial territories. *See* colonies
colonialism: arbitrary violence and, 101; benign, 37–38; characteristics of, 64; class and, 63; colonial governors, 18; decline during twentieth century, 68; dependency and, 8; economics of, 67, 72, 86, 96–97
—GOVERNORSHIP ACTIVITIES: enforced demographic change, 129–130; politicians, support of, 127; rewards and sanctions, 125–126; great powers' national security goals and, 66; humanitarianism of, 16; inattention in, costs of, 98–101; justifications for, 70, 71; misfits in colonial service, 99; outside control of

sovereignty as, 52; paternalism of, 87; riot control, 124–125;

— AND PEACEKEEPING (See also peacekeeping): commonalities, 64–66; comparisons, 15–16; differences, 62–64; political will, great powers' lack of, 147; similarities, 38. See also colonies; foreign control; imperialism; occupations; sovereignty

colonies: change in great powers' attitude to, 69; Christian missionaries in, 74; control of, 71–73; development, lack of attention to, 99; economic development, 69, 74; educational systems, 73; governance, 68; resources. See also colonialism; sovereignty

complex military peacekeeping, 33–37

complex peacekeeping operations: control of, as basis for, 18; evolution of, in 1990s, 21–58; foreign societies, goals, 4, 5; humanitarianism and, 81–85; international legitimacy, bases for, 12; military tasks, similarities to colonial era, 123–124; moral dilemma of, 13; motivations for, 34, 38, 80; multiple multilateralisms in, 10; need for, 5–6; nonpriority of, 101–104; Owen on, 6; political will in, lack of, 97; problems of, 41, 82; successful instances, 38; U.S. military's view on, 45. See also colonialism, and peacekeeping; complex military peacekeeping; national self-interest; political will, and security; security-keeping

Congo, 26

consistency in complex peacekeeping operations. See political will

Contact Group (U.S., Great Britain, France, Germany, Italy, Russia), 46–47, 50

control. See foreign control

Coppola, Francis Ford, 108–109

cordon and search missions, 108, 109

Cosgrove, Peter, 141

Cote d'Ivoire, 182n20

Council of Ministers (Bosnia and Herzegovina), 48

Coxhead, Andrew, 136

Crawford, Neta, 38

Croat Democratic Union (HDZ) party, 132

Croatia, 39–40, 46–47

Croatian independence movement, 132–133

Curtin, Philip D., 66, 72

Dallaire, Romeo, 31

David, William C., 116–117, 139

Davis, Lance E., 67, 68

Dayton Accords (General Framework Agreement for Peace, GFAP), 46–47, 49, 91, 127–129

democracy, in Philippines, emergence of, 63

democratic imperialists, 159

democratic international community. See international community

democratic states, nonliberalism, possibility of, 23

demographic change, enforced, 129–133

Department for International Development (DFID) (Great Britain), 84–85

deployment gap, 112

DFID (Department for International Development) (Great Britain), 84–85

Dili, East Timor, 53, 56

displaced people. See refugees

Displaced Persons Property Law Implementation Plan, 130

Dodson, Michael, 132

Doyle, Michael W., 6, 37–38, 66, 72

Drljaca, Simo, 128

Duvall, Robert, 108

Dziedzic, Michael, 112

East Timor (Timor Leste), 53–56; complex peacekeeping operations in, goals of, 5l; economic hardships, 55–56; foreign control in, 54–55; future of, 57, 58; Indonesian sovereignty over, 79; Indonesia's actions in, 53; liberal democratic peacekeeping operations in, failure of, 14; peacekeeping operations in, context of, 40–41; role in intervention in, 19; social system, 55; UN withdrawal from, 164. See also Australia; INTERFET

Eastern Slavonia model, 39–41

economic aid policies, as rewards and sanctions, 126

economic development in colonies, 69, 74

economics of colonialism, 67, 72, 86, 96–97

educational systems, colonial, 73

empire, definition of, 6

enforced demographic change, 129–133

ethics, national interests and, 65

ethnic cleansing, 78. See also genocide

ethnic separatism, 24

EU (European Union), 45, 51, 84, 115

European Commission, 84

European Union (EU), 45, 51, 84, 115

evacuation missions, 142

Evans, Mark, 142

FADH (Force Armée d'Haiti), 76
Faidherbe, Louis, 72–73
fear, role in keeping order, 39–40
Feaver, Peter, 113–114
Feith, Douglas, 14
Feith, Peter, 115–116
flash a red card (political refusal of NATO orders), 136–137
force, 35–36, 124–125
Force Armée d'Haiti (FADH), 76
force protection, 106, 137
foreign control: as characteristic of colonialism and complex peacekeeping operations, 146–147; class and, in colonialism, 63; colonial, 66–70, 70–74; complex peacekeeping operations as basis for, 17; dilemma of, 56–58; humanitarian peacekeeping missions and, 92; institutionalization of, 73; international law and justification of, 85–91; liberalism vs., 49; NATO's, of BiH society, 129; political, 65, 71–73; psychological, 72; self-determination vs., 52; of sovereignty, as colonialism, 52; of territory, great powers and, 68. See also colonialism; great powers; sovereignty; individual countries
France: Africa, goals in, 73; colonial army, problems of lines of control of, 133–134; colonial rewards and sanctions, 125; colonialism, 60, 71, 86; colonies, inattention to, 98–101; in Haiti, 161; Iraq and, 90, 119–120, 146; Morocco, activities in, 127; NATO plan in Balkans, reluctance to follow, 137; Sudan, activities in, 129–130; as UN Security Council P-5 member, 88
Front for Haitian Advancement and Progress (FRAPH), 76

Gardez, Afghanistan, 93
Gelb, Leslie, 162
gendarmerie (France), 111
General Framework Agreement for Peace (GFAP) (Dayton Accords), 46–47, 49, 91, 127–129
genocide, 30–32
Germany, 40, 84, 112, 149–151
GFAP (General Framework Agreement for Peace) (Dayton Accords), 46–47, 49, 91, 127–129
Gong, Gerrig, 73
good will, colonialism and, 69
Gore, Al, 75
governorships, temporary military, 40
Great Britain: Afghanistan, peacekeeping operations in, 94; Australian cooperative security arrangement with, 141; colonial actions, moral justifications for, 71; colonialism, 57, 60, 86; colonies, inattention to, 98–101; Department for International Development (DFID), 84–85; empire, economic analysis of, 67; India, riot control in, 124; Iraq, troops in, 119, 120; Malaya, forced relocations in, 129; military, 109, 110, 124–125; as UN Security Council P-5 member, 88
great powers (United States, Great Britain, France): colonial policy, political choices shaping, 65; colonialism, 66, 133–134; colonies, changing attitudes toward, 68–69; competition among, 66, 67–68; humanitarianism, 70; peace operations, control of, 88–90; rewards and sanctions, 125; United Nations, domination of, 88–90. See also colonialism; France; Great Britain; international community; United States
green box activities, 137
Gusmao, Xanana, 54

Haiti, 41–45; complex peacekeeping operations in (1994), goals of, 5; future, 58; instability, history of, 41–42; judicial institutions, 44; lessons learned in, 156; liberal democratic military peacekeeping operations in, 13; peacekeeping operations in, context of, 40–41; police, citizen's avoidance of, 43–44; security-keeping, as model for, 161; social problems, 44–45; UN intervention in, 146; U.S. activities in, 41, 42, 75–77, 83, 106, 177n55
HDZ (Croat Democratic Union) party, 132
hearts and minds campaigns, 73, 100, 142
helicopters, in peacekeeping operations, 120–121
Herbst, Jeffrey, 162
High Representative (HR), 47–49, 83. See also Office of the High Representative (OHR)
Hillier, Rick, 136
Hobbes, Thomas, 157
Holocaust Memorial Museum (U.S.), 177n56
Human Rights Chamber (Bosnia and Herzegovina), 48
human rights violations, 62, 64
humanitarianism: Afghanistan, aid to, 94; aid decisions, multilateralism and, 138–139; aid delivery, 124, 139, 142; colonial control and, 70–74; of colonial imperialism, 16; colonialism, as domes-

tic justification for, 70; complex peace-keeping operations and, 81–85; of great powers, 70; interventions, goals of, 18; limits of, 75–81; in nineteenth-century international agreements, 86–87; in peacekeeping era, 61; as political control, 72; religious support for, 71
Huntington, Samuel P., 110–111
Huttenback, Robert A., 67, 68
Hutus, in Rwanda, 30–31

IFOR (implementation force), 49, 134, 135
Ignatieff, Michael, 7, 16
impartiality of peacekeepers, 29, 31, 32, 33
imperial soldiers, tasks of, 17
imperial states. See great powers
imperialism, 6–8, 9, 60. See also colonialism; great powers
implementation force (IFOR), 49, 134, 135
inconsistency in complex peacekeeping operations, 10. See also political will, and security
India, 25, 29, 57, 119–120, 124, 146
indirect rule in colonialism, 72
Indonesia. See under East Timor
induced consent, 37
information technology, 151
INTERFET (International Force in East Timor), 7, 53–54, 102, 123, 140–143. See also East Timor (Timor Leste)
international community: Afghanistan, approach to problems in, 94–95; and Bosnia and Herzegovina, 47, 48, 49; civil conflicts, views on, 27; complex peacekeeping operations, goals of, 5–6, 23; East Timor, actions in, 54; foreign interventions, 35, 36–37; Haiti, actions in, 41–45; humanitarian control of foreign territory, dilemma of, 56–58; induced consent, use of, 37; international security, views on, 38; Kosovo, intervention in, 49, 51–52; military force, use of, 23–24; multilateralism, problems of, 133; political will, lack of, 157. See also great powers; multilateralism
International Criminal Tribunal for the Former Yugoslavia, 128
International Force in East Timor (INTERFET), 7, 53–54, 102, 123, 140–143. See also East Timor (Timor Leste)
international law: African sovereignty and, 87; Berlin Conference General Act, 86; and foreign control, justification of, 85–91; national self-interest and, 90; power structure of, 91; two-tiered sys-

tem of, 88–89; and UN Security Council, 88–90
international police missions, 112–113
International Police Monitors (IPMs), 42, 43
International Police Task Force (IPTF), 135
international political system, 81
International Security Assistance Force (ISAF), 94
International War Crimes Tribunal for Yugoslavia, 129
investment, colonial humanitarianism and, 74
IPMs (International Police Monitors), in Haiti, 42, 43
IPTF (International Police Task Force), 135
Iraq: complex peacekeeping operations in, goals of, 5; as democracy, U.S. interests in, 155; dispute over intervention in, 90; Marsh Arabs, 126; multinational peacekeeping force in, 3, 12; new government, 160; occupation, cost of, 120; security situation, post-Saddam, 96; UN intervention in, 146; U.S. and, 12, 13, 15, 104, 119–121
ISAF (International Security Assistance Force), 94
Italy, 40

Jackson, Robert H., 87
Jakobsen, Peter Viggo, 104
Jammu and Kashmir (Indian province), 57
Janowitz, Morris, 111
Japan, 149–151
JCS (Joint Chiefs of Staff) (U.S.), 103
Jelavic, Ante, 48, 132
Jewish-American lobbying groups, 78
Joint Chiefs of Staff (JCS) (U.S.), 103
judicial institutions, 44, 48, 55, 160, 161–162

Kabul, Afghanistan, 94
Kamenica, Kosovo, 126–127
Karzai, Hamid, 95, 160
Kaufmann, Chaim, 162
KFOR (Kosovo Peacekeeping Force), 51, 115, 130–131, 135
Khalilzad, Zalmay, 160
Khmer Rouge, 28
Khost, Afghanistan, 93–94
Kinzer, Joseph W., 42
KLA (Kosovo Liberation Army), 115
Klein, Jacques Paul, 39, 137–138, 141
Komusina, Bosnia and Herzegovina, 124
Kosovo: Albanians in, 22, 50, 78; Camp Bondsteel, 115, 117; complex peace

Kosovo (*continued*)
keeping operations in, goals of, 5; ethnic integration, U.S. interests in, 155; ethnic separatism, 23–24; forced relocations in, 130; future of, 57, 58; international oversight of, 14; international peacekeeping operations in, 50–52; international protectorate, status as, 52; Kamenica, 126–127; lessons learned in, 156; Mitrovica, 107–108, 130–132, 137, 155, 156; NATO intervention in, 78–79; peacekeeping operations in, context of, 40–41; Podgorce, 22; Serbs in, 22, 50; sovereignty, 45, 91; Strpce, 126, 127, 138–139; UN intervention in, 145–146; U.S. military activities in, 108; U.S.-Russian cooperation in, 127; Vitina, 21–22
Kosovo Liberation Army (KLA), 115
Kosovo Liberation Front, 127
Kosovo Peacekeeping Force (KFOR), 51, 115, 130–131, 135
Kotor Varos, Bosnia and Herzegovina, 126, 138
Kuwait, 104

Laughland, John, 7
law. *See* international law; rule of law
League of Nations mandate system, 87
legal systems, 44, 48, 55, 160, 161–162
liberal democracies: colonialism of, 16; foreign control and, 146–147; imperialism, reasons for, 6; military peacekeeping operations, 13–14, 24; peacekeeping, difficulties with, 117, 118; security interests, 18; successful foreign operations, lack of political will for, 17. *See also* France; Great Britain; international community; United States; western liberal values
liberal democratic international community. *See* international community
liberal democratic society, 9, 11
liberal international community. *See* international community
liberal states. *See* liberal democracies
liberalism. *See* liberal democracies; western liberal values
Liberia, 151
Little Bosnia (Mitrovica), 131
lobbying groups, 76, 78
loya jirga (grand council, Afghanistan), 95
Lyautey, Louis-Hubert, 127

Macedonia, 78–79, 114–118
Mackenzie, Lewis, 26
Malaya, 129

man-on-the-spotism, 99, 148
Manila, Philippines, 62
Marines (U.S.), 45
Marsh Arabs, 126
Marshall Plan, 150
Martin, Lisa L., 9
Mazar-e-Sharif, Afghanistan, 93
Meille, Robert, 137
military: colonies, inattention to, 98–99; doctrinal innovation, need for, 153–154; imperial soldiers, tasks of, 17; military police (MPs), 111–112; occupation duties, view of, 152; peacekeeping operations, effects on, 17; U.S., post-September 11 presence in, 2. *See also* complex military peacekeeping; Peacekeeping activities; United States, military
Military-Technical Agreement, 51
Mill, John Stuart, 37–38
Millennium Report (Annan), 90
Milosevic, Slobodan, 40, 50, 51
Mindanao, Philippines, 62
minority returns, 85
mise en valeur (improvement of colonies), 69
Mitchell, Timothy, 73
Mitrovica, Kosovo, 107–108, 130–132, 137, 155, 156
MNB(E) (Multinational Brigade East), 126, 127
MNF (Multinational Force), 42
models: for complex peacekeeping operations, 39–41; for occupations, 149–151; for peacekeeping operations, 19, 158–164; security-keeping, 160–161, 162–163
Mogadishu, Somalia, 30, 105, 106, 120
Morocco, 127
MPs (military police), 111–112
multilateralism: and Australia in INTERFET, 140–143; difficulties of, 8–13, 19, 122, 133–134, 143–144; difficulties of, solutions for, 157–158; and humanitarian aid decisions, 138–139; Martin on, 9; and troops for policing, 134–138; U.S. and, 121, 145–146. *See also* international community
Multinational Brigade East (MNB[E]), 126, 127
Multinational Force (MNF), 42
Muslin/Croat Federation, 47

Nadelman, Ethan A., 87
National Guard (U.S.), 1, 104
national interests. *See* national self-interest
national security, 65–66

National Security Council Deputies Committee (U.S.), 103

National Security Strategy (Bush), 151

national self-interest: in Balkan peacekeeping operations, 77–79; colonial control and, 66–70; complex peacekeeping and, 74–81; in East Timorese peacekeeping operations, 79–80; ethics and, 65; in Haitian peacekeeping operations, 75–77; humanitarianism and, 70–74, 81–82; international law and, 90; in peacekeeping operations, summary of, 80–81. *See also* political will, and security

NATO: in Afghanistan, 12, 95, 158; in Bosnia and Herzegovina, 46, 78, 127–129; in Kosovo, 78–79; in Macedonia, 115–116; orders, political refusal of, 136–137; in Yugoslavia, 32, 51

— IN BALKANS, 123–138; enforced demographic change, 130–133; intervention in, 77–79; multilateralism, problems of, 134–138; politicians, support for, 127–129; rewards and sanctions, 126–127; riot control, 124–125

new empire builders, 14

New York City, 1–2

New Zealand, 141

NGOs (nongovernmental organizations), 83, 122, 138–139, 141, 144

Northern Ireland, 110

occupations: colonial, 69–70, 71–72, 133–134; Germany, 149–151; Iraq, cost of, 120; Japan, 149–151; length of, 41; models for, 149–151; Philippines' resistance to, 62; progressive, 125; by U.S., 42, 120. *See also* foreign control; sovereignty

Office of the High Representative (OHR), 47–49, 91, 130, 136

O'Neill, Barry, 89

ONUC (United Nations Operation in Congo), 26, 168n8

Open Cities program, 84, 126, 138

Opération des Nations Unies au Congo (ONUC), 26, 168n8

Operation Essential Harvest, 116

Organization for Security and Cooperation in Europe (OSCE), 45, 50, 78

Owen, Robert C., 6

P-5 members (UN Security Council), 36, 88–89

pacification campaigns, 61

Pakistan, 57

paramilitary forces, in Bosnia and Herzegovina, 46

Paris, Roland, 9

PDDs (Presidential Decision Directives), 82, 103–104

peace-building, 27

peace enforcement. *See* peacekeeping

peace maintenance operations. *See* complex peacekeeping operations

peace process, local ownership of, 10–11

peacekeepers: impartiality, 29, 31, 32, 33; military tasks, similarities to colonialism, 16; tasks, 17, 26

peacekeeping: as colonial heritage, 60; failures, 29–30, 31–32; imperialism, differences from, 61; initial conceptualization of, 25; peacekeeping fatigue, 14; political change and, 37–39; term, use of, 168n2; as war-fighting, 33. *See also* colonialism, and peacekeeping; complex peacekeeping operations; military, peacekeeping activities; peacekeeping operations; security-keeping; United Nations, peacekeeping missions

— ACTIVITIES: appropriate tasks, 152–155, 156; colonial era, similarities to, 123–124; colonial humanitarianism, role in, 73; enforced demographic change, 129–130; multiple roles, 23; nontraditional duties, 59–60, 141–142; policing, professionalism and, 109–113; policing activities and, 104–105; policing duties, reward system and, 113–114, 152, 154; political outcomes, influencing of, 3–4, 23; politicians, support of, 127; promotions, conquest and, 100; rewards and sanctions, 125–126; riot control, 124–125; in UN operations, coordination problems, 34

— OPERATIONS: colonial military actions, differences from, 62; evolution of, 24–27; future interventions, 164–165; lack of priority on, costs of, 101–104; limiting goals of, 155–157; models for, 19, 158–164; multilateralism of, 64; purposes, 12; sovereignty vs., 90–91; UN control of, 34. *See also* complex peacekeeping operations; military, peacekeeping activities; United Nations, peacekeeping missions

Permanent Five members (United Nations Security Council), 36, 88–89

Petritsch, Wolfgang, 132, 136

Philippines: forced relocations in, 130; political reforms, 63; social structure, 63; U.S. and, 60, 62–64, 125, 127, 130, 134

Philpott, Daniel, 70–71, 80

Plavsic, Biljana, 128–129, 137

Podgorce, Kosovo, 22
policing duties: dangers of, 97; importance,
need for recognition of, 114; in Iraq,
120; military professionalism and,
109–113; military reward system and,
113–114, 152, 154; military's view of,
152; successful, requirements for, 107;
U.S. military and, 43, 104–109; use of
troops for, 134–138
political change, 37–39, 42. *See also* regime
change
political control, 65, 71–73. *See also* foreign control
political development, security and, 96
political favoritism, 63
political sovereignty, 11. *See also* foreign
control; sovereignty
political transformation, 18
political will: fickleness, 118; importance,
34; lack of, 146–149; military peacekeeping duties and, 152–153
—AND SECURITY, 93–118; in Afghanistan,
93–95; in Aracinovo, 114–118; and
colonial inattention, 98–101; in Iraq,
93–95; military professionalism and,
109–113; military reward system and,
113–114; peacekeeping operations, costs
of lack of priority on, 101–104; U.S. and
policing, 104–109
Poplasen, Nikolai, 48
Porch, Douglas, 125
positive sovereignty, 87
Powell, Colin, 120
Powell Doctrine, 153
Presidential Decision Directives (PDDs),
82, 103–104
Priest, Dana, 108, 109, 113
private trading companies, 68
progressive occupation, 125

Rambouillet peace agreement, 50–51
Ramos-Horta, José, 54
RAND Corporation, 150
raw materials, importance of access to,
67–68
refugees: Balkan, 78, 84; Bosnia and
Herzegovina, return to, 47; Haitian,
76–77; minority returns, 85; Open Cities
program, 84, 126, 138; as political
problem, 80; under security-keeping
model, 163
regime change, 15
relocations, forced, 129
"Report of the Panel on United Nations
Peace Operations" (Brahimi Report,
United Nations), 4–5, 27, 148

Republic of Somaliland, 169n18
Republica Srpska, 47, 48, 128–129
reserve troops, 104
Resolution (UN Security Council), 41
rewards and sanctions, 125–127
riot control, 124–125
Rollins, John, 139
Roosevelt, Theodore, 62
Royal Canadian Mounted Police, 112
Ruggie, John Gerard, 9
rule of law, 48
Rumsfeld, Donald, 116
Russia, 51, 89, 90. *See also* Soviet Union
Rwanda, 30–32, 75, 78, 82
Ryan, Alan, 140

Sadr City, Iraq, 120
sanctions, rewards and, 125–127
Sanderson, John, 28, 142
Sarajevo, Bosnia and Herzegovina, 48,
134–135
Saudi Arabia, 178n77
Schmidl, Erwin A., 26
security: definition of, 157; in Haiti, problems of, 43–44; for medium term,
achievability of, 155–156; military
reward system and, 113–114; national,
65–66; security rings, 124; U.S.,
post–September 11 terrorist attacks,
1–2. *See also* political will, and security;
security-keeping
Security Council. *See* United Nations, Security Council
security-keeping, 19–20, 158–164,
164–165
self-determination, 52, 87, 162. *See also*
sovereignty
self-interest. *See* national self-interest
September 11 terrorist attacks, 1–2
Serbs, 22, 46–47, 48, 50
services-protected personnel evacuation,
142
SFOR. *See* stabilization force
Sierre Leone, 182n20
Skopje, Macedonia, 115, 116
slavery, 71, 72, 86
Smith, Jeffrey, 108
Smith, Tony, 63
Snyder, Jack, 9
social systems, 55, 63
societal change, 39, 44
The Soldier and the State (Huntington),
111
soldiers. *See* military
Somalia, 29–30, 176n50
Somaliland, Republic of, 169n18

sovereignty: Annan on, 90; of Bosnia, 45, 48–49; in colonial Africa, 87; of East Timor, 140; of Kosovo, 45, 52; non-universality, 87; outside control of, as colonialism, 52; peacekeeping operations vs., 90–91; political sovereignty, 11; positive sovereignty, 87; state sovereignty, 36. *See also* foreign control; occupations
Soviet Union, 88. *See also* Russia
Spain, 136–137
Special Operations Forces (U.S.), 42, 153
spoiler problem, 35
spotlight effect, 157
Srebrenica, Bosnia and Herzegovina, 32–33
stabilization force (SFOR) (Bosnia): counterinsurgency raids, participation in, 106; Croat independence movement, actions on, 132–133; ethnic evictions, participation in, 130; force, reluctance to use, 135, 136; Plavsic and, 128–129; policy, 84; role, 49; security rings, creation of, 124
state security interests. *See* national self-interest
state self-interest. *See* national self-interest
states, 11. *See also* liberal democracies; individual countries
Stedman, Stephen John, 35
Stolac, Bosnia and Herzegovina, 124
Strpce, Kosovo, 126, 127, 138–139
Sudan, 129–130
Sun Tzu, 72
Supreme Court (Bosnia and Herzegovina), 48

Taiwan, 89
Taliban, 95
Tata, Anthony J., 116, 117
technology, 68–69, 81, 99, 151
temporary military governorships, 40
terra nullius, 87
territorial competition, 63
territorial control, 68
territorial divisions, 162, 163
Tieszen, Randal, 126, 127
Timor Gap, 80
Timor Leste. *See* East Timor
trade, colonial humanitarianism and, 74
trusteeship, 71, 88
Tudjman, Franjo, 40
Turkey, 94
Tutsis, in Rwanda, 30–31

unified command, of UN peacekeeping operations, 36

Unified Task Force (UNITAF), 142–143
unilateral action, 12, 144. *See also* multilateralism
United Nations: Charter, 35–36; Commissioner on Human Rights, on Bosnia and Herzegovina, 48; High Commissioner for Refugees, Open Cities program, 84, 126, 138; peacekeeping successes, 39; Secretary General, selection of, 89, 90; security-keeping model, role in, 162–163; Trusteeship Council, 87; U.S.-led activities, follow-up for, 146
—PEACEKEEPING MISSIONS: changing nature, 3, 23; Eastern Slavonia, 39–40; impartiality, 25; initial conceptualization, 25; Rwanda, 31–32; Somalia, 29–30; unified command of, 36; United Nations Interim Administration Mission in Kosovo (UNMIK), 51, 52, 91, 126; United Nations Mission in East Timor (UNMET), 53; United Nations Mission in Haiti (UNMIH), 42–44; United Nations Mission of Support in East Timor (UNMISET), 55; United Nations Operation in Congo (ONUC), 26, 168n8; United Nations Preventative Deployment Force (UNPREDEP), 115; United Nations Protection Force (UNPROFOR), 32, 46, 78; United Nations Transitional Administration for East Timor (UNTAET), 54–55, 143; United Nations Transitional Administration for Eastern Slavonia, Baranja and Western Sirmium (UNTAES), 39–40, 141; United Nations Transitional Authority in Cambodia (UNTAC), 28–29, 142; Yugoslavia, 32
—SECURITY COUNCIL: Haiti, action on, 76; implementation force, authorization of, 49; Kosovo, authorization for mission in, 51; operation of, changes in, 81; peacekeeping operations, authorization of, 35–36; Permanent Five members, 36, 88–89; power structure, 89; Resolution 940, 41; resolution 1511, 12
United States: Afghanistan and, 94, 95; Cambodia and, 29–30; Central Intelligence Agency, 118; colonialism, 60, 71, 86; colonies, inattention to, 98–101; empire, lack of political will for, 145; isolationism, 154; leadership role, 95–96, 102; Macedonia and, 115; multilateralism, need for, 145–146; National Security Council Deputies Committee, 103; peacekeeping operations, lack of will for, 97–98, 145–146; peacekeeping

United States (*continued*)
  operations, political arguments over,
  102; Philippines and, 60, 62–64, 125,
  127, 130, 134; and policing, 104–109;
  Somalia and, 105–106; as UN Security
  Council P-5 member, 88; unilateralism,
  12, 13. *See also* Haiti; Iraq
—MILITARY: Army, 153; doctrinal innovation, need for, 153–154; domestic policing activities, 109–110; force protection
  policy, 137; interventions by, 145; in
  Macedonia, 115–118; military police
  (MPs), 111–112; National Guard, 1,
  104; peacekeeping operations, 103;
  policing activities and, 104–109; pres-
  ence, post–September 11, 1; reserve
  troops, 104, 153; in Somalia, 29–30;
  Special Operations Forces (U.S.), 42,
  153
UNMET (United Nations Mission in East
  Timor), 53
UNMIH (United Nations Mission in
  Haiti), 42–44
UNMIK (United Nations Interim Adminis-
  tration Mission in Kosovo), 51, 52, 91,
  126
UNMISET (United Nations Mission of
  Support in East Timor), 55
UNPREDEP (United Nations Preventative
  Deployment Force), 115
UNPROFOR (United Nations Protection
  Force), 32, 46, 78

UNTAC (United Nations Transitional
  Authority in Cambodia), 28–29, 142
UNTAES (United Nations Transitional
  Administration for Eastern Slavonia,
  Baranja and Western Sirmium), 39–40
UNTAET (United Nations Transitional
  Administration for East Timor), 54–55,
  143
Uphold Democracy mission. *See* Haiti
"U.S. Policy on Reforming Multilateral
  Peace Operations" (Presidential Decision
  Directive [PDD] 25), 82

violence, 32–33, 43–44, 100–101
Vitina, Kosovo, 21–22

Wagner, Richard, 108, 109
war crimes, 128, 129
warfare, colonial, causes of, 101
warlords, in Afghanistan, 93, 95
wars, origins of, 34–35
Westendorp, Carlos, 48, 138
western liberal values, 6, 49
Wolfowitz, Paul, 14, 159
Wood, Leonard, 62, 134
World War II, 149

Yugoslavia (former), 32, 46, 51. *See also*
  Bosnia and Herzegovina; Kosovo

Zakaria, Fareed, 23
Zaranj, Afghanistan, 93